"*Psychiatry has labored too long under the delusion that every emotional malfunction requires an endless talking out of everything the patient ever experienced.*"
—Dr. Nathan S. Kline

Dr. Nathan S. Kline, whose method of treating depression has achieved an astonishing rate of cure, believes that in most cases it is a physiological condition that *should* and *can* be treated accordingly. FROM SAD TO GLAD explains fully—

- symptoms of depression
- the varied nature of the illness
- tracing causes and cures
- the mechanisms of mood and emotion
- severe depression and suicide
- drug therapy and psychotherapy
- Marsilid, lithium, reserpine and other psychotropic drugs
- much, much more.

Read it—it really could change your life!

NATHAN S. KLINE

CURRICULUM VITAE

B.A.   Swarthmore College
M.A. (Psychology)   Clark University
M.D.   New York University College of Medicine
F.A.C.P.   Fellow, American College of Physicians
F.A.P.A.   Fellow, American Psychiatric Association
F.A.P.A.   Fellow, American Psychological Association
F.A.C.N.P.   Fellow, American College of Neuro-
   psychopharmacology (former president)
F.A.M.A.   Fellow, American Medical Association
F.R.C. Psych.   Fellow, Royal College of Psychiatrists

Formerly Clinical Professor of Psychiatry, Columbia
   University
Clinical Professor of Psychiatry, New York University
Permanent Visiting Professor of Psychiatry, University
   of California, San Diego

Director, Rockland Research Institute, New York State
   Office of Mental Health, Orangeburg, N.Y.
Medical Director, Regent Hospital, New York, N.Y.
Consultant Physician, Lenox Hill Hospital, New York,
   N.Y.
Consultant, McLean Hospital, Belmont, Mass.
Expert Advisory Panel on Mental Health, World Health
   Organization, Geneva, Switzerland

Hon. F.R.C. Psych.   Honorary Fellow, Royal College
   of Psychiatrists
Albert Lasker Clinical Resarch Award, 1957 and 1964

From
SAD
to
GLAD

Kline on Depression

REVISED AND UPDATED

NATHAN S. KLINE

BALLANTINE BOOKS • NEW YORK

The author acknowledges his indebtedness to George Groh for his valuable assistance in the preparation of this work.

ACKNOWLEDGMENTS
Page 158 from "East Coker" in FOUR QUARTETS by T. S. Eliot, copyright 1943, by T. S. Eliot; copyright 1971, by Esme Valerie Eliot. Reprinted by permission of Harcourt Brace Jovanovich, Inc.

From "Ash Wednesday" in COLLECTED POEMS 1909–1962 by T. S. Eliot, copyright 1936, by Harcourt Brace Jovanovich, Inc.; copyright © 1963, 1964, by T. S. Eliot. Reprinted by permission of the publishers.

Library of Congress Catalog Card Number: 74-79652

ISBN 0-345-33419-1

This edition published by arrangement with
G. P. Putnam's Sons

Manufactured in the United States of America

First Ballantine Books Edition: October 1975
Eleventh Printing: October 1985

Dedicated to those individuals (and their families) who have expressed their confidence in us by generously contributing to the financial support of our research over the last quarter-century, including:

Mr. and Mrs. Franz Denghausen

Victor Gettner and Anita Stein

David Heyman

Mary Lasker

The Raible Family

Mr. and Mrs. Walter J. Schloss

Mr. and Mrs. Kent C. Withers

I will now say my piece,
I will declare what I know.
—JOB 32:17
THE ANCHOR BIBLE

For you were not born to be depressed and unhappy.
—EPICTETUS

Gladness of the heart is the life of man,
and the joyfulness of a man prolongeth his days.
—ECCLESIASTES

Contents

1

Are You Depressed?

How weary, stale, flat, and unprofitable
Seem to me all the uses of this world.
— HAMLET

MENTAL depression is the most common of all psychologic ills. Fortunately it is also one that as a rule responds quite readily to treatment. That statement may surprise many, including some who now suffer from the malady. In the course of a varied psychiatric practice I have treated more than 5,000 depressed patients, and the majority of them have achieved good recoveries. In many instances one can recognize depressives on sight. The inner anguish that afflicts them is signaled in many ways by small, outward signs such as dress, posture, gait, and manner. Sometimes it makes it easier for the patient, when he or she is first seen, to ask directly, "Are you depressed?"

I am beginning this book in the same fashion because I assume that for many readers it will constitute a kind of long consultation about a problem that affects them or someone dear to them. Let us consider, then, some of the basic attitudes and approaches that I try to establish from the first moment of an office consultation.

When I say to a patient, "You seem depressed," I am trying to convey that I am thoroughly familiar with the problem, that I see in it nothing odd or unusual, and certainly nothing to occasion guilt or shame.

Depression in my view is an inherent part of the human condition, a price we pay for those infinitely

1

complicated physical mechanisms and emotional patterns that make us sensitive, intelligent, and aware. I assume that nearly everyone suffers from some degree of the condition at one time or another. It becomes an illness when this ordinary human reaction takes on severe symptoms and chronic form.

I believe that it is a specific disorder, one that in most cases is very probably triggered by some disarray in the biochemical tides that sweep back and forth within the body. Thus when a depressed patient enters our office, he or she is seen by a psychiatric nurse and one or more physicians, and has blood and urine taken for laboratory tests.

There are few clinicians who still depend completely on the psychotherapeutic couch. For nearly all depressed patients I prescribe medications designed to correct or compensate for the chemical imbalance. In simple, uncomplicated cases this eventually relieves the symptoms and ends the matter. The patient no longer suffers, and for all practical purposes we may regard him or her as successfully treated. In more complicated cases the medication relieves the depressive symptoms but does not resolve the deeper-rooted psychic problems. As the consultation develops, some other problems may emerge. The patient may have some conflicts with his parents, his spouse, his children, indeed with himself. He may be neurotic, though not necessarily so. He may need psychotherapy, though again not necessarily so. I recommend psychotherapy to certain of my depressive patients. There are other people who could benefit but for whom psychotherapy is impractical because of the time and expense involved. Even for these people, however, effective chemotherapy can be of the utmost importance if it permits them to mobilize the mental and emotional resources that they need. It pulls them out of the "blues"—and not incidentally it overcomes their preoccupation with symptoms—and so helps them confront the problems they have to face.

Within that context I regard depression as one of the most treatable of the serious ills. In my experience a large percentage of my patients have been able to obtain very satisfactory relief. The treatment period varies widely, but typically a substantial start toward recovery is made in some four to eight weeks, with periods of progressive improvement back toward normality in subsequent weeks.

For a small percentage of depressive patients the recovery is only partial. They show definite improvement but continue to experience some distress. And finally there is a small, intractable core of all cases in which the medications do not provide significant relief.

One could provide psychodynamic reasons for those patients who respond slowly, only partially, or in rare cases not at all. In my opinion, however, the most likely reason is biochemical. I believe that either some anomaly prevents the patient from metabolizing the drug properly, or that the biochemical deficit in these patients is not corrected for some other reason. As there are more than fifty transmitters and enzymes involved, it may be that the drugs currently available do not affect some of these substances. This, of course, is a phenomenon observed quite commonly in other branches of medicine. Thus when we treat an ordinary infection, we often find that a particular antibiotic serves quite well for one patient but not for another. The practitioner may now resolve this by bacterial cultures whereas previously he had to proceed essentially by a process of trial and error, altering his prescriptions until he found a combination that worked.

Psychopharmacology specialists like myself do much the same in the chemotherapy of depression except that the laboratory tests are not yet available for diagnosis. We can, however, measure the concentration in the blood plasma of many of the drugs. In some cases there is a correlation with clinical response. This can help us to tell whether we have given too little or too much of these drugs. The other good news is that medical science is providing us with an increasingly diversified array of agents. Some of the latest additions appear to offer high promise of helping patients who could not be reached before.

The chemical agents that I usually use—singly or in combination—various monamine oxidase inhibitors, tricyclics, tetracyclics, minor tranquilizers, phenothiazines, and lithium (all to be discussed later). I must add at once that these are not, and should not be, medications that the patient can prescribe for himself and buy like aspirin over the counter. Altering the body chemistry is a delicate procedure, not to be undertaken lightly; it should be attempted only when necessary and only under a physician's strict supervision and control. That is a complex subject, one I shall develop later, but here I wish to stress one simple, fundamental point. The really important thing is that in most cases the medication works.

Interestingly, the medication for depression appears to be equally effective whether the patient believes in it or not. He cannot fight it. I have had occasion to observe this phenomenon many times. Often severely depressed patients feel so utterly abject, so trapped in a swamp of despair, that they think their case is hopeless. They may inform me on the first visit that they have come at the insistence of their families while knowing full well that "it's a waste of time." Naturally I try to give reassurance, but I do not place inordinate faith in my powers of persuasion. What I do place great faith in is results. I expect that the patient's attitude will improve when his condition does. I am willing to put off psychologic counseling until that day when the patient comes in and says: "Doctor, I don't understand why, but I'm feeling better."

Curiously enough, some patients feel guilty about achieving that kind of recovery. They have been thoroughly indoctrinated in the idea that emotional disturbance must reflect psychic ills, and they expect the treatment to require a prolonged, painful search through deeply buried layers of their unconscious. When they obtain relief without that effort, they feel that they didn't earn recovery because they haven't paid the psychic price. However, that is a disappointment that most can adjust to readily enough.

I recall a particular patient, a prominent radio personality, who was a manic-depressive. For fifteen years he sought a remedy in psychoanalysis, all the while enduring moods that swung erratically and irrationally from elation to despair. "I think the analysis was valuable," he told me later. "I gained a lot of insight into myself. I was probably the most insightful manic-depressive you ever met. But I was still a manic-depressive and had all my symptoms." I placed him on chemotherapy, and the problem was cleared up in about two months.

I am aware, of course, that I am treading here on controversial ground. I want to state clearly that I have no quarrel with psychotherapy and no doubt about its efficacy in many situations. In most cases of clinical depression, however, I doubt that neurosis lies at the base. I believe it is fundamentally a biochemical disorder, one that may or may not be complicated by neurosis in particular patients.

The reader will note some careful qualifications in the foregoing statements. I say that "I doubt" and "I believe." I do not say, "I know." In fact, no one knows. The interaction between the psychic and the somatic is an immensely complicated process, one we are just beginning to unravel. There is no computer sophisticated enough to read out the myriad biochemical reactions and interactions that take place in a human being every day. If we had such an apparatus, we would not have nearly enough data to feed it.

And if we were able to define and trace every physical reaction, we would still have to interpret it all in terms of the infinitely varied responses of the human spirit. We would somehow have to define and trace all the colorations that an individual brings to his experience by virtue of psychic history, cultural background, existential circumstances, all the elements that make up life-style.

The search for a better understanding of these things

is an important and intriguing quest, one in which I have been privileged to play some part. When a patient enters my office, however, I must put aside the theoretical speculations and deal with the pressing and immediate problem of a man or woman in pain.

The psychoanalytic clinician is, of course, in exactly the same position. I know, because for many years I practiced psychotherapy. In some circumstances the differing theoretical views sometimes merge into quite similar therapeutic approaches. We borrow freely from each other whatever we find useful in insights and techniques, and that is as it should be. It would be a poor physician indeed who would let a theory stand in the way of treatment.

This whole question of psyche and soma is another matter that I will explore more fully at a later point. Here I will state my view that the opposing schools represent not irreconcilable opposites but merely different approaches to the same goal.

We all know that biochemical processes can trigger psychological reactions and, conversely, that psychological stress can produce biochemical fallout. We physicians may disagree sometimes on cause and effect, but we are all looking for ways to correct the process when it malfunctions. In the end, all our theories must give way to the practical question, "Did it help the patient?"

In these matters I believe we do well to apply to medicine what Tennyson wrote about life in general: "And God fulfils himself in many ways,/Lest one good custom should corrupt the world."

In these first few pages I have ranged broadly over very complex matters, in order to give the reader some preliminary view of my medical attitude and general approach. Now I would like to begin at the place where the physician must always begin—with the patient's problems.

Depression might be defined as the magnified and inappropriate expression of some otherwise quite common emotional responses. That, of course, is true of many another disorder. By way of analogy, one expects to find heart palpitation in a person who has just run up a steep hill. Something is decidedly amiss, however, if such palpitation occurs during a sedate walk. So, too, with depression. All of us experience moments of sadness, loneliness, pessimism, and uncertainty as a natural reaction to particular circumstances. In the depressed person those feelings become all-pervasive; they can be triggered by the least incident or occur without evident connection to any outside cause. At times there may be a sudden burst of tears that the person cannot explain—or more or less constant weepiness.

The level of psychic pain varies widely. Some patients are only vaguely aware that they feel blue most of the time. They lack the emotional energy to make friends and enjoy activities; they have a flat response to situations that stimulate others. If they are preparing for a picnic, they glance up at a slightly overcast sky and assume that it will probably rain. For such victims chronic depression is felt not so much as overt pain but rather as the inability to experience pleasure.

For others the pain is acute. They may feel like bursting into tears when someone so much as looks at them. Some, indeed, do weep openly at the least provocation. Some withdraw deeply into themselves, becoming dull and lethargic, hiding the pain behind a mask that seems to exhibit no emotion at all. Some become frightened and irritable. These reactions are often mistaken for anxiety states.

Sometimes the person is not aware that he is depressed. He may displace his reactions, insisting that his moods result entirely from the tribulations of his job, his family situation, or other such circumstances. If he is severely and chronically depressed, he may indeed develop real problems in those areas, but he cannot face the fact that his illness is creating difficulties in his dealings with others. He regards it as a question of blame, and he feels impelled to shift it to someone else.

At the root of such defense mechanisms there is usually the feeling that psychic illness is somehow shameful. At the very least the victim regards it as a failure of nerve and will, a mark of inadequate spirit. If he could assign his complaints to something he regards as purely physical—to arthritis, for instance— he could accept much more readily the fact that he is not functioning well. The irony is that the depression may be at base a physical malfunction, but he hides his illness from himself because he has a fearful image of anyone having a "mental disorder."

Some victims displace their symptoms to other forms of physical ailment. This is easy to do, because depression has numerous physical side effects. The depressive who does not admit to such illness can find any number of medical disguises; most frequently he ascribes it to recurrent, inexplicable headaches, backaches, stomachaches, weakness, generalized aches, pains, and particularly the complaint that he is easily fatigued.

At the opposite pole are those depressives who earnestly seek out psychological reasons for their distress. Again this is perfectly natural, for depression has its psychologic side effects, too. If the depressive was not emotionally disturbed, he may begin to feel that he is, and he may even become so if the depressive episodes occur frequently.

Who wouldn't become upset if he woke up every morning not knowing whether he would be able to function that day or not?

One can produce the appearance of neurosis in so simple a creature as a rat just by frustrating the animal constantly, continually changing the signals so that he never knows whether a particular situation is likely to produce pleasure or pain. It is not surprising that the far more intricate human mechanism should be distressed by not knowing whether tomorrow will be a good day or a bad one.

Depression, then, is an affliction that wears many faces. For the knowledgeable physician, however, the recognition is simple enough. There are a host of companion symptoms that help us identify the affliction. Not all of these symptoms are found in every case, but together they make up a classic syndrome. Many of these affiliated complaints are things the ordinary person might not associate with depression. Years ago I drew up for my own patients a list of such symptoms, so that they might have a better understanding of their ills. Below are some of the major reactions the patient may experience. Please note that it is unusual for all of them to be present in a particular case. As a rule, only a few are necessary to make the diagnosis:

Reduced enjoyment and pleasure: The one universal symptom of every depression is the loss of pleasure and joy in those things and activities which under normal circumstances make life worth living. Oddly, the feeling of depression need not always be present, but in every depressed patient it is the lack of enjoyment that is the touchstone of recognizing the condition.

Boredom: Often the lack of enjoyment bcomes deepened and you may find yourself bored most of the time. Time seems to pass very slowly so that both the days and the nights seem endless.

Rejection of opportunities: Job promotion, the opportunity to meet new people, the chance to go somewhere, are turned down. There is no spirit of adventure or excitement.

Poor concentration: If you are depressed, you may have difficulty concentrating. Perhaps you often read a newspaper or listen to a television program only to find you have not been able to retain anything of what you read, saw, or heard.

Difficulty making decisions: Not only major decisions but even minor ones seem almost unreachable. A housewife may fluctuate for several minutes, trying to decide which brand of soap to buy. A businessman may stare at his tie rack and then try on a dozen ties before selecting one to wear and then spend an hour wondering whether he made the best choice.

Memory: Often memory of recent events becomes progressively worse. Memory of remote events is not affected to the same degree.

Neglect of personal appearance: The patient's usual level of neatness and cleanliness begins to deteriorate. Dirty clothes are ignored and bathing occurs less frequently.

Retarded thinking: Your thought processes may be slowed down and seem to move in circles, so that you can't complete an idea. In addition, there just aren't any new and creative thoughts.

Social withdrawal: There is no desire to be with other people, and frequently even good friends are avoided. There is often a preference to be alone and isolated.

Fatigue: You are quite likely to get tired very easily and lack the drive to get things done the way you used to. It becomes impossible to cope with relatively minor difficulties, and really not worth the effort.

Insomnia: You may want to sleep a great deal—but at the same time, when you go to bed you may not be able to get to sleep, or else you may fall asleep rapidly but awaken after only an hour or two. It is also common to awaken very early, feeling exhausted, frightened, and depressed.

Ruminations: At times there is an irresistible need to chew over past events and to think of how they might have turned out differently. This can become so severe that it cannot be turned off. Often, under such circumstances, ruminations not only prevent sleep but interfere with thinking and experiencing.

Remorse: It is not unusual to feel deep regret about things in the past that you think you should have done and did not do—or the opposite, about things you did do and feel you should not have done.

Guilt: Because of your illness there are many things you cannot do that would ordinarily be easy for you. This inability to function as well as you feel you should is apt to produce feelings of guilt. You may feel that you are being unfair to your family, your friends, those who depend on you, and those to whom you are important. At other times feelings of guilt are out of all proportion to the circumstances.

Financial concern: People in depressions are concerned about using up their resources. Their judgment about financial matters is often defective, and some tend markedly to underestimate what they can afford to spend.

Loss of appetite and weight: Eating becomes a chore; weight losses of ten, twenty, or thirty pounds are not rare.

Reduced sexual activity: Interest in sex and sexual performance usually declines to a remarkably low level for the depressed patient. Not only loss of libido but often impotence or an inability to reach a sexual orgasm is common. So are menstrual irregularities.

Decreased love and affection: You may feel shocked to discover that you feel little or no love anymore for those persons among your friends and family who have always been extremely close to you in the past.

General loss of interest: You may well find yourself indifferent to all sorts of people, things, and ideas that were once of great importance to you.

Over-responsiveness: Trivial events may precipitate a flood of uncontrollable emotion.

Tearfulness: At times you may find your eyes brimming with tears, although nothing has happened to explain the crying.

Gloominess about the future: The conviction exists that things will not improve and are likely to get worse. The patient's feeling that nothing will help is one of the very most painful symptoms.

Anxiety: Besides being depressed, you may be tense, anxious, or frightened. These feelings are so strong in some patients as to cover up the underlying depression.

Irritability: All sorts of trivial things may irritate you, and you may not be able to control your annoyance and impatience. You may hold a grudge long after it should have been forgotten.

Suicidal thoughts: Almost everyone thinks of committing suicide at one time or another, but naturally such ideas are more frequent during a depression. Often this seems the only escape from an intolerable situation. Even when the idea of suicide is rejected you may simply wish that you wouldn't wake up tomorrow.

Unusual thoughts and urges: Frequently there is fear of someone near and dear to you dying. Oddly enough, there are also times when depressed patients have the urge to harm those near and dear to them. Feelings that the world is unreal are not unusual; or at times you may feel unreal yourself.

Physical changes: Changes in bowel habits, particularly constipation, are not unusual; neither is dryness of the mouth. Some patients overeat. Many patients find themselves plagued by all sorts of aches and pains, some of which may be new and some of which may have been present before but were seldom noticed. Other physical reactions that may accompany depression include nausea, chest pains, stomach cramps, rapid breathing, sweating, coldness of the extremities, numbness, or tingling of the hands and feet—and particularly headaches or other odd feelings of pressure in the head, ears, or neck.

Concern about dying: Because of the physical symptoms (or even without them) you may feel that a terrible and untreatable disease process is destroying some part of your body or brain. If medical attention has already been sought, you may believe that doctors fail to recognize the illness or will not tell you the truth about it. Despite the concern you may do all sorts of self-destructive things—overeat or starve yourself, neglect yourself, and not take necessary medication.

Need for relief: The feeling is so uncomfortable that you have tried all sorts of things to get away from it. At first there is usually an effort to find distraction in trivial things like movies or games. Later this no longer works, and the use of alcohol or any kind of drug that will make escape possible becomes very attractive.

This will be discussed at greater length in a subsequent chapter.

Such are the afflictions, whether physical or emotional, that beset the depression victim. There are also characteristic behavioral traits that provide a clue to this condition. A knowledge of such traits would be useful to the depressive's friends and family; it would help them to recognize the problems involved.

At times, the depressive speaks in a retarded fashion. He may exhibit even more difficulty on the reception end of communication. In general his responses tend to be either evasive or flat. Often I will chat socially with a patient for a few minutes and drop in a casual joke. One can observe much from the quality of the responding smile or the lack of it.

Sometimes, a patient displays a slack posture and a seemingly hesitant gait. Facial expressions may be flat and nonresponsive. On occasion severe depressives become downright clumsy, bumping into large fixed objects they might easily avoid. Of course, interpretation of such signs requires some knowledge of a person's usual style and manner. A particular individual may be by nature reserved in conversation, untidy in dress, or clumsy in movement; that does not mark him as a depressive. When such small signs accumulate, however, and when they coincide with other common symptoms, it provides a clear warning.

The four criteria for major depressive syndrome in the latest statistical manual of the American Psychiatric Association are:

1. Has, for *at least a week,* been bothered by depressive or irritable mood or had pervasive loss of interest or pleasure (i.e., anhedonia).
2. Has sought or has been referred for help from someone during the *dysphoric** period, has taken medication, or has had *impaired functioning* so-

---

* Dysphoria: a state or condition marked by feelings of unease or mental discomfort.

cially, with family, at home, at work, or at school.

3. *Has had at least four* of the following symptoms associated with the most severe period of dysphoria.

   (i) poor appetite or weight loss; increased appetite or weight gain.
   (ii) trouble sleeping or sleeping too much.
   (iii) loss of energy, easily fatigued, or feeling tired.
   (iv) loss of interest or pleasure in usual activities or sex.
   (v) feeling guilty, worthless, or down on self.
   (vi) difficulty with concentrating, thinking, or making decisions.
   (vii) thoughts of death or suicide.
   (viii) inability to sit still and had to keep moving, or felt slowed down and had trouble moving.

4. Has shown *no* evidence of delusions or hallucinations that are not congruent with the existing mood disorder, *nor* shown marked formal† thought disorder.

Those individuals with a history of drug abuse and/or alcoholism that antedated a history of depressive illness, and in whom chronic use of these drugs/alcohol accompanies recurrences of depression, even if the above criteria are met, are excluded.

I have also prepared tables that I use in discussions with fellow psychiatrists and other professionals. They, too, may be of help if you are concerned about a particular situation. Keep in mind two things:

1. It is unusual for *all* the symptoms to be present.
2. The severity of the condition is *not* always related to the response. Neither is the duration. Patients with "late" symptoms that they have had a long time may respond rapidly and completely.

---

† Primary.

Early Symptoms	*Midway Symptoms*	*Late Symptoms*
Anhedonia (absence of joy and pleasure)	Gloominess about the future	Retarded physical movements (thick speech, etc.)
Loss of interest in usual activities	Rumination + guilt about past mistakes	Weakness
Poor concentration	Defective recent memory	Delusions of fatal illness
Indecisiveness	Insomnia (especially in early morning)	Suicidal preoccupation
Chronic fatigue	Loss of appetite, or the reverse (bulimia)	Isolation
Decreased sexual activity	Constipation	Depersonalization
Carelessness about personal appearance	Psychosomatic symptoms (headache, cramps, etc.)	Nihilism
Anxiety, irritability	Weight loss + anorexia	Hallucinations + delusions
	Autonomic lability	Hopelessness

Feelings of sadness and depression increasing →   Feelings of sadness and depression increasing →

Feelings of sadness and depression increasing →

Over the years I have had a substantial number of patients come to consult me from other parts of the world. Most such patients came from Europe, and for a few years I used to travel back and forth across the Atlantic to see them—or have them come to see me several times a year. This was not a very convenient arrangement for either the patient or for me. Therefore, I referred these patients to Dr. Jules Angst, professor of clinical psychiatry and director of psychiatric research of the University Hospital in Zurich, Switzerland. Both the patients and I were pleased with how well things went. Then one spring Dr. Angst and I spent a week together at a meeting in the Caribbean, during the course of which we discussed how we decided what medication to give to which patient. We eventually figured out that what we were doing was making the decision as to which medication to use, not on the basis of diagnosis alone, or just on the basis of symptoms.* Rather we made use of what are referred to in medicine as syndromes: groups of symptoms that go together in time. Over the next three years we reviewed both our own patients and those described in the literature. Obviously not all patients fit into these categories.

The syndromes that we identified are:

1. Retarded Depressive Syndrome
   The patient complains of reduced capacity for enjoyment, loss of interest in work and family, reduced productivity, disorders of attention and immediate memory. Thinking is inhibited, retarded, restricted, or even blocked. Appearance is depressed, hopeless, sometimes anxious, and the patient complains of inner restlessness or fatigue, lack of drive and energy. Thought is heavily loaded with depressive content. Guilt feelings or delusions of guilt, feelings of impoverishment or

---

* N. S. Kline, and J. Angst, *Psychiatric Syndromes and Drug Treatment* (New York and London: Jason Aronson, 1979).

delusions may be present. At times there is suffering from pressure in the head and throat. Vital feelings are disturbed. Characteristic also are diurnal fluctuations of the symptoms, in which the patient feels worse in the morning. Usually there is early morning awakening, loss of appetite for both food and sexual activity. Suicidal tendencies must be looked for. Autonomic symptoms include constipation and dryness of the mouth. In severe cases, the condition progresses to stupor, with complete blockage of speech and motor activity.

2. Agitated Depressive Syndrome
   The patient feels hopeless, desperate and anxious, suffering from agitation, motor restlessness, sleep disturbances, and lack of concentration. He is full of complaints, constantly appealing to others for help. Delusions of poverty, guilt or hypochondriasis are frequently present, and the need for increased contact leads to his clinging to others in his anxiety. Diurnal rhythm is such that he may show improvement in the evening.

3. Affective Hypochondriacal Syndrome
   The affective hypochondriacal patient always observes himself more carefully than the normal individual. He worries about his physical or mental condition, with frequent concentration on his bowels, his constipation, his autonomic functions, any paresthesias, dryness of the mouth, and so on. His hypochondriacal anxiety may increase to the point of a delusion that he is suffering from cancer or some other incurable disease. The patient insists upon being examined by many different doctors, and in general is very unstable. He is full of complaints, anxiety, and hopelessness. His thinking is almost restricted to bodily functions.

4. Depressed Obsessive-Compulsive Syndrome
   The patient suffers from a clearcut depressive state, most frequently of the retarded type, but

additionally he suffers from obsessive thoughts, compulsive impulses and actions. In contrast to an obsessive-compulsive *neurosis,* these symptoms increase or decrease in accord with fluctuations in the depth of the depressive state.

5. Depressive Syndrome with Delusions and Hallucinations

In contrast to schizophrenic reactions, the content of delusions and hallucinations is congruent with the depressive affect; for instance, voices accusing the patient because he feels guilty, or hallucinations of being in hell or in prison are "deserved" as a punishment for his guilt. Sometimes the patient believes the police are persecuting him because of his sins. The whole content of the delusions and hallucinations is synthymic* with the thought content, i.e., depressed. In older patients one often hears expressed ideas of poverty in respect to money, clothes, and food, plus the conviction that not only the patient but also his family is dying. Such patients often express the idea that their spouse is already dead.

6. Syndrome of Simultaneous Manic and Depressive Responses

Although some of the manifestations of the manic and the depressive phase are mutually exclusive, other symptoms can coexist. Unless the clinician is aware of this, the picture can be very confusing. Not only can the mood swing rapidly from one extreme to the other, but a patient under pressure of speech, hyperactive and euphoric, may suddenly burst into tears but otherwise continue to behave in a hypomanic manner. All sorts of odd combinations are possible.

Depression also appears frequently as a symptom in the neurotic- and personality-disorder syndromes. Two

---

* Compatible in respect to mood.

of these are described for comparison with the affective syndromes.

1. Anxiety State or Syndrome

   The anxiety state is characterized by excessive anxiety, often amounting to panic. It can manifest itself in the psychic sphere or in the somatic field with autonomic reactions. The patient often suffers from free-floating anxiety with cardio-vascular symptoms (tachycardia, palpitations, feelings of faintness), dryness of the mouth, lack of appetite, dyspepsia, fullness of the stomach, gastric pain before or after meals, nausea, and oc-casional vomiting. The anxiety may be increased under certain circumstances such as crowded surroundings. The patient is agitated to varying degrees.

   Anxiety states tend to be overdiagnosed; the true underlying diagnosis of depression is very often missed. Many depressive syndromes show marked symptoms of anxiety and even agitation. There is rarely depression without anxiety, so what appears to be an anxiety state must be very closely examined to determine whether it is ac-tually an agitated depression. At the end of one to two months of treatment, if the patient diag-nosed as having an anxiety state experiences no relief, one ought to reexamine the case to see whether there is not an underlying depression. Look for basic symptoms of a depressive state: symptoms worse in the morning and better in the evening, early awakening, and so on.

2. Depressive Neurotic Syndrome

   The depression follows some acute psychic trau-ma or develops as a result of chronic psychologi-cal conflict. The symptomatology shows rapid changes dependent on the external situation and is often linked with symptoms of aggression or appeals to others. The symptoms tend to be worse in the evening, and the patient has difficulty falling asleep. Mixed in with symptoms of anxiety there is often hostility.

It should also be recognized that certain cycles and episodes in life are accompanied by increased susceptibility to depression. Certain traumatic life events may precipitate a true depression. A death in the family, divorce, cancer, and similar misfortunes may result in far more than the normal reaction if the biologic predisposition is present.

Many women experience some degree of depression as a side effect of premenstrual tension, and postpartum depression is very common and sometimes quite severe. In my judgment it is not coincidental that these are both events involving marked changes in the biochemical processes. Other profound events that may trigger depression are the great life-cycle changes involved in adolescence and aging.

In all, depression is a very common affliction, one that besets many people at some point in life; for considerable numbers it is a chronic condition. According to National Institute of Mental Health figures and other sources, some 1,500,000 people are being treated for depression today. This sounds like a large number until we realize that certainly 7,000,000 and possibly 15,000,000 are in need of such treatment but are not receiving it.

Some of these people resist treatment because they are prey to old superstitions. The idea of any mental or emotional malfunction inspires in them nameless dread and so they push it aside, refusing to recognize the damage it is doing to their lives and the lives of those close to them.

There are also some ensnared in what might be termed a new superstition. They have acquired some knowledge of the great insights contributed by psychology and psychiatry, and they have embraced it with the total commitment that was reserved in other times for religious faith. Believing as they do in psychologic absolutes of cause and effect, they have clanged down a kind of interior iron curtain that separates psyche and soma. They may accept the fact that what happens in psyche can affect soma, but they resist stubbornly the notion that there is a busy two-way traffic, with the cause located now here and now there.

Currently there is also resistance to the very idea of using medication for treatment, because it is not "natural." But then, neither is depression. Fear of addiction to the medication is the result of misinformation. The worst that can happen if drugs used in treating depression are discontinued prematurely is that symptoms will recur. It is *not* true that if you take medication you will have to continue it indefinitely.

In the chapters that follow I will document my own conviction that in any particular case of depression the cause arises in the somatic area in at least the great majority of cases. In proper course I will also outline the somatic therapies, but here let me reaffirm my assertion that I regard as valid any treatment that proves effective for the individual patient. Considering the great unknowns in the equation of human emotion, it would be presumptuous to dismiss any method that brings substantial relief to the patient.

Before there can be treatment and relief, there must be recognition that the problem exists. I will regard this book as valuable if it helps depressives and those near them to know that they suffer from a recognized medical disease and to confront the condition with both inquiring mind and hopeful spirit.

2

Of Men and Melancholy

Men become heroes because they do not traffic with Inevitables. They understand the plasticity of history and are at home with its sudden turnings. They also know something of the art of creating such turnings where they might not otherwise exist.

—The Saturday Review

DEPRESSION is an ancient malady, one probably present at the dawn of history. It appears today in all societies from the most primitive to the most complex. And when we turn to the past, we find this illness running like a dark thread through the whole fabric of man's recorded experience.

A brief historical scan of depression is instructive for more than mere academic reasons. It clearly demonstrates that this is a natural illness, something inherent in the human condition, and not just a by-product of the anxieties created by modern times. A view of the past is useful also in providing some perspective on how man has tried to explain and cope with this common problem through the ages.

One of the ancient case histories we encounter is that of Nebuchadnezzar, a king of the Babylonians more than 2,500 years ago. He is familiar in Judeo-Christian lore as the man who cast Shadrach, Meshach, and Abednego into the fiery furnace. Historically he was also an important monarch, a great builder and doer, who presided over a mighty empire.

The old chronicles inform us that Nebuchadnezzar

suffered intensely from insomnia. His moods were wildly erratic, peaks of intense, probably manic activity being interspersed with what appears in retrospect to be sloughs of profound depression.

For those who now suffer from similar but less severe attacks it may be heartening to know that Nebuchadnezzar eventually recovered. He went on to a long, successful regime in which the Babylonian empire reached its zenith.

Nebuchadnezzar had to endure his crisis without the aid of modern therapy. He had no psychoanalysts at his command and, for that matter, no effective drug treatments. How, then, does one account for his recovery? To those who share my view of the illness there is no great mystery about it. I believe that he was overwhelmed by a biochemical storm that raged through his system, and that the storm finally blew itself out in the cyclic fashion nature sometimes exhibits. That sort of "spontaneous remission" is part of a classic pattern that frequently occurs in this disease.* Modern drug treatments reinforce the healing process and speed it along, assisting nature to correct itself.

The case history just cited is not an isolated historical fragment. One can trace similar depressive patterns in the lives of Saul, Herod, and other ancient personages. No doubt the common people were afflicted too, though that was usually not recorded. The significant point is that this was from the very beginning a quite common disease, one that occurred independently of the pressures produced by any particular civilization or historic age. Society has played a decisive role, however, in shaping man's reaction to the illness.

Most of the ancients thought of depression in magical or religious terms. The Babylonians saw it as demonic possession, while the Hebrews ascribed the manifestations to the combined forces of divine retribution and human guilt. Interestingly, neither civilization

---

* Nothing in the universe is strictly "spontaneous." The phrase "spontaneous remission" simply reflects the fact that we do not know the causal links involved.

developed any specific terms for the malady, presumably because they did not see it as a specific problem. Life to them was full of random supernatural interventions, and there was really no accounting for the trials and punishments the gods might inflict.

Most of the Greek physician-philosophers related emotional disturbance to basic physical mechanisms. Hippocrates, the father of Western medicine, stated the premise that behavior is related to the brain:

> Men ought to know that from nothing else but the brain come joys, delights, laughter and sports, griefs, despondency and lamentations. . . . And by the same organ we become mad and delirious, and fears and terrors assail us, some by night and some by day, and dreams and untimely wanderings, and cares that are not suitable. . . . All these things we endure from the brain.

Hippocrates ascribed madness to humidity of the brain, postulating different types of secretions that gave rise to mania and depression. The theory was later expanded to include four bodily substances called humors, whose ebb and flow supposedly determined physical and mental health. Each of the humors was considered vital, but an excess of any one upset the balance and created disturbance. Depression was blamed on a surplus of *melan cholē,* the Greek term for black bile; thus derives our word "melancholy."

The old Greek theory was crude, of course. Today we know that the brain alone contains some 10 billion cells, each of them an intricate life form in itself and each interconnected with the other through an enormously complicated network of chemical secretions, electrical impulses, and neural pathways. The brain, moreover, is but one component of a much larger system, and it responds continually to signals relayed from all the glands and organs. We are just beginning to unravel the myriad biochemical reactions involved, but we do know that they are profoundly related to all of our physical, mental, and emotional responses. Four humors, indeed! Perhaps four thousand?

Nonetheless, the original Greek concept was deeply insightful on two counts. It assumed that emotions are rooted in our physical makeup, and it introduced the idea of mechanisms attuned to a balanced interplay of natural forces. Today physicians like myself have come back full circle to what might be called a modern "humoral theory." Once again we seek to isolate and identify some "black bile" of melancholy, only now we are examining biochemical constituents so small that their very existence was not suspected until recent decades. Later in this discussion I will describe some of the intriguing clues we have begun to uncover.

The original belief in humors persisted for many centuries, being passed on from Greeks to Romans, then through the Moslem civilization to medieval Europe. Of course, the ancients were not all of one mind on the matter. One of the early Greeks, Soranus of Ephesus, viewed the cause of melancholy as being not humoral secretion but tension and stricture in the nerve fibers. That was quite an astonishing shot in the dark: modern research on the problem is heavily focused on those biochemical reactions that activate the nerve endings.

Aretaeus of Cappadocia was still another ancient who anticipated some modern views. He suggested that melancholy really involved two separate illnesses whose differences were masked by common symptoms. The first type, he thought, was simply an organic illness, occurring without relationship to external situations. The second type was psychologic in origin, emotional stress somehow setting in motion the same reactions as physical malfunction. In the medical literature today one still finds discussion of those supposed two forms of the malady; they are now called, respectively, the "endogenous" and "reactive" types. Whether the two types require distinct treatments remains a controversial question to be discussed later.

* * *

The early physicians attempted to treat depression with every remedy that came to mind. They tried bloodletting, opiates, sleep therapy, hot baths, cold baths, and special diets of every kind. They offered also a variety of counseling, much of it conflicting.

Some advised the patients to seek soothing music, and some recommended stimulating conversation. Some thought vigorous exercise was called for, and some advocated complete bed rest. It was all very crude and empirical, and no doubt confusing to the patients, but then they were groping in the dark as best they could.

Medieval attitudes eventually regressed all the way back to the old idea of demonic possession. A severe depressive was likely to be considered bewitched or, worse yet, be cast in the witch's role. Such are the powers of belief and suggestion that many condemned witches concurred in the verdict, believing that they were in fact guilty of casting satanic spells.

The demonic view of the illness persisted for a long time and cut across all religious movements of the period. In the sixteenth century Martin Luther declared, "In cases of melancholy I conclude it is merely the work of the devil." That was about the high-water mark for diabolic diagnosis, but even so, the physician-priest Saint Vincent de Paul was risking an advanced position a century later when he stated that physical and mental disturbance arose from similar causes.

Psychiatric diagnosis and treatment began to appear at the end of the eighteenth century. A notable pioneer was Philippe Pinel, a great French physician and medical reformer. He is known to the general public as a man who won immortal fame by striking the chains from the wretched asylum inmates. He also contributed a theory of melancholy, a malady with which he was much concerned.

Pinel believed that it was a two-layer illness, caused by mental aberration at the base but overlaid with severe physical symptoms. He advocated a corresponding two-level treatment, applying *remèdes simples* to the physical problems while attempting to root out the mental problem with a *traitement moral*.

Traitement moral was a far cry from psychoanalysis, but it did attempt to cure the illness by talking it out with the patient. Pinel hoped at first that he might overcome the depressive's morbid sentiments by his reasoning with the patient. That didn't work and so he turned to what he called "the pious fraud." He would pretend to share the depressive's fantasies, entering into the dark labyrinth of the patient's suspicions and fears, so that he could by gentle stages lead him out. That too, however, proved unavailing, for the deeply depressed are immune alike to cajolery and reason.

Pinel turned next to methods that anticipated modern encounter therapy. The patient was induced to feel strange objects, listen to odd music, engage in argument, and act out his emotions in free play. The idea was to stimulate him to amusement, surprise, pleasure, or if necessary even anger and rage—anything at all that would shake him out of his lethargy and allow him to open the floodgates on the dammed-up stream of his emotions.

When all else failed, Pinel and his followers resorted to some early forms of "shock" treatment. Depressives were whipped with stinging nettles, thrust into ice-cold showers, and subjected to other forms of "harmless torture." Pinel himself was a humane man, and he cautioned against using such methods too freely. Some others, however, went at it with what seems to have been quite literally a vengeance. They had a medical rationale, of course—they were trying to shake the patient out of his illness—but a good deal of the old punitive attitude seems to have lingered on.

A widespread view at the time was expressed by one practitioner who said the most important thing was to "make the patient reasonably responsive . . . cost what it may." Another praised the disciplinary virtues of the ice-cold shower, saying: "A patient who has once experienced the shower is not inclined to want to do it again; and if you make him aware in advance of what awaits him, and if he knows that you keep your word, he will be restrained without the use of a single drop of water."

Today we would call that "aversive conditioning." This is one technique of behavior therapy or modification; nowadays more sophisticated approaches are available.

Thirty years after Pinel died, Sigmund Freud was born.

The general outline of Freud's theory and practice is surely too familiar to require an extensive treatment here, but in brief Freud and his followers saw the depressive patient as one trapped by some trauma in an unresolved childhood phase of ego development. Through psychoanalysis they attempted to take the patient back to the scene of the accident, psychiatrically speaking, so that the old injury could be repaired.

The Freudian approach to depression was never universally accepted, but it is fair to say that it dominated medical thinking through the first half of the twentieth century. It still has powerful defenders. In recent decades, however, it has been increasingly challenged by those who believe depression's basic cause in at least some cases is a biochemical disorder. Interestingly, such was Freud's own view at one time. That development is a fascinating story, one I will save for more detailed treatment in succeeding chapters. Suffice it to say here that the recent biochemical era began by chance and accident, with bits and pieces of discovery, and is only now producing some theories that seem to fit the facts.

Such, then, in brief, is the case history of this elusive illness we call depression. For some 2,500 years physicians have turned the question around and around, seeking the cause and cure.

Must the long quest be considered still a failure? Not at all. We have not yet settled the "why" of the disorder, at least not to everyone's satisfaction, but we are making long strides on the "how" of treatment. We have learned more through trial and error than through application of any theory, but the important thing is that we have learned. The great medical advances proceed in that groping fashion more often than most laymen know.

Depression has also a social history, including a long roster of famous people and whole societies that seemed especially prone to the affliction. That, too, is revealing, for it sheds some light on the questions of how or whether the disease interacts with particular modes of life.

Depression has been omnipresent throughout history, but there have been particular times when the incidence appeared to rise to epidemic proportions. Note that I say "appeared"; the issue is one that goes deeply to the essential nature of the disease. Elizabethan England was known as the great age of melancholy. It was in some ways a time much like our own and so bears particular examination here.

Queen Elizabeth's long reign spanned roughly the last half of the sixteenth century, and it saw England emerge from a relatively minor nation to a world power. The change was accompanied as always by tumult and strife, the abandonment of old social moorings, and the restless groping toward an uncertain future.

It also produced a great outpouring of melancholic literature. There are those who see a direct connection. They believe such convulsive eras are conducive to creating a climate in which individual depressions flourish. Perhaps so, but I view the theory with moderate skepticism.

I suspect that the social influence was more subtle in nature. In fact, I suspect that the beruffled and bejeweled gentry of the Elizabethan salons were no more and no less depression prone than were the buckskin-clad frontiersmen of the American West. The difference, I believe, was in the attitude toward the disease. The Elizabethans brought it out in the open and talked about it. Many even preened themselves on being melancholy, for they came to consider it a superior malady, a mark of refined sensibility among those deeply touched by the pathos of life.

Self-proclaimed melancholics advertised their elegant suffering by adopting a sad, languid air and ostentatiously dressing all in black.

In *Hamlet* Shakespeare presents the malady in a very different vein. Here is a character caught up in a deep, fearful melancholy. He knows his reactions are irrational, and he would fight them off if he could, but thought and will are both powerless against the emotions that grip him. The physician meets that kind of patient often, and Shakespeare saw it with a perceptive eye. It is all said in a scene in which Hamlet and the queen discuss death:

QUEEN: Thou know'st 'tis common; all that lives
        must die,
        Passing through nature to eternity.

HAMLET: Ay, madam, it is common.

QUEEN: If it be,
        Why seems it so particular with thee?

HAMLET: Seems, madam! Nay, it is; I know not
        'seems.'
        'Tis not alone my inky cloak, good
        mother,
        Nor customary suits of solemn black,
        Nor windy suspiration of forced breath,
        No, nor the fruitful river in the eye,
        Nor the dejected 'haviour of the visage,
        Together with all forms, moods, shapes
        of grief,
        That can denote me truly: these indeed
        seem,
        For they are actions that a man might
        play:
        But I have that within that passeth show;
        These but the trappings and the suits of
        woe.

It is all there: the exaggerated nature of the emotion, its overwhelming power, and its ultimate irrationality. Hamlet is quite right when he brushes the reasons aside, saying that it does not matter if his mood seems inappropriate to others. To him the mood does not seem, it simply "is."

Many other writers have explored this affliction. One, indeed, devoted his entire life to it. The author was Robert Burton, a shy, diffident English librarian who was Shakespeare's contemporary.

Burton spent more than twenty years writing and rewriting *The Anatomy of Melancholy,* a classic work that ultimately stretched out to more than 500,000 words. He put into it almost all that was then known about the illness, along with his own endless musings and speculations about it.

He was, in fact, a lifelong victim of the malady. The mood for him seems to have been pervasive and lingering rather than overpowering, and he developed an ironic humor about it. He took refuge in work. He wrote of melancholy, he said, in a busy effort to avoid it.

The pain of depression has been transmuted into art by such other writers as Dostoevski, Poe, and Hawthorne. Their haunting sense of tragedy and horror expressed some of the inner anguish of their own lives.

For Hawthorne melancholy was like a prison cell, and it was all the more frightening because the bars were invisible. In a letter to his friend Longfellow he described it thus: "I have secluded myself from society; and yet I never meant any such thing. I have made a captive of myself and put me into a dungeon, and now I cannot find the key to let myself out."

It was worse for Dostoevski, becoming at times an ordeal of sheer terror. He described one attack in a letter to his brother:

As soon as night began to fall, I lapsed into a state which I call *dread.* It is a cruel, unbearable fear in face of something indefinable, something inconceiv-

able, and quite outside the natural order of things.
. . . [It] comes and dogs me like some inescapable
fate, terrible, hideous and implacable it is. This
dread becomes stronger and stronger, despite all
attempts to reason it away, so that in the end the
mind is deprived of every means of fighting against
sensation.

For Poe it became a fatal illness; he destroyed himself with alcohol and opium. Here is a friend's description of Poe as he teetered on the brink in his last days:

He walked the streets, in madness of melancholy,
with his lips moving in indistinct curses, or with his
eyes upturned in passionate prayers (never for himself, for he felt, or professed to feel, that he was
already damned) . . . with his glance introverted to a
heart gnawed with anguish, and with a face shrouded
in gloom, he would brave the wildest storms and at
night, with drenched garments and arms wildly beat-
ing the wind and rain, he would speak as if to spirits.

The depressive may be a scientist, coldly rational in
his professional thought processes and yet inwardly
threatened by the most irrational fears. Charles Darwin
was like that. As a thinking man, he was able to construct the grand epic of evolution from the painstaking
study of thousands of fossils. As a feeling man, he all
but collapsed in the midst of his task. Before he set
out on his fossil-collecting voyage, he became "inex-
pressibly gloomy and miserable" and was beset with
such physical symptoms as chest pains and heart palpitations. When he returned from the voyage, he had to
lay the work aside for a year and a half because he
became so depressed that he could not even read.

One of the most fascinating historical cases is that of
Winston Churchill. There were periods in his life when
he was beset by what he called his "black dog" of
depression. The fact that he gave it such a name suggests how familiar a companion it was. He was prey

also to the small phobias that can at times be characteristic of the illness. The indomitable leader who defied the blitz was, in his secret heart, a man afraid of leaning over a balcony. "I have no desire to quit this world," he said, "but thoughts, desperate thoughts, come into the head."

A hereditary strain of the illness ran through Churchill's family, as he well knew; he wrote perceptively about its effects on his great ancestor, the first Duke of Marlborough. His own affliction was something he usually concealed beneath a gruff exterior, saying, "I can look fierce whenever I like."

In fact, he practiced that look in front of a mirror and learned to assume the expression like an actor playing a role. Occasionally he let the mask slip and confessed to intimates the hidden things behind the pose. One such conversation was recorded by his friend and personal physician, Lord Charles Moran, in 1944. Lord Moran's account:

"The P.M. was in a speculative mood today.

" 'When I was young,' he ruminated, 'for two or three years the light faded out of the picture. I did my work. I sat in the House of Commons, but black depression settled on me. It helped me to talk to Clemmie [Mrs. Churchill] about it.' "

Churchill went on to admit that he had never wholly conquered his fears:

"I don't like to stand near the edge of a platform when an express train is passing through," he told Moran. "I like to stand right back and if possible to get a pillar between me and the train. I don't like to stand by the side of a ship and look down into the water. A second's action would end everything. A few drops of desperation. And yet I don't want to go out of the world at all in such moments. Is much known about worry, Charles?"

Moran replied, "Your trouble—I mean the black dog business—you got from your forebears. You have fought against it all your life. That is why you dislike visiting hospitals. You always avoid anything that is depressing."

"Winston stared at me," Moran added, "as if I knew too much."

Some famed depressives have been seen on the American political stage. George Washington suffered from numerous psychosomatic ills that appear to have been depression-linked. It was probably a depressive episode, rather than philosophical doubts, that caused him to refuse the presidency when it was first offered him.

An even clearer case is that of Abraham Lincoln, whose drawn, haggard face is the very portrait of melancholy. No doubt those pain lines were etched deep by the Civil War, but for Lincoln the knowledge of suffering began long before that; as a young man he was so withdrawn and brooding that his friends feared he might take his own life.

Only recently depression made front-page headlines in the now celebrated case of vice-presidential candidate Thomas Eagleton. Probably no one who saw him give his acceptance speech suspected that he had ever harbored such illness.

Here was an accomplished political figure, a seeming extrovert, who stood before the nation with every appearance of total self-confidence. Then he was revealed as a former depressive, and many were surprised and shocked. They should not have been. The disease is no respecter of eminent persons, and it can attack a variety of personality types.

Once Eagleton's diagnosis was known there were, of course, all sorts of explanations. I read with skeptical interest one long account that traced his breakdowns to the psychologic pressures placed on him in childhood. Supposedly he was strained beyond endurance by the image of a demanding father.

Such a cause-and-effect rationale often seems plausible in the individual instance, but the explanation never covers all cases. Thus no one was more ambitious for his sons or more demanding of them than Joseph

Kennedy. There was not the least evidence of a depressive personality in President John F. Kennedy. Why the difference?

I firmly believe that some men give way more readily under emotional stress for the same reason that some athletes are more injury prone than others. It is a question of constitutional difference, be it neuroamines in the one case or bones and cartilages in the other.

The human being is an infinitely complex creature, and his responses do not always follow form charts. The point is illustrated by still another famous patient. I refer to Edwin "Buzz" Aldrin, Jr., the second man to set foot on the moon.

If there is any least-likely habitat for depression, it is surely a spaceship capsule. Here, after all, are men thrice tested in the most rigorous fashion. They are selected in the first place because they stand out for their cool competence even in such company as professional test pilots. Second, they are subjected to the most exhaustive battery of physical and psychological examinations that medical science can devise. And finally they are wrung out in simulation flights while wired with electric sensors that pick up every flicker of heartbeat, blood pressure, brain wave, and nerve-end skin response.

Before they go up, we know them almost literally inside and out, or think we do, and their performance shows how good the screening is. When something goes wrong on that blazing rocket far out in space, we hear about it from a calm, controlled voice saying, "Houston, we have a problem."

Nonetheless, they are only human. When they splash down at flight's end, they frequently experience a depressive letdown, much as more ordinary men after any strenuous and demanding experience.

With Aldrin the letdown was more than that. He became suddenly terrified of the attention and demands that were thrust upon him. He has said since that he was on his way toward having "a good old American nervous breakdown."

It sounds, in fact, like a severe depressive episode, one serious enough that he was secretly hospitalized for a month. To his credit he has now disclosed it, saying that knowledge of his problem may help other people to face theirs.

If Aldrin was not immune to such attack, then who is? Perhaps no one. As with other ills, it strikes all manner of people, in all kinds of circumstances, and all we know for certain is that some individuals are somehow rendered more susceptible than others.

It is a most paradoxical ill. It wears the face of fear and yet it has nothing to do with lack of courage, for brave men have been attacked. It is also a disorder that subverts the brain and yet has nothing to do with lack of insight or understanding. Brilliant, insightful men have been its victim.

Interestingly enough, one of its historic victims was that great master of insight, Sigmund Freud. One episode seemed particularly significant to him because it occurred at a critical time, when he was writing his classic work, *The Interpretation of Dreams*. He recorded it thus:

> I am now experiencing myself all the things that as a third party I have witnessed going on in my patients—days when I slink about depressed because I have understood nothing of the day's dreams, fantasies or mood, and other days when a flash of lightning brings coherence into the picture, and what has gone before is revealed as preparation for the present.

He was so depressed at times that he tried cocaine, on which he was doing research, and widely recommended its use before it was realized how dangerous the drug could be.

The depression of William Pitt played a role in preventing the reconcilement of the American colonies to England [Kline, N. S., *British Journal of Psychiatry*, accepted as a monograph in preliminary form, publication scheduled for 1981/82].

Many creative artists have put their individual depressions to essentially the same use, working through it to glimpse some larger truth about the tragic side of human experience. Such insights are no less valid for being rooted in a biochemical accident. Some others arrive at insight through the equally accidental experience of surviving a war.

Depression is to its victims a kind of internal war, one all the more trying because each combatant feels condemned to fight it alone.

3

The Disorder: What Is It?

I'll change my state with any wretch,
Thou canst from gaol or dunghill fetch;
My pain's past cure, another hell,
I may not in this torment dwell.
Now desperate I hate my life,
Lend me a halter or a knife,
All my griefs to this are jolly,
Naught so damn'd as melancholy.
—ROBERT BURTON,
The Anatomy of Melancholy

THUS far in the discussion I have attempted to simplify matters by using depression in the most general meaning of the term. Some readers may have assumed that this is today a well-defined medical condition, one in which modern psychiatry has established firm guidelines on such questions as the diagnosis, classification, and general nature of the illness. Unfortunately it is not that clear cut and simple. Depression is still a mysterious affliction, and it presents many baffling questions.

If we could assemble a great conclave of psychiatrists, we would hear intense, sometimes furious, and often many-sided debates on all of the following questions:

Does depression arise from physical causes or psychological factors, or some combination of both?

Is it a single disease, or might it be two or more diseases masquerading behind a similar set of symptoms?

If it is two or more diseases, what are the major types?

Do the supposed different types arise from separate and quite different causes, or are they merely variations on a basic pattern? Do they respond to the same or different treatments?

On all these matters there are numerous theories that we shall explore shortly. For the moment let us merely accept the fact that there are broad disagreements as to the basic description of the illness. Beyond that, psychiatrists often disagree even on such matters as the diagnostic criteria and terms.

There is an immense medical literature devoted to the perplexing questions of terminology alone. To the casual reader the mere idea of sorting out the labels probably induces, if not depression, at least a mild ennui. For the depressed patient and his or her family, however, this is no small matter. Here, after all, is a person in pain and often in danger, heavily besieged by confusion and doubt. When he turns to medical science for help, he is not reassured to discover that his illness changes names almost as often as he changes doctors. In his frustration and despair he may conclude that we psychiatrists do not know what we are talking about.

At the risk of professional heresy I must concede my sympathy with such a complaint. This preoccupation with naming the condition is destructive. The arguments about categories are not relevant because decisions about what to do are based upon our knowledge of the patient and not upon a factor of largely theoretical concern. It is sufficient to recognize that an individual is depressed—and in what ways. We can, however, offer effective help. There are numerous conditions in medicine that we manage to treat quite successfully though we are still uncertain as to the basic nature of the illness.

Interestingly, most of the big questions about depression have arisen in the last twenty years. Before that most psychiatrists thought they knew. Recent scientific advances have so altered the picture, however, that we have been forced to rethink the whole matter, as has occurred periodically in the past. Previously we were accustomed to regard "mental" and "physical" ills as quite separate and different matters. Now, rather belatedly, we are again accepting the fact that the brain is involved and it is, after all, a physical organ. Like any other organ, it is subject to breakdown from purely physical reasons. Of course, mental breakdowns can occur also as a result of repressed and unresolved emotional conflicts. The great thrust in psychiatry today is the attempt to redefine the borderlines while integrating the old views and the new. The effort has necessarily produced much controversy, but the questioning spirit is a healthy sign, both for the psychiatric profession and for the patients we serve.

The intensity of current psychiatric debate reflects the fact that we are in the midst of an ongoing quest. There are few fields in medicine more alive with exploration and discovery. In the particular area of depression, every year produces dozens of new reports that range from psychological depth studies to biochemical analyses to statistical surveys. All this has inevitably produced an array of intriguing theories. By definition, however, a theory is not a proven fact. When all the facts are finally in, the need for theories will disappear. As the philosopher Leucippus wrote 2,000 years ago, "Where there is ignorance, theories abound."

The situation is analogous in many ways to a problem that confronted another branch of medicine in earlier times. It is worth a brief glance back at that page in medical history to obtain some perspective on the dilemmas of psychiatry today.

Until the latter half of the nineteenth century physicians simply did not know what caused many contagious diseases. Outbreaks came and went mysteriously, sometimes striking individuals at random, at other times devastating whole communities, and all for no apparent reason. The human mind abhors such uncertainty, however, and so the doctors constructed theories. For a long time one principal theory attributed many contagions to something called miasma, roughly defined as a deadly gas generated by putrefaction from swamps, rotting garbage heaps, and the like. Many people slept with their windows closed so that the miasma could not get in. The theory was logical enough, it just happened to be wrong, but it contributed, nonetheless, to some great advances in medicine. Physicians of the miasma school became crusaders for public health and led the early-day campaigns to clean up filthy, germ-ridden places.

In due course the miasmal doctrine was challenged by technological discovery. Science produced the microscope, and peering through it, physicians saw a world swarming with strange little organisms they called "animalcules." That, of course, led to another theory. This one happened to be essentially right, but there was a long period before anyone could prove it. In the interval the miasmal and animalcular theorists had at each other so hotly that they sometimes forgot how much they held in common.

The human element that distorts such scientific controversy is illustrated by an odd and touching story from the medical archives. During the late nineteenth century the role of bacteria was finally established, and science tracked down and identified the particular microorganism responsible for cholera. There remained one eminent physician who could not accept it. He was a grand old man of European medicine, a public-health pioneer who had devoted much of his life to fighting the terrible cholera outbreaks of his time. He was also a miasma advocate, and at an international medical convention he made a last stand for his theory. Mounting the rostrum, he brandished a beaker of water containing millions of cholera germs and then slowly, deliberately, he drank it to the last drop. So much, he said, for your damned bacteria!

Fortunately his immunity was strong. He survived the demonstration, as did the science of bacteriology and the important contributions of public hygiene.

I cite the incident as a cautionary tale for our times. I believe that psychiatry is now just beginning to emerge from its own miasmal era, and I think we must be willing to reexamine all the old theories in the light of new discoveries. Of course, the new theories must also be questioned rigorously, for the process of discovery is still far from complete. I expect that in the twenty-first century psychiatrists will look back on some of our present controversies in much the spirit that we view the old contagion disputes.

Happily, the depressive patient need not wait that long for effective relief. It happens quite often in medicine that we arrive at useful clinical procedures long before we have settled all the ultimate questions about the basic nature of the illness. Sometimes we hit on remedies through sheer luck or simple trial and error. A combination of those factors produced for depression a series of chemotherapy breakthroughs beginning about twenty-five years ago.

At first we used the new medicines empirically without knowing how or why they worked; they just did. Now we believe that we are beginning to unravel some of the mechanisms. It is to be hoped that this will lead us to even more effective measures of both prevention and cure. We have already reached the point where the condition is manageable for the great majority of patients.

Meanwhile, we continue to pursue the theoretical questions. The one quest, in fact, is closely intertwined with the other, for the more we learn of the disease, the better our chances to combat it. Now let us turn to the theories, to consider what is known, not known, and merely conjectured about the nature of this illness.

The first major question is whether depression consists of a single disease or, alternately, a number of different conditions concealed behind a superficial resemblance. Probably most psychiatrists today would agree that there are different kinds of depression, but we then proceed to disagree as to what types are chiefly involved. It is a complex question, and to follow it one must understand the general rules of medical evidence.

Ideally we like to identify a disease with a flat statement of cause and effect. If we can demonstrate that a specific medical condition arises from a particular cause —and only from that cause—then we think we know with what we are dealing. We can go on from there to an orderly and logical search for medical solutions. If we can't prove the cause, however, then we have to attempt an identification based on circumstantial evidence. We compare case histories, searching for some reliable pattern that marks the illness. Typical checkpoints include such matters as the type of persons who are either most subject or most immune, the circumstances surrounding the typical attacks, the pace and manner of onset, the common symptoms, the duration and course of the illness, and the response to treatment. If it appears that the cases all fall into a consistent, well-defined framework, then we can make at least a working assumption that it represents a specific condition.

The difficulty lies in that word "appears." Two quite different and entirely unrelated ills can produce symptoms so similar that to the untrained eye they are easily mistaken one for the other. Contrarily, two attacks of the same illness may not look alike at all because the symptoms may range all the way from very mild to extremely severe. The symptoms may also manifest themselves in quite different ways. The problem is further compounded by the fact that in depression many of the symptoms are highly subjective and thus susceptible to widely varying interpretations.

Faced with such problems, we might do well to simply admit that there are large gray areas on our diagnostic charts. In my judgment psychiatry quite often errs in the opposite direction, by attempting to define too precisely conditions that do not yield to an exact formula. There is a resulting tendency to make up new terms and even whole new diagnostic categories for cases that may well be merely variations on a general pattern. Fortunately the types of depression have little to do with the methods of treatment used and the effectiveness of results.

The lack of standard diagnostic criteria has long been recognized as a perplexing problem in psychiatric medicine. In the particular matter of depression both the American Psychiatric Association and the World Health Organization have attempted to resolve the dilemma by drawing up suggested guidelines for description and classification of the disease. The eventual ability to design exact categories may be useful, but fortunately it will serve primarily to improve upon an already effective capacity to treat the disorder.

I have said earlier that I believe psychiatry is still emerging from its miasmal stage, and the facts just cited constitute supporting evidence for that view. It is an interesting parallel that medicine had precisely the same problem in classifying contagious diseases in the old days when specific causes were not known. Physicians then often fell back on such vague designations as "swamp fever," and even when they began to sort out one fever from another, they were frequently misled by vagrant symptoms. Typhoid fever, for instance, sometimes looks a lot like malaria or cholera, though the three are very different ills.

Numerous other contagions can assume such diverse disguises as to deceive even the skilled observer if he must rely on symptoms alone. The epidemiologists never completely solved the problem until they were able to link each major contagious disease to a specific microorganism. But today, of course, it's no problem. If a physician suspects typhoid, he can extract a culture, send samples to any number of laboratories anywhere in the world, and get back the same answer every time. It's either typhoid or it's not; there is no ambiguity about the verdict and no room in the question for differences in individual opinion or national style.

I believe that someday we'll get to that kind of place with depression. I expect that we'll find a biochemical test or series of tests that will prove highly specific to a particular depressive condition. It may emerge as a single test indicating the presence of a single basic disorder. Or, more probably, it may prove to be several tests suggesting a group of abnormalities that meet along a common behavioral path. We don't know yet. When we do know, we won't have any trouble devising a system of classification and terminology that will convey the same precise meaning to all physicians all over the world.

We are now searching earnestly for such tests. At the Rockland Research Institute, Office of Mental Health, New York State Department of Mental Hygiene, where I am director, the investigations related to devising ways of diagnosing schizophrenia and depression consume a substantial part of an annual $4 million research budget. Other hospitals, foundations, and government agencies are working on the problem all around the world. The technical difficulties are extraordinarily intricate and complex, as was true in the earlier search for microorganisms, and we may well have to devise new kinds of apparatus and techniques before we can complete the task. We are still very much in the pioneer stage. Nevertheless, I am confident that we are on the right track, and I'm hopeful that we may even come up with the beginnings of a practical testing system soon.

Meanwhile, we have to make as much sense as we can of the classification systems that now exist. My own practical response is to await further evidence. I do distinguish between four types of the illness.

In my judgment the principal type is what used to be referred to as "endogenous" depression, the term meaning "to come from within." The present system prefers the terms "unipolar" and "bipolar." The unipolar patient has only depressions and when recovered returns to normal mood. The bipolar patient also has periods of euphoria ("highs") as well as episodes of depression. The term *affective* refers to emotional state whether depressed, normal, or elevated. Thus "bipolar affective disorder" (already in general use in England) is probably the best way to describe what used to be called manic-depressive psychosis. Neurotic depressions are those characterized by an excessive reaction to environmental misfortunes (e.g., death of spouse, loss of job), or arise from severe internal psychological conflict.

A purely physical type is "secondary" depression, occurring as a side effect of certain medicines, or as an accompaniment or a sequel to particular illnesses. It has symptoms quite similar to other depressions, but medically it presents much simpler problems.

Somewhere along the diagnostic borderline there occurs a schizo-affective disorder. That's a condition that presents mixed and confusing symptoms, resembling both schizophrenia and severe depression. In some rare cases it is difficult to distinguish between the two ills, but it is my general opinion that the schizophrenia label is overused. On occasion antidepressant drug therapy has been successful when used to treat patients previously diagnosed as schizophrenics.

So much for diagnostic classifications and terms. To the patient and his family it may seem a confusing clutter, but it all comes down to a few basic facts. A depressive illness is either bipolar (such as manic-depression) or unipolar (purely depressive). If it's a unipolar depression, it may result variously from biochemical disorder, neurosis, or the secondary effects of medication or illness.

Manic-depressive reactions offer the most dramatic symptoms. Sometimes the mood swings are so extreme that the patient seems to undergo a complete personality reversal between his high and low periods.

In the manic phase he is bursting with energy, full of plans and projects that he often pursues with reckless enthusiasm. If he's a stock market investor, he may suddenly abandon all caution and begin to plunge wildly. Or he may borrow to the hilt to finance some highly dubious business venture. Or then again he may desert his business, leave his family, and run off with his secretary. One very depressed patient arrived at my office for his first visit accompanied by three brothers, a sister, and a wife. When I discovered that he had been that way for almost a year, I asked why they hadn't sought treatment before then. They said he had been treated for depression once before and had gone directly into a manic state. He came from a very wealthy family, and the day he suddenly felt better he began making up for lost time by phoning various brokers he knew and buying almost half a million dollars' worth of stock. The oldest brother discovered what was happening by accident when he called one of the same brokers. He dashed home and found the patient totally high and almost out of touch with reality. He was able to cancel all the stock transactions, since they had all been made that day, but before submitting the patient for treatment he wanted me to guarantee that the patient wouldn't take off again in a similar fashion. Of course I couldn't make such a promise, but I did explain that I would give medications "to cover" in case this were to happen. The family was satisfied, and as they left the office I couldn't resist asking what had happened to the stock. It had skyrocketed, which proves, I guess, that even though someone is euphoric his intelligence, knowledge, and luck may remain intact even though his judgment (in buying such a large quantity) is bad.

Sometimes manic behavior becomes truly aberrant. While preparing this book, I read a newspaper account of a midwestern museum director who suddenly and unaccountably absconded with a suitcase full of stolen pictures. From a practical standpoint the crime didn't really make sense. One cannot diagnose on such evidence, of course, but what I suspect is a manic episode. Manics do take off, literally and figuratively. Trying to elicit from a depressed patient whether she had ever had a manic episode, I asked if she had ever spent more money than she really intended. Yes, a few years before, she had gone to Bloomingdale's department store for some dish towels and had spent six thousand dollars. I didn't need to ask further.

The opposite, depressive, pole is likely to present equal or even worse dangers. Aggressive action is replaced by extreme withdrawal, chronic excitement gives way to listless torpor, and in extreme cases the patient becomes unable to manage the simplest matters. In his despair he may ponder suicide. Indeed, he may attempt and even succeed in committing suicide if not properly and correctly watched.

Actually, there are three major types of persons who carry out suicidal acts: those who intend to kill themselves; those who hope and expect that the gesture will provoke sympathy, anger, or some other emotion from those learning of the act; and finally, those whose existence has become so harried that they simply must have some intermission even though it entails a risk of life. For this last group, medications are particularly effective. For the first group (those who wish to kill themselves, not because of the reality situation, but because they are so pathologically depressed) medications, by correcting the illness, restore the patient to a desire to live. The second group (those putting on an act) never really intend to do away with themselves, although occasionally they do succeed accidentally.

Typically, manic-depressive conditions are recurrent, cyclic illnesses. In my opinion they result from biochemical tides that rise and fall within the body, the onset of high and low periods being quite independent of other circumstances in the patient's life. Such highs and lows may occur in a variety of sequences, but one sees patients whose next episodes can be predicted quite accurately on the basis of their cyclic history. In some rare cases one can almost set one's watch by it, knowing that the next high tide of manic excitement or depression will sweep in within a particular hour on a given day. To me such cyclic occurrence seems clearly linked to a basic physical disorder. The biochemical involvement is further indicated by the fact that generally manic-depressives respond very well to drug therapy, and in many cases the medication either prevents or softens subsequent attacks.

Manic-depressive episodes often manifest themselves in ways so marked as to leave little room for diagnostic dispute. When we turn to depression, however, we encounter a far more elusive illness. The symptoms are more diffuse, the attack patterns more irregular, and the general course of the illness is more uncertain.

The classic depressive condition is a flat emotional response that blocks all expressions of pleasure. In particular cases it may descend into a deep, protracted gloom. Other indications that may or may not be present include guilt, anxiety, hostility, indecision, the inability to concentrate. There are also numerous physical effects—headaches, backaches, and the like—that sometimes confuse the picture.

The severity, duration, and general sequence of the attacks all vary widely. Some patients experience a depression as a single, isolated episode, and others are subject to recurrent bouts. Some come out of depression through spontaneous remission, while for others the condition hangs on indefinitely unless properly treated.

All this inevitably produces a good deal of medical debate over the nature of the illness. Indeed, there is only one area in which we are in general agreement. We now know that depression can appear as a secondary effect of certain drugs and virus infections.

Drugs that may induce secondary depression include certain agents, such as reserpine, used for treating high blood pressure, at times some of the hormones, and many sedatives. In some sensitive individuals it can also be triggered by oral contraceptives or certain antibacterial preparations used for treating infections. Such depressions can be painful and debilitating for patients already suffering from other ills, but medically the problem is not too difficult. Once the offending drug is identified, the condition can usually be cleared up quite quickly by changing the medication inducing the depression.

Drug-induced depressions seem logical enough to those of us who are biochemically oriented. Why virus infection should cause depression is more obscure, but it happens. Mononucleosis and infectious hepatitis are especially notorious for bringing depression in their wakes. Any virus infection, in fact, may induce depression, and it is quite common to feel "under the weather" for one or two months after the flu or even a virus type of gastrointestinal upset. In most cases the best antidote is to let nature take its healing course. Like the physical weakness that follows disease, the depression should be regarded as a disagreeable but temporary condition.

True depression is quite another matter. It requires treatment, and that brings us right back to the question of what kind of illness it is. I am convinced that it's usually a biochemical disorder, and I find that in most cases it responds well to drug therapy.

I believe that some cases probably do truly arise from a neurosis, but I consider these to be exceptional instances. I estimate neurotic depression to constitute a very small percentage of the truly severe cases.

The position just stated is, of course, not universally accepted. Some of my psychiatric colleagues would reverse the equation, ascribing all or almost all depressions to neurotic causes. The question is fundamental to one's whole approach to the disease, so let's look at both theories.

The familiar analytic view is that depression results from inverted hostility, an unresolved anger being turned inward against oneself. The source of such anger is sought most basically in the early relationships between parent and child.

One supposed mode of development is that a child somehow fails to receive from the parents the love and support it needs. The child resents this bitterly but cannot express it openly because of guilt and so turns the anger inward. In effect, the child enters into a kind of subconscious alliance with the parents, rejecting himself as he believes they reject him and forming toward himself feelings of inadequacy and unworthiness. Thus created is a pattern of responses that becomes deeply embedded in the individual's personality. He will be plunged into depression, so the theory goes, whenever some stress situation brings out his buried feelings of rejection and failure.

There are various elaborations on this theory. Thus the depressive individual is said to be one who is trapped in an early, oral stage of development. He has remained dependent on others for emotional support, just as he was once dependent on the mother for food. He is constantly seeking some reassurance for his fragile, ill-developed ego, and he lapses into depression when those around him fail to meet his endless, insatiable need. Again the root problem is presumed to be the fact that he is reliving over and over the anxiety created when he was denied proper support at a critical stage in his development.

I do not doubt that some neurosis arises in such fashion. I also do not doubt that many depressives have serious neurotic problems. In particular cases neurotic anxiety may even be a stress factor that contributes to the depressive breakdown. I remain quite skeptical, however, when it is cited as depression's most frequent cause.

My view is best expressed by way of analogy. If I were to tour a cardiac ward, I would expect to find there numerous patients who suffered from neurotic problems. With some, anxiety may have contributed to the attack, though just how much is problematical. We could go out on the street and find others even more neurotic who didn't have heart attacks. Moreover, beyond neurosis, we'd find that heart attacks happen to all kinds of people under all kinds of circumstances. Some get heart attacks while shoveling snow or sprinting for a train. But some others risk physical strain and don't get heart attacks. And there are a good many who are suddenly stricken in the midst of a

placid day, without apparent relationship to any unusual physical or emotional stress.

When we run the cardiac patients through an EKG
and other tests, we find just one thing they all have in
common. All suffered a specific physical breakdown
in the heart itself or its supporting blood vessels. That's
the fundamental cause of the heart attack. As to other
factors, stress certainly plays a role, but the strength
or weakness of the heart itself is often more decisive.
All life is a stress, and individual hearts vary widely in
ability to carry the load.

The brain, too, is a physical system and is subject
to breakdown. In a later chapter we'll examine the
particular biochemical failures that appear to cause
depression. Suffice it to say here that in any given case
an overload of emotional stress may or may not be a
significant contributing factor.

I say "may or may not" because there is simply no
one-to-one relationship between the type and degree of
stress and the type and degree of emotional breakdown.
Depression may occur, in fact, in three separate and
entirely different emotional settings.

Consider first a neurotic. We'll call him John. He
is burdened with anxieties and insecurities that seem
clearly a product of emotional conflict. In effect, he
never successfully shed his security blanket, and thirty
or forty years later he is still grasping for all kinds of
inappropriate support. We can predict easily enough
that the steady, insistent pressure of such anxiety will
take an emotional toll. What we can't predict at all
is the behavioral outcome. Not all neurotics become
depressives. Some are habitually aggressive and hyperactive. There are differences, moreover, not just in the
kinds of neurotic reaction but in the degree. Some
neurotics are so overwhelmed by anxiety that they become functionally crippled. Others manage to contain the threat and live quite normal lives. Some even
channel their emotional turmoil into quite productive
outlets. Why the difference?

One can construct elaborate psychological rationales,

but I am convinced that much of the answer lies in the fact that individuals vary widely in their constitutional ability to absorb or handle emotional stress. Beyond that, there is the fact that depression often occurs in cases where marked neurosis is simply not an important factor. In my practice I judge that to be the case more often than not. Obviously, then, we must look elsewhere for the basic cause.

There is probably a biological predisposition, some factor that provokes a particular individual to respond to stress with depression. As indicated elsewhere, we have some clues as to how persons who will become depressed under pressure differ biochemically even when they are not in an actual depression. Such tests are not yet well enough established to be of practical use, but a beginning has been made.

Without a great deal of knowledge it is difficult to tell whether John is a neurotic who suffers from a common form of depression that strikes neurotics and non-neurotics alike or whether the depression is part of the neurosis itself. The attempts to list the characteristics of true neurotic depression as opposed to the types in which there is a strong physiological element have not, in my estimation, been too successful. A skilled clinician can usually, but not always, distinguish between the types, but it is on the basis of his own intuition or reaction to a set of behavior patterns, emotional responses, and thought processes that are not too clearly spelled out as yet.

Let us consider now a second kind of emotional stress, one in which the pressures arise not from neurotic causes but from the actual circumstances of life. Take the case of a woman we'll call Sue. She was married at nineteen and proceeded to have four babies in rather rapid succession. In her mid-twenties she finds herself tired, harried, beset by problems and demands that severely tax her physical and emotional capacities. Her husband is heavily taxed, too, in his efforts to support the growing brood. The two of them are so enmeshed in the daily struggle that they have little time or energy for the loving attentions that were once so important to the marriage. Sue feels that loss and feels, too, the rapid fading of her youth. She bottles up the frustration and anxiety, and then one day the dam bursts. Some trivial little accident results in a cracked dish and she breaks down and weeps. It is not surprising. She is overloaded and she has, so to speak, just blown a fuse. She is depressed.

Some people are plunged into severe depressive episodes by that kind of pressure. Some others manage it remarkably well, exhibiting, to be sure, some signs of stress but generally maintaining a healthy balance. It is again a matter of individual ability to absorb the strain. The surprising fact is that there is only a minor correlation between life circumstances and the degree and frequency of depressive breakdowns.

Certainly life circumstances can provoke severe depression. In the case of Sue the question is how long the reaction lasts. There is no absolute figure. Surely a few hours would be one thing, whereas months of severe depression with immobilization would be quite different.

If the depression did persist for several months, we would almost certainly eventually conclude that Sue was a lot more neurotic than appeared on the surface, and that she was one of the relatively rare cases of true neurotic depression or, more likely, that the depression was of the usual type and by coincidence appeared at a time when there was "justification" for it. In the case of John, there was internal stress. With Sue the reason for the depression appears—and note that I use the word "appears"—to be external stress.

We turn now to a third case we'll call Mary. There is nothing particularly remarkable about either her life situation or her neurotic responses. And she may have to cope with some day-to-day pressures and problems, but again that is the common lot. The uncommon factor in Mary is an aberrant, totally inappropriate response. She suffers frequent, prolonged depressions under circumstances that might prompt others to mere worry or concern. I encounter this type of patient much more often than the other two.

In the hypothetical instances just cited I have separated the patients into three distinct and separate categories, deliberately oversimplifying in order to make a point. There was John, whose problems were presented as almost wholly neurotic. There was Sue, responding to entirely circumstantial stress. And there was Mary, conveniently isolated from either sphere. In actual medical practice, as in life generally, things are often not that clear cut. All of us suffer in some degree from subconscious tensions, and certainly all of us encounter real problems in the course of life. Often the biological, neurotic, and existential elements weave in and out across shadowed borderlines.

Moreover, the severity of any particular pressure is obviously not the same for every person. One individual might accept business or professional setbacks with relative equanimity and be devastated by a marriage or family problem. With another individual it might be just the opposite. When we deal with human beings, we cannot pretend to measure either stress loads or breaking points with the precision an engineer applies to a steel beam. Nonetheless, and with all exceptions duly noted, John, Sue, and Mary do represent valid archetypes of depressive patients. Depression may occur under existential stress, and it may not. It may also occur, and often does, without any important relationship to obvious pressure. Once we are able to identify the biological element,* we should be in a much better position to clarify the role of various pressures (e.g. fatigue, malnutrition, job loss, divorce, etc.) in bringing on the depression, the types of individuals who are depression prone, and even which

* Carroll describes the overnight dexamethasone suppression test, which measures the hormone cortisol. He found that patients with endogenous (biological) depression had abnormally high levels. As of early 1981 the test is still not specific, since it identifies only about half of the subjects but even that is very exciting.

symptoms are most likely to go with which type of depression.

Why should the emotional system break down if there is no particular stress? I would turn the question around and ask, why not? We accept readily enough the fact of functional deficiency in other spheres. If we meet a man with defective eyesight, we do not assume automatically that he has subjected his eyes to unusual strain or, alternately, that he is suffering from some form of hysterical blindness. Either of those explanations may apply to a particular case, but the more probable cause is some mechanical defect in the optic system. The same holds true for malfunctions of the heart, lungs, liver, kidneys, blood vessels, and all the supporting apparatus. Nature operates on a rather broad tolerance for error and may bestow on us disorders large or small in any of the vital life-support systems. Why should we assume that there is a special exception for the apparatus that regulates emotional response?

Of course, emotion is not just a matter of apparatus. It involves deeply personal reactions to all things in life that we find most moving, most poignant, most joyous or terrible. It embraces our memories of what we have been, our hopes of what we may become, our view of life itself, and the value we place on our own existence. There are those who find it appalling, perhaps almost unthinkable, that so fundamental a part of the human spirit might be deranged by a random "mechanical" accident. And yet, that risk is a matter of common knowledge in another closely related area. Consider what can happen in the case of a stroke. A brilliant mind—a brain in fact as well as in metaphor—can be profoundly changed and damaged by the constriction of a blood vessel that is a mere tube to convey nourishment and carry off waste. All of existence depends in fact on quite delicate and fragile arrangements of nature.

We are just beginning to understand the biochemical networks that play crucial roles in regulating both thought and emotion. Much still remains to be learned, but we know already that the systems are extraordinarily complicated and delicate. When we examine these systems closely, there is no cause for wonder that they sometimes malfunction. The wonder really is that anything so complex and intricate could prove so durable and serve so well.

4

In Search of Causes—
A Medical Detective Story

*He was systematical, and, like all systematic rea-
soners, he would move both heaven and earth, and
twist and torture everything in nature to support his
hypothesis.*

—LAURENCE STERNE, *Tristram Shandy*

MEDICAL research is a lot like detective work. It involves a great deal of patient plodding, collecting facts,
and checking small details that may or may not fit a
suspected pattern. Sometimes we don't even have a
decent theory to go on, and we are reduced to gather-
ing random information in the hope that if we learn
enough, the pieces will begin to fit. And then, occasionally, we stumble onto something quite unexpected
that breaks a case wide open. One of those instances
occurred some twenty-five years ago, when an accidental discovery helped to usher in a new era of psychiatry.

At the time, science had just begun to explore the
basic mechanisms of brain chemistry. It appeared that
an immense amount of work lay ahead before we could
establish the cause of particular malfunctions, let alone
find remedies. And then suddenly we made a drug
discovery that jumped over all the intervening steps of
investigation. This chapter is written for those interested in the biochemistry involved. Skipping it will not
spoil the "story."

The drug was reserpine, and curiously enough, it
derived from the tribal medicine of ancient witch

doctors. Through chance circumstances I played a pioneer role in its modern development. It was my peculiar distinction to "discover" a drug that was 2,000 years old.

I would be pleased to say that I tracked down this long-neglected drug through historical research. Or, alternately, that I deduced its properties by shrewd chemical analysis. Or even that I just hit on it by some brilliant intuitive hunch. In fact, however, it was none of these. It was mostly luck.

The discovery fell in my lap in quasi-accidental fashion, and the chief credit I can claim is that I was able to recognize an important event when I saw it happen. Probably my willingness to recognize it had something to do with my educational background. I came to medicine by a roundabout route, taking up psychiatry after earlier interests in English, philosophy, and psychology, and I had no particular commitment to the established dogmas of my profession. Perhaps also my role in the discovery had something to do with personal style. I can capsule that aspect by explaining that I paid my way through medical school in part by playing the horses. It was an unorthodox training for later scientific research, but still it had its merits; it taught one to study the form charts closely while remaining ever mindful that now and then a long shot comes in. When I encountered reserpine years later it was rated as a very long shot indeed, but when I saw the first real clinical trial run I knew we had a big winner. I was prepared, if necessary, to back that judgment by betting my professional reputation.

Reserpine is a drug extracted from *Rauwolfia serpentina,* a plant that grows wild in the hill country of India and in many other parts of the world. The plant root bears a striking resemblance to a snake—hence the name *serpentina*—and it is the root that provides the active pharmacological ingredients. Its medicinal powers were chronicled in ancient Sanskrit and Hindu manuscripts, and it has ever since been used by the native healers of the region.

Like many folk medicines, it is wrapped in myth and associated with magic powers. One legend asserts that the mongoose chews the root to gain strength and courage against the cobra. In Hindu medicine it was used to treat a long list of ills including snakebite, fever, stomach ulcers, high blood pressure, and complications of pregnancy. It was noted especially for its soothing effects and so was employed also as a sleeping potion and as a remedy to quiet crying infants. And finally, its calming powers proved so great that it was sometimes used as a treatment for the insane.

At first glance it might seem improbably romantic that such a witch-doctor potion should bob up in the twentieth century to change the course of psychiatric history. Romantic or not, however, that is the way it happened, and on closer inspection, it is not really so improbable. Nature operates a vast, rich, endlessly creative chemical laboratory, and among the many millions of plant species there occurs every now and then some particular type that produces powerful effects. Early men discovered such plants by sheer trial and error, testing everything they found for possible value as food, medicine, or magic brew. Thus they found and used a long list of potent botanical drugs.

It is instructive to glance briefly at Western medicine's historic attitude toward such jungle concoctions. In general our medical forebears accepted quite readily the native remedies that would heal a wound or reduce a fever. They balked, however, when confronted with anything that seemed to touch the mind or spirit. The point is illustrated by two Indian plant medicines that the Spanish found when they came to South America.

One medicine was the bark of the cinchona tree, used by the Indians to treat malaria. The Spanish found it highly effective, and the Jesuit missionaries spread the use of it wherever they traveled. It became known all over Europe as "Jesuit's bark." In the nineteenth century a chemist extracted the active ingredient and came up with quinine. It was one of the most important medical discoveries of the era, and it was borrowed unabashedly from the empirical wisdom of native healers.

The other drug was cocaine, brewed from the leaves of the coca tree. The Indians used it variously as a mood drug, as a stimulant and energizer for periods of sustained labor, and as an anesthetic. One ancient Indian sculpture shows a primitive surgeon opening a patient's skull with a stone chisel while leaning over to spit pain-deadening coca-leaf juice into the cranial incision.

It was, in fact, a far more effective anesthetic than anything then known to the West. Unfortunately it was also associated with mystical rites that the Spanish saw as dark magic and demon worship. As a result, they would not even consider its medical applications. In 1567 a council of bishops declared that all uses of the drug were contrary to dogma, and two years later Spain's King Philip II issued a royal decree stating that cocaine's pharmacologic effects simply did not exist. All evidence to the contrary was dismissed as being "merely the illusions of the devil." When the Spanish found that the natives would not or could not work without coca leaves, they rescinded their prohibition. However, another 300 years passed before Europe accepted the fact that it was a powerful though dangerous drug that could be used for either good or ill.

Oddly enough, when cocaine was finally "discovered" by Europe, it briefly became a medical fad. In the late nineteenth century it was hailed as a cure-all for nearly all human ills.

One of those caught up in the rash enthusiasm was Sigmund Freud. For about three years he regularly dosed himself with cocaine to ward off depression and combat fatigue. He found the results "magical" and enthusiastically recommended the drug for a medical friend who had become a morphine addict because of a chronic pain condition. Instead of curing the morphine addiction, as Freud claimed in a hastily published paper, the patient became dependent on both drugs. Freud was horrified at his inadvertent part in the affair. Thereafter he opposed not only cocaine but also any other drug that affected mental processes. When he was dying of cancer, he refused all sedation, saying he would rather endure physical agony than blunt the control of his mind. The choice was both heroic and foolish, and it had some unfortunate consequences. It probably reinforced in psychiatry certain almost mystical taboos that were already embedded in Western medicine.

In such a climate of medical opinion it was easy enough to ignore a drug like rauwolfia. Psychiatrists were certain that where mood drugs existed at all, they were merely narcotics or sedatives, generally harmful in action, and of no possible value in treating emotional ills. If the healers of India thought otherwise, that was just another curious aspect of the exotic East. And if sometimes those healers seemed to get results that, too, was easily explained. It merely illustrated how susceptible people are to the power of suggestion. Rauwolfia in particular was wonderfully adapted to that explanation. Its appearance evoked the snake—a powerful magic symbol in almost every culture—and snake references were thickly intertwined in its legend and lore. No wonder the native healers prescribed it, and no doubt they achieved excellent results when they applied it to hypochondriacs and those suffering from a momentary touch of hysteria. The explanation was so complete and so convincing that it seemed pointless to inquire further. Thus it was that generations of British doctors came and went through colonial India and no one thought to test the properties of the native remedy. Or, at least, if some did think of it, they were careful to keep such vagrant notions to themselves. One can imagine the raised eyebrows at the officers' club if an army doctor had suggested that India's folk medicine just might be 2,000 years ahead of the West in treating insanity.

The first break in such resistance appeared in 1931 when Drs. G. Sen and K. C. Bose published a medical paper claiming successful rauwolfia treatments of several violently disturbed patients. They reported that in some cases the "senses are restored within a week though the patient may show some mental aberrations." It created scarcely a ripple of reaction, but still the drug's existence was now a matter of medical record. The next twenty years brought a trickle of other accounts, many of them by Western-trained Indian physicians who helped to bridge the medical gap between the two cultures. Names such as Siddiqui, Chopra, Gupta, Chakràvarti, and Kohali appear as contributors to these pioneer reports, along with such British and American physicians as Arnold, Wilkins, and Judson.

By the early 1950's there was a small but growing medical literature attesting promising Rauwolfia experiments with patients suffering from a variety of psychiatric disorders. The evidence fell short of conclusive, however, and the papers appeared mostly in the back pages of obscure journals. To the extent that the psychiatric profession took note at all it greeted the claims with profound skepticism.

Fortunately the Rauwolfia experimenters also recorded some lesser virtues of the drug. It was an effective sedative and appeared to have particular value in treating hypertension. That sort of claim seemed a good deal more probable to Western observers, and a few pharmaceutical companies began to display a mild interest. Such were the circumstances in 1953 when I agreed to give Rauwolfia to a group of hospitalized patients.

I got into it in the most accidental way. As a mental-hospital research director I was involved in other, quite unrelated inquiries, and I badly needed a $500 piece of laboratory apparatus. There was no money for it in the hospital budget, and in those days you had to hustle to raise a $500 grant from outside sources. So, I hustled. I got in touch with a friend who was medical director at Squibb, and I asked him if the two of us couldn't think up some passable excuse for obtaining an equipment gift from his company. My friend was obliging; his firm was then testing Rauwolfia for the treatment of high blood pressure, and we decided that the drug's alleged psychoactive qualities warranted additional trials in a psychiatric hospital.

On looking back, I find that my first view of the project was pretty cautious. I was then chiefly concerned with the problem of schizophrenia, but I didn't really expect any big breakthrough on that. When I wrote my first Rauwolfia report, I took note of the alleged schizophrenia cures, assessed the various doubts and objections, and then prudently qualified the scope of my own investigation. I have that twenty-eight-year-old paper before me as I recall the event, and it is interesting to see how carefully I hedged the bet. My introductory report read as follows:

> We felt that there was not sufficient evidence to undertake a large scale investigation of the effectiveness of Rauwolfia as a treatment for schizophrenia. There was both clinical and experimental evidence, however, that Rauwolfia had marked sedative properties. There was also strong evidence that Rauwolfia altered psychic states, even if its effect on schizophrenia was somewhat questionable. We, therefore, designed an experiment to evaluate the sedative action of the drug, feeling certain that if any schizophrenics were cured in the course of the research we should soon hear about it.

In a manner of speaking, we were setting sail to explore a small island, and if it just happened to be the tip of a psychiatric new world, why, we'd claim it.

As a preliminary step four assistants and I took the drug for several weeks to test for safety. We tried both a preparation made from the plant root and a refined alkaloid extract called reserpine, which had been isolated in the interim by the CIBA pharmaceutical company. When we were reasonably sure that it would have no serious ill effects, we began a small trial with four patients. Two of them were schizophrenics and two were manic-depressives. The first results were not at all remarkable. There was clearly some sedative effect, but aside from becoming a little quieter, the patients showed no marked behavior change.

At the next stage we enlarged the experiment to some 700 patients, taking in a broad range of cases from schizophrenics to psychoneurotics, and we started to increase the doses a bit at a time. Now some intriguing things began to happen. We found that in some cases the drug did affect behavior patterns.

One of the patients studied in my private practice was a neophyte salesman who was so bound up by anxiety that he couldn't call on his customers. He hid out in movie theaters day after day in order to spare himself the humiliation of being turned down on an attempted sale. He knew that neglect of his job would catch up with him pretty fast, and that only increased his anxiety, but he couldn't force himself out of the self-defeating pattern.

Under Rauwolfia medication he got the tension under manageable control and began to function. He wasn't transformed suddenly into a successful salesman—indeed he was probably ill-suited for that calling—but at least he was able to get out on the street now and find out whether he could make sales or not.

Another anxious patient was a young attorney who seemed to be forever pleading guilty to his own abject existence. His wife bullied him unmercifully, and he was so timid and browbeaten that he would eat something he didn't want rather than inform a waitress that she had brought him the wrong order.

The drug treatment released him from his emotional handcuffs, and he asserted himself by throwing a dish of tomatoes at his nagging wife. I don't know what that did for the marriage, but for him it was a healthy gesture.

There were other cases of a similar nature. What

intrigued us most was a fascinating paradox—the drug was clearly a sedative, and yet its practical effect was to make some patients more active. Apparently the sedation was confined to particular centers in the nervous system, damping down anxiety reactions without impairing other responses. In the early trials, however, that kind of result was limited to patients who suffered from fairly mild disturbance. We still weren't reaching the severe cases. Accordingly, we decided to be a bit more cautiously bold with a psychotic patient. Our plan was to administer a larger dose of the concentrated reserpine extract, injecting it directly into the muscles for maximum effect. I was sufficiently uncertain about it to invite Dr. Henry Brill, the deputy commissioner of the New York State Department of Mental Hygiene, to sit in as witness to the trial.

The patient was a woman who would be described in popular parlance as a "raving maniac." She did, in fact, rave incessantly. She believed that she was burning in hell, and she cried out at the torments that demons inflicted on her body and soul. In the presence of Dr. Brill, I injected her with what was then considered a large dose of reserpine. Then we sat back and waited.

I was torn between anticipation and doubt. The drug had shown surprising promise, but what we were reaching for now was something very far out, and I really didn't know what to expect. Over the next hour all those doubts were swept away by an astonishing transformation in the patient. Visibly and measurably, the mania began to ebb away. She was not suddenly cured of her delusion, but the terror had gone out of it. One had to question her closely now to draw out of her the fact that she still thought she was in Hades. And over the days that followed, the delusion itself began to fade as we continued the drug treatments.

We repeated the treatment with two other psychotics and the results were much the same. Then we published the findings and the storm broke. There was a large and adamant body of theoretical opinion that held that such a drug simply could not exist. So intense were the feelings that some good friends and respected colleagues took me aside to warn me that I was making a fool of myself. I was told that if I persisted in pursuing such an eccentric course, it could jeopardize my career.

Such warnings, of course, were both well meaning and sincerely motivated. They came from men who believed that drug treatment of mental disturbance was, by definition, a dangerous quackery.

I had not set out to make so controversial a discovery—indeed I had more or less stumbled upon it—and if I can claim any particular credit, it was simply that I did persist. The judgment was later vindicated by the course of events. Reserpine proved an enormously important drug in itself, and it stimulated a massive search for other so-called psychotropic drugs. The almost simultaneous discovery in France of chlorpromazine, with similar chemical effects, lent enormous support to acceptance of the chemical approach to mental illness. Today there is a great variety of such medications, and they account for approximately one third of all current drug prescriptions in the United States.

The effect on patient treatment was truly revolutionary. A before-and-after comparison of mental-hospital case loads reveals that drug therapy allowed hundreds of thousands of patients to leave the institutions and return to relatively normal lives. For those who remained under hospital care it permitted in most cases a far more tolerable existence. The locked cells and straitjackets of the past have been almost entirely discarded, since the violent behavior that necessitated their use now occurs only rarely.

This in turn brought about the beginning of a second revolution, which is still continuing. Patients were no longer regarded as subhuman or inhuman. More "nice people" became involved with patient care. Because they were treated in this manner—that is, given medications that relieved many of the underlying symptoms, and then dealt with more like patients with physical diseases—they responded well. This second revolution still has a way to go.

Still other benefits have accrued to hundreds of thousands who are not sick enough to require hospitalization and yet suffer from emotional disturbance. Depression victims have benefited especially from the new therapy. Later in this account I will describe particular antidepressant drugs that developed out of a great research thrust in this field.

The ultimate benefits are still to come. When we discovered this old snakeroot remedy, it was a curious phenomenon, something we hit on by chance and used empirically without having any idea of how or why it worked. Later, as we explored the mechanisms, we found strong evidence that the drug interacts with chemicals produced in the body itself for the purpose of regulating nerve impulses. We have not yet proved how this relates to mental and emotional states, but we think we are getting pretty close. If we can trace the exact mechanisms, then we will be on the threshold of still greater advances in both treatment and prevention of psychological disorders.

The great breakthroughs in drug therapy do not render obsolete the old analytic techniques of psychotherapy. On the contrary, the new drugs have greatly extended the range of the classical treatment. One really cannot analyze or even counsel a patient who is seized by wild delirium or frozen in deep, trancelike withdrawal. Even the lesser disturbances of the typical depression can render a patient highly intractable to treatment that requires enough psychic energy to bring about change. Drug therapy breaks through such resistance and allows the analyst to help patients he could not reach before.

Many medical psychotherapists now employ drug therapy but regard it as a kind of psychiatric first aid. They acknowledge that it controls symptoms but believe that the treatment is not complete until the psychiatrist has rooted out the underlying emotional causes. There are others of us who believe that in many cases the underlying cause is primarily a physical malfunction that the drugs correct. It is a disagreement that the profession has now learned to accommodate while seeking to expand our knowledge of both aspects of the problem.

On both the psychologic and biochemical fronts we may yet have much to learn. The recent years have brought other research that suggests that whatever the mechanisms, there may be numerous routes to emotional breakdown.

In one intriguing experiment the neurophysiologist Dr. John Lilly demonstrated that mere isolation and boredom can have effects as devastating as a hallucinogenic drug or a psychotic seizure. Dr. Lilly put on a blacked-out breathing mask and lay submerged for three hours in a tank of warm water. At first he floated pleasantly as though on a cloud. Then panic crowded in on him, he felt the conscious control of his mind slipping away step by step, and finally he was overwhelmed by vivid and terrifying three-dimensional hallucinations. And all this because for three brief hours he had shut himself off from the usual busy flow of sights, sounds, and perceptions to which his nervous system was attuned.

In a less severe trial of the same type some college students were offered twenty dollars apiece to shed all work and worry and just lie in bed for twenty-four hours. The experimental conditions required them to wear goggles that masked the light, and cuffs that deprived them of touch. About fifty student volunteers signed up. They thought it would be a cinch—a bit boring perhaps but an easy way to pick up a little spending money while catching up on their sleep. In fact, it proved an ordeal. Nearly all gave up before the experiment ended, and one fourth of them suffered sensory disturbances and hallucinations comparable to the effects of mescaline. Mescaline is an active ingredient of the peyote plant used for religious purposes by many American Indians.

The experiments are interesting because they add a new dimension to the factor of psychologic stress. In searching for stress causes, we tend to think in terms of positive force, as in particular events that create a trauma. The evidence now indicates that stress can also be a negative event, a nonhappening, occurring through the mere absence of normal stimuli and responses. To put the matter simply, we know that the muscular system improves with healthy exercise but wastes away with disuse. It may be that similar principles apply to the neurological system, which regulates both sensory perceptions and emotional response. If the outer world does not supply stimulation, the inner world makes up its own.

If such is the case, then convicts who speak of going "stir crazy" would appear to be using an apt expression. So, too, the alienated youth, slack-jawed and droopy-eyed, who talks of being "turned off." One would seek social and psychological reasons as to why the youth is alienated, but what I am suggesting here is that a mental and emotional attitude of alienation may set in motion a chain of neurological consequences. Habitual boredom may descend into profound depression if postures of passive withdrawal are carried too far.

The question is worth looking into because there are millions of people who in one way or another are constrained or imprisoned by the circumstances of their life. The blind, the deaf, the bedridden invalids, and the aged who sit alone in furnished rooms are all deprived of the normal flow of stimulation. We need to know a lot more about both the psychological problems involved and the biochemical changes that may result.

There seems little question that particular animals may become "depressed" at the loss of their masters, but the occurrence of similar behavior in other animals is extremely rare. Despite considerable effort, we have been unable to create satisfactory animal models of depression. Perhaps the biological equivalent shows itself in other ways. One of the characteristics of depression is the concern that it will go on and on indefinitely. Concern for the future requires not only consciousness but also self-consciousness, which is perhaps one of the reasons why depression as we know it seems largely limited to humans. Also typical is rumination about the past, so that to some degree depression and those parts of the psyche and possibly the brain itself that are involved with time may be the crucial ones.

Some studies show that brain-chemistry changes may well occur as part of a conditioned reaction to protracted stress. One interesting example emerged from a series of animal experiments that were specifically designed to induce depressive behavior patterns.

The experiment began with a familiar observation on the way animals learn to avoid or manage a painful experience. In a typical demonstration a rat is placed in a specially contrived cage, is there given a mild electric shock, and is allowed to flail around until it touches a bar or crosses a barrier that turns off the irritating current.

In the usual reaction the laboratory animal thrashes around in a random manner until it accidentally achieves relief. On subsequent exposures the rat continues to flail around, but it obtains relief a little quicker each time, and eventually it learns to perform almost immediately the action that turns off the current. Thus obviously—and whatever the "mental process" involved—the rat does learn in rudimentary ways to control its environment.

The question then arises, what happens if the control efforts don't work? A researcher tackled that by rigging the cage so that random electric shocks were administered no matter what the rat did. The animals at first reacted just like the others, frantically thrashing around, attempting to escape. The efforts grew progressively more feeble, however, and after a while they submitted passively, lying there silently. They had acquired what the researcher called "learned helplessness," and its manifestations correspond closely to depressive behavior patterns. Even when not experiencing the shocks, they were torpid and listless, even losing interest in food and sex.

The researcher concluded that the rats were demoralized not by the painful experience itself but rather by repeated lessons that they could not escape their unhappy fate. Moreover, they tended to become fixed in that response. When the experimental conditions were changed, the rats were very slow to discover that they could now control the shock. The researcher would drag them through the motions, showing them how to turn off the current, but still they lay there silently, caught in a trap of their previous conditioning. A parallel was drawn with human depressives who regard themselves as born losers, reacting to a history of past failures in a way that perpetuates the misery.

Still another researcher now took up the subject and repeated the experiment with new rats. He obtained essentially the same results, but he went a step further. After inducing chronic-depressionlike reactions in the rats, he performed autopsies on them and found abnormally low levels of norepinephrine, a body chemical that serves transmission functions in the central nervous system. It was particularly interesting because it cross-checked with other evidence that makes norepinephrine deficiency one of the prime suspects in the biochemistry of depression. I will describe the supposed mechanism in the next chapter, but the point I want to make here is that severe and protracted stress may well leave a kind of biochemical scar.

If this is true, then physical repair through drug therapy is probably useful even in cases in which the original problem was primarily psychological. By the same token, of course, drug therapy alone will not suffice if the patient has acquired fixed psychologic attitudes that predispose toward a continued depressive reaction. In such instances rival theories give way to complementary insights, and both contribute to a cure.

Finally there are those animal experiments that suggest powerfully that biochemical malfunction can serve as an overriding cause when other factors are not present in any significant way. By the use of both drugs and electrical stimulation we can investigate brain processes, producing remarkable behavior changes. It is important to add that we do not merely tamper at random. Rather we direct the experiments to specific mechanisms, attempting to exaggerate or minimize natural processes in order to observe the course of resulting malfunction. The results are often quite dramatic. I have seen a cat cower submissively before a mouse, the sole cause being a drug calculated to suppress certain brain-chemical functions.

The case is further buttressed by the fact that the diverse chemical and electrical experiments yield to a common interpretation. We believe that a prime function of the biochemical system is to regulate electrical impulses that in turn activate nerve-cell responses. Thus it makes sense that intervention could be accomplished by either the one method or the other.

There have been innumerable such experiments, but I'll cite just one more that especially intrigued me. This one employed an electrical signal to reverse an ingrained, apparently instinctual pattern of animal response. The animals involved were monkeys of a species that has developed a highly structured power system in their relationships with one another. Specifically, one monkey asserts himself as ruler, proves his claim in combat if necessary, and thereafter claims royal prerogatives in matters ranging from a preferred perch to first choice of a desirable mate.

The other monkeys tamely submit, bowing and scraping, actually bending over to display their buttocks in placating gestures. All this is their natural and ordinary behavior, presumably developed over thousands of years. It became subject to instant change, however, when an experimenter implanted an electrode in the brain of a submissive monkey. The device possessed a remote control, allowing an impulse to be switched on or off in a brain site that controls expressions of aggression and rage.

Thereafter when the experimenter pressed the switch, the submissive monkey would fly from his perch, chattering and screaming, swarming over the surprised boss monkey to cuff him around. The aggression was always directed at the same object and always began and ended precisely on the electric signal. A flick of the switch ignited ferocious challenge in the monkey's brain; at another flick of the switch he retired immediately to his corner and resumed the humble, submissive mien of a Caspar Milquetoast.

The fact that aggression can be so stimulated is no longer a novel finding. What interested me was the other side of the matter, an aspect that Sherlock Holmes would have called the clue of the dog that didn't bark in the night. Or in this case, the clue of the monkey that didn't normally assert itself. What are the mechanisms of such habitual submission, and what might that suggest about the nature of depressive reactions?

I'll offer a tentative conclusion. The natural behavior of the monkeys may exhibit merely a stylized and highly specialized expression of aggression-submission patterns that serve necessary functions for both animals and men.

Let's take aggression first. The boss monkey's habitual aggressions are obviously highly functional for him, but beyond that some measure of aggressive instinct is probably necessary for all of the higher life forms. Without it we could not face challenge and conflict, and we would never have survived the long evolutionary struggle. The human species, of course, is notably well equipped in this area. We have aggressions to spare, and it is provided for in our very glands. The adrenal glands, which produce adrenalin, are psychic energizers of the first order, providing us with massive doses of emotion and energy when we confront a danger.

Now consider that complex of depressive reactions

that is bound up in such responses as submission, passivity, withdrawal. That, too, at times can be highly functional. In the case of the subordinate monkey it saves him from being beaten up every time he challenges the powerful and dominant head of the band. For the rats in the shock cage one can also see a survival value; if they really are trapped and helpless, then at least they conserve energy by ceasing to struggle. Similarly, a man imprisoned for many years may fare better if he resigns himself rather than pace the cage and beat his fists against the wall. In a larger sense many of us may feel imprisoned at times by circumstances we can neither overcome nor escape; in such situations some damping down of emotional response may well serve as a protective device.

Such a rationale would explain why depressive mechanisms exist in the biochemical system. They may have evolved because they were needed as a valuable counterbalance in a functioning whole. They are probably linked to the proper and healthy expression of such emotions as grief, sadness, and resignation. But they can also malfunction, creating exaggerated and aberrant response, to cause the disorder we call depression.

We know that other systems do malfunction in that fashion. Thus the blood contains a complex brew of chemical elements that provide for clotting, protecting us from bleeding to death every time we suffer a minor cut. When that same system goes awry, it can cause internal clotting, leading to a heart attack. Depression may be a disease of the same order, a kind of emotional clotting that occurs through some mishap in a necessary protective system.

All that is speculation. The case for specific depressive mechanisms does not depend on such a premise, however, and the search for particular biochemical causes did not grow out of concerted attempts to prove a theory. It was quite the other way around. The quest developed because scientists kept finding unexpected things, and each discovery led to another. It could be described as a collection of random facts that went in search of a reasonable explanation. Now, after some three decades of accelerating research, we are beginning to glimpse the broad outlines of the systems involved. We think we know what the principal mechanisms are, and we've made some informed guesses on how they probably work.

5

The Mechanisms of Mood and Emotion

I see men ordinarily more eager to discover a reason for things than to find out whether the things are so.
—*The Autobiography of Michel de Montaigne*

It is a thing of no great difficulty to raise objections against another man's oration—nay, it is a very easy matter; but to produce a better in its place is a work extremely troublesome.

—PLUTARCH, *Of Hearing*

WE have really just begun to explore the inner world of our own mental and emotional being. What we have learned is still far outweighed by what remains a mystery. Nonetheless, we now stand on the threshold of a great age of discovery. It compares, I believe, to that earlier scientific era when men first began to probe the laws of light, energy, and motion, preparing the way for an Einstein who would put it all together in a grand equation.

There is something splendidly fitting about our present quest. Since man first walked the earth, he has poked and pried at his universe, attempting to puzzle out the nature and meaning of all things around him. Now the human mind is attempting to comprehend the human mind and brain. It will take some doing, but we have made a good start. Specifically, we have outlined by now the broad principles of the brain's structure and function, and we are tracing, examining, and testing the component mechanisms one by one. So far we have found three particular mechanisms that appear to be heavily involved in mental and emotional breakdowns.

I say these mechanisms "appear to be" involved in breakdowns. Actually, I'm convinced that they are involved, and the whole thrust of current research strongly supports that view. I have qualified the initial statement to forewarn the reader that some of the evidence is still circumstantial and to acknowledge that there remains some room for conjecture and controversy in the interpretation of particular data.

Even those of us who endorse the findings will acknowledge readily that the evidence is not all in. Thus we see direct cause-and-effect connections between depression and particular biochemical breakdowns, but we do not claim to have traced the full chain of events. We do not know, for instance, whether the different kinds of breakdown occur independently or whether they are all interconnected in some subtle and still unknown way.

We recognize also that further inquiry may extend the whole sequence of events, implicating other mechanisms that are not now suspected. These and other questions are pursued intensively in many laboratories, and a full discussion of the subject would fill a large volume.*

Here I will treat it in highlight form, sketching the evidence in broad strokes while describing the mech-

_____

* I did, in fact, edit *Factors in Depression* (New York: Raven Press); co-edit *Endorphins in Mental Health Research* (London: Macmillan Press, Ltd.); *Lithium* (Amsterdam: Excerpta Medica); and contribute to *Handbook of Experimental Pharmacology, Psychotropic Agents* (Berlin: Springer Verlag); and *Alcoholism and Affective Disorders* (New York: Spectrum Publications). The field is moving so rapidly that at least 100 books have appeared since then, and what was new at that time may now be out of date. As we learn more, the publications dealing with endorphins or the relationship between depression and alcoholism become more specialized.

anisms involved. The information is both intriguing and important in its own right, and it provides an essential background to an understanding of how and why drug therapy works.

One of the mechanisms involves particular chemical compounds that regulate nerve-cell responses in the brain. These compounds which are produced in the body belong to a chemical grouping known as amines and hence they are known as biogenic amines (bio= bodily, genic=produced, thus "biogenic"). Their biochemical role is to assist in the transmission of electrochemical impulses from one nerve cell to another.

When a nerve ending is stimulated, the reaction is carried up the nerve by a difference in chemical composition between the inside and the outside of the nerve. As with an electric battery, the difference between these two chemical substances produces an electrochemical current that transmits the impulse.

One biogenic amine, norepinephrine, has already been mentioned briefly in the previous chapter. Two other biochemical substances, dopamine and serotonin, are also important biogenic amines. To explain how they act, we must first inspect the brain cells that they serve.

A typical three-pound brain contains some 10 billion neurons, or nerve cells. They are so densely packed that at some critical brain sites 100 million cells are crowded into one cubic inch. One one-millionth part of the brain contains 10 million neurons. Each cell operates, in effect, as a short-wave radio station, broadcasting and receiving coded messages.

In any given situation hundreds of millions of cell stations may be transmitting simultaneously. The total network would be overwhelmed by its own static were it not for an exquisite system of channelization and console control. In fact, without the controls we would be so bombarded with signals that we would probably have something like an epileptic fit every time we opened our eyes.

Much of the message traffic is managed by channelization. Particular clusters of nerve cells are specialized to handle those impulses that convey sight, sound, touch, taste, and smell. At a second level of specialization there are clusters of "executive cells" that process message units as they flash up the line. In effect, all signals are sorted and classified in terms of priority and then are amplified, sped through, delayed, muffled, or simply discarded as situations require.

Consider those functions in terms of a commonplace situation. A man driving at night on a typical two-lane highway is sorting out literally thousands of signals and making hundreds of decisions. If he is a reasonably competent driver, however, he does much of it so easily and automatically that he is only half aware of the process.

He could not tell you afterward how many cars he encountered along the way, and yet with a portion of his brain he monitored every one of them. Every time a headlight struck his rearview mirror he was aware that a car was coming up from behind, probably preparing to pass. He was watching, too, the taillights of the car ahead, judging its distance and noting any change in its speed. And he was watching especially the oncoming stream of headlights that hurtled by in the opposite lane. Each such meeting represented potential disaster, and yet each was but an ordinary and quite manageable occurrence so long as the traffic streams remained separated by a narrow strip of pavement.

Ordinarily the brain handles such problems so smoothly that the experienced and confident driver does not even give it his complete attention. If he has a passenger, he may be enjoying an animated conversation. Otherwise he may be listening to the radio, mulling over the day's business problems, or anticipating the pleasures of a weekend fishing trip. The driving is no problem, and his thoughts seem free to wander.

But all that changes instantly if he sweeps around a

blind curve and meets a pair of headlights bearing down on him in the wrong lane.

In a split second all extraneous thoughts are obliterated, as though he had reached up and unplugged those circuits of his brain. Simultaneously, another half-dormant circuit is fully activated to meet the crisis. Millions of brain cells are transmitting innumerable signals—but all to one urgent purpose. In an instant the foot moves from gas pedal to brake, the hand hits the horn, the eyes measure the remaining distance and estimate the closing speed. The decision-making cell clusters are already calculating the relative hazards of riding it out or hitting the ditch.

This driver is lucky, however, and the danger is over almost as quickly as it appeared. The other motorist manages to squeeze back into his proper lane, and the two cars pass each other safely with some seconds to spare.

"Damn fool!" our threatened driver exclaims.

He rolls on, a little jittery and angry, too, but then he calms down. It was a bit too close, but such things happen, and it came out all right. Probably he reminds himself that there are a lot of reckless people on the road, and for the rest of the trip he may consciously and deliberately intensify his attention.

It is a commonplace observation that immense reserve powers of both body and mind can be mobilized quickly to meet an emergency. I have cited the small highway incident to illustrate a somewhat different point, namely, that we regularly tune the system both up and down as situations require. In fact, both kinds of response are needed for survival.

Put it this way: If a driver viewed every oncoming auto with equal alarm or anticipated a collision on every curve, he would be emotionally exhausted before he was an hour on the road. But if he couldn't summon alarm reactions as needed, he would become all too literally a physical wreck.

How does the brain mediate between such conflicting needs? By what means are the circuits turned up and by what means turned down? How exactly are all those innumerable signals muffled or amplified as the case may require? Above all, what goes wrong so that responses sometimes become stuck at one or another extreme end of the spectrum? A good part of the answer seems to lie in the operating principle of the individual nerve cell.

Earlier I compared these cells to tiny broadcasting stations, and the analogy extends to both structure and function. The illustration on page 83 should help to clarify this. Sprouting from the top of each cell is a cluster of antennae, formed by a bushy crown of fibers that is called the dendrite. It is through these that impulses arrive. The cell's transmission cable trails from the other end and takes the shape of a single fiber called the axon.

Nerve signals are transmitted in the form of electrochemical impulses. When the dendrite picks up an incoming signal, it automatically creates an electrical imbalance within the cell body by altering the sodium-to-potassium balance, triggering a discharge by the axon. In such fashion the signals are relayed from cell to cell throughout the system.

Each cell communicates with the next across a narrow gap that is known as the synapse. The close packing of the cell bodies and their convoluted design allow a single cell to transmit to as many as 10,000 others, thus amplifying messages as they are sped along.

The entire circuit embraces many complexities, and yet the basic principle is one of elegant simplicity. At a specific instant any given cell is either turned on or turned off, transmitting or not transmitting. Always, however, some are transmitting and some not. The ramifications of those "go–no go" signals reach astronomical, almost unimaginable proportions when one considers how many combinations may arise among the 10 billion cells. By lightning calculation of all those on-off signals the brain sorts out information and determines responses. Incidentally, that's exactly the same principle that is employed in computers, but the brain is adapted to a far more sophisticated range of choices.

Obviously the key to the entire operation is the ability to accept or reject any given signal. In the brain the control mechanism is an on-off switch attached individually to each of the nerve cells. That is the apparent function of the biogenic amines.

Tiny sacs (vesicles) are found in the nerve cell axons. In these various nerve cell sacs are stored serotonin, norepinephrine, and dopamine, as well as other

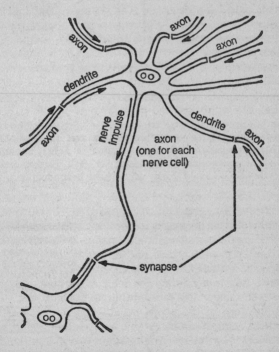

Nerve cell (neurone). There are about 10 billion nerve cells in the brain, and most are connected to a number of other nerve cells. For each nerve cell there are 10 "supporting" cells that furnish nutrition or serve other related functions.

The synapse is 1/500,000 of an inch wide. The nerve impulse is carried across the synapse (also called the synaptic cleft) by chemical neurotransmitters in 1/300 to 1/1,000 of a second.

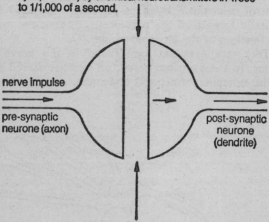

nerve impulse

pre-synaptic
neurone (axon)

post-synaptic
neurone
(dendrite)

Among the major neurotransmitters are: norepinephrine (NE), serotonin (5 hydroxytryptamine = 5HT), dopamine (DA), acetylcholine (AC), histamine (H), gamma-amino-butyric acid (GABA). Many others have been identified.

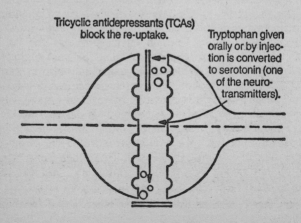

Tricyclic antidepressants (TCAs) block the re-uptake.

Tryptophan given orally or by injection is converted to serotonin (one of the neurotransmitters).

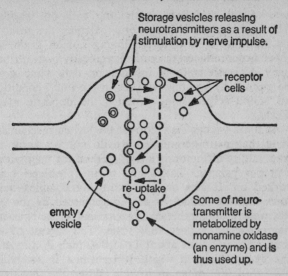

Storage vesicles releasing neurotransmitters as a result of stimulation by nerve impulse.

receptor cells

re-uptake

empty vesicle

Some of neuro-transmitter is metabolized by monamine oxidase (an enzyme) and is thus used up.

Monamine oxidase inhibitors (MAOIs) retard certain types of metabolism. Thus, all of these antidepressants may act by increasing the quantity of neurotransmitters in the synapse.

neuro-regulators. The regulators are released by the electrical disturbance which occurs as a signal pulses through. These molecules then flash across the intervening synapse and sensitize the receiving apparatus of the adjacent cells. That, in effect, provides the "on" switch. After performing their task, the vast majority (ca 80%) of these molecules return to station, ready to repeat the operation. This is referred to as re-uptake.

The "off" switch is provided by a set of antagonistic compounds. Some of these compounds destroy the biogenic amines, and some merely block the amine action, but the immediate practical effect is much the same. If the biogenic amines are neutralized, then sensitizing does not take place at the receptor site, and for the moment the cells involved are turned off.

The competing biochemical forces are in a constant

state of ebb and flow, interacting with one another. When the system is in general balance, the result is the harmony of a well-functioning human brain. An imbalance produces discord. Specifically, we attribute many depressions to amine deficits that damp down the circuits by locking switches in the "off" condition. An amine surplus may produce the opposite manic effects.

At times we can now correct the switch mechanisms when they malfunction, but we do not yet know the exact nature of the brain's own method for maintaining a proper balance. That's one of the problems being worked on. It gets us into extremely complex questions, and the difficulties are compounded by the fact that we are attempting to observe and measure events that occur on a very tiny scale. The largest of the brain cells measures about 1/25,000 inch in diameter. The synapse across which it transmits is something like 1/500,000 of an inch wide. When the sensitizing chemical agents are released, they flash across that tiny gap, perform their function, and return to station in about 1/1,000 second.

The quantity of biogenic amines involved is on the same minuscule order. I have noted before that the biochemical scales are "delicately balanced."

We have not yet learned how to measure exact biogenic amine levels in the living human brain, but we have arrived at pretty good rough estimates. We believe that the typical brain probably contains about 1/30,000 ounce of the compound norepinephrine. Dopamine quantities are about the same, while serotonin is present in about 1/90,000 ounce.

The reader can put his own brain cells to work as he calculates the distribution of those totals among the 10 billion cells. And finally, bear in mind that these are the estimated norms and that a fractional difference plus or minus creates an imbalance.

In more ordinary usage we really need a term to convey something finer than just "delicately balanced." The abiding marvel is that the system can operate on such small tolerances while ordinarily performing so well.

Having inspected the mechanisms, let's go back to that highway motorist and take another look at the brain circuits in action. This time we'll add a stress element to the mundane problems of driving a car. Specifically, our motorist is driving home on the night he was summarily fired from his job.

This man has a lot on his mind. His swirling thoughts and emotions may comprise strong mixtures of anger at his boss, guilt or self-reproach at his own failure, and anxiety about his future. Other reactions crowd in as he thinks about breaking the bad news to his family. Perhaps he's been having some problems with his teenage son but thought he was getting it straightened out. Now this happens. He may not be able to afford that college he had persuaded his son to enter. How will that look, the old man failing at his own game, after all that talk about getting ahead? And what will his wife say? What will she think about the failure even if she doesn't say it? And how can they manage if he's out of work for months?

Such are the thoughts that might occur as the man tries to deal not only with his actual problem but also with his own reactions and the anticipated reactions of others. All of it is transmuted into storm signals that flash through his brain circuits. Meanwhile, his auto is moving along a narrow strip of pavement at eighty feet a second, and his brain has to go on sorting out and dealing with all those traffic signals along the way.

The problem is still well within the brain's capabilities, and if our subject is reasonably stable he will be able to handle it. A lot of people do manage to perform well at routine functions while under heavy stress of one kind or another.

There are others, however, who habitually blow up when confronted with a crisis. If our driver is one of those, he had better get off the road. He may be so flooded with angry reactions that he takes out his aggression on every car he meets. Or he may be so confused and overwhelmed that he's just not able to deal with the task at hand.

Why can one person handle stress and another not? There are, to be sure, many factors in personality development, but I am convinced that one critical element is biochemical. Among those who habitually blow up I suspect that a marginal, quite dithery brain chemistry is overwhelmed when stress situations introduce a flow of unmanageable pressures. And I am convinced that many suffer from a poorly organized biochemical system that simply functions only marginally even when external pressures are not a factor.

I have noted that we now have practical ways to correct some of these malfunctions. Simply stated, we accomplish it through drugs that adjust the biogenic amine levels up or down as the case may require. I will treat that in more detail when we come to therapy, but here I'd like to glance back briefly at the amine effects of some drug agents already cited. It completes the picture of what was learned from the early experiments.

We now know that such hallucinogens as LSD and certain of the mushrooms produce dramatic increases in biogenic amine levels. Once again the drug users employ an apt expression when they speak of being "turned on." From a medical standpoint, however, employing such agents to combat depression is both uncertain and far too drastic.

One of the first effective medically acceptable mood drugs was reserpine. It decreases certain amine levels, thus acting as an antidote to some highly agitated forms of behavior. It is not a drug for depressives, however, as it may push them into deeper withdrawal.

We have since found other drugs that increase biogenic amine activity in the same moderate way that reserpine lowers it. Such drugs have proved highly successful in practice, thus offering strong circumstantial evidence that amine malfunction is one of the basic mechanisms of the disorder.

*   *   *

Two other types of malfunction are also suspected in addition to the biogenic amines. Having sketched the general system in some detail, we can describe these breakdowns in a rather brief fashion.

One of the suspected mechanisms involves the biochemical roles played by various salt compounds, most notably sodium and potassium. They are known as electrolytes because the chemical particles of which they are composed can carry an electron that enters into an electrical reaction.

Most of the potassium found in the nervous system is concentrated within the cell bodies, while most of the sodium circulates in the spaces between cells. Charged particles of the two salts interact through the cell's thin walls in a manner that helps to determine the cell's electrical behavior. When the balance is upset, the cell becomes either more or less excitable, thus creating a malfunction not at the synaptic junction but in the transmission along the nerve fiber itself.

The particular mode of this malfunction is still a little puzzling. There are a number of studies on what happens to sodium, and although the research is somewhat different in each of them there is general agreement that depressed patients retain more sodium. Certainly, more than sodium and potassium are involved. Perhaps these electrolytes interact with the biogenic amines, which in turn alter the switch system.

A third suspected malfunction points to a group of hormones called steroids. They differ both in structure and function from the amines cited earlier.

The steroids are fatty, waxlike compounds secreted by glands and involved in a multiplicity of body functions. Essentially they are chemical activators and regulators, and they operate most notably in connection with the adrenal cortex and the sex glands.

Several steroids are implicated in depressed-patient studies, but the one that shows up most markedly is cortisol. Numerous investigations disclose a sharp rise in cortisol production by depressive patients and a corresponding decrease as recuperation sets in. There is

also some intriguing evidence that the amount of increased cortisol output may be an index to the severity
of the case. One study found a close correlation between suicide attempts and surging cortisol levels. The
biochemical chain of events is not entirely clear, however, and there is still some question as to whether
this phenomenon is a mere symptom or a basic cause.
Nature has performed one such experiment by creating Cushing's disease, in which the adrenal gland produces an excess of cortisone. Depression is often one
of the symptoms of this disorder.

Some researchers note that cortisol output also rises
in stress situations where depression is not involved. It
can thus be considered a general symptom, a reaction
to stress rather than its cause, and the high level in
depressive patients can be viewed as merely confirming
the fact that they do suffer severe anxiety. However,
there are those who suspect that cortisol plays a much
more basic role, at times perhaps triggering decisive
changes in either the sodium-potassium balance or the
amine activity.

The differing views are not necessarily in total contradiction. It may well be that different kinds of stress
reactions flow along common biochemical pathways,
with the predominant role played on different occasions by different mechanisms. Thus a surge of cortisol
might trigger a depressive chain reaction in one case
while in another case it might flare up and subside
without leaving any large consequences in its wake.

The difference might lie in the intervention of some
other agent we have not yet identified. Or it might lie
in the total interplay of all the forces. Perhaps there is
even some element of random outcome that comes
close to chance. When a spark falls in the forest, it may
smolder briefly and die. Or it may be fanned by a
vagrant breeze, and then be blown into a pile of dry
leaves, and from there catch hold and feed on itself
until it becomes a roaring blaze.

One plausible, but unproven, theory is that the biogenic amines act to regulate the production rate and

release of other hormones in the brain and in many other parts of the body. In 1977 and 1978 Dr. Heinz Lehmann and I gave beta-endorphin, a substance produced by the anterior pituitary gland, to a few depressed patients in my private practice. The results were dramatic, with substantial relief of the depression within minutes. Professor Jules Angst, using the same material, confirmed our findings in six patients at the famous Burghöltzli Hospital in Zurich, Switzerland. This is described in detail in a later chapter. There are so many possible interactions that years ago I wrote of the necessity of building specific models of the delicate interrelationships, and of testing them out by computer-derived predictions of what would happen with measurable changes in a variety of the elements involved. This field is in its very infancy.

At the outset of this discussion I warned the reader that the presumed biochemical mechanisms are subjects of considerable controversy. To avoid a tangled welter of point and counterpoint I have proceeded to describe the forces involved from one standpoint without pausing to note every shade of contrary view. Now I would like to look briefly at the other side and assess the objections, again as I see them.

The first point of controversy is the amount of evidence required for a valid scientific conclusion. It is not quite so clear-cut a matter as the reader might assume. When young researchers ask me what it takes to prove a medical finding, I sometimes reply that it depends on what one is trying to prove. As a whimsical illustration, let's suppose that a reputable man comes to me and says he has found a drug that will revive a cadaver. My reply would be, "I'd like to see it."

Let's then suppose that I watch a demonstration and see a corpse arise and walk. For me, that one demonstration would be proof enough. A purist might require two demonstrations. One might say to the purist, "Very well, you select the next cadaver and satisfy yourself as to all conditions of the test." If it worked again, not even the purist would demand a third proof!

Of course, in the case of depression the matter is not that simple, and the purists do have a good deal of room for further questions. The very first difficulty is that the depressive victim cannot be identified and labeled with anywhere near the certainty that applies to a corpse. The reader will recall the immense confusion and disagreement that applies to the problem of diagnosis alone. Thus when particular results are claimed for particular studies, the question left dangling is, How can one be sure the subjects were depressives? Perhaps such-and-such results really indicated some entirely different condition. In the present state of the art it is an almost unanswerable objection, and so I will not dwell on it.

A more cogent line of objection is that researchers who use common methods sometimes do not obtain the same results. Thus I mentioned the sodium-potassium imbalance as a finding that bears the seal of scientific observation. It was, indeed, a finding arrived at by a brilliant scientist after long and careful study, and some backup evidence is now coming in. Nonetheless, it is not yet a discovery confirmed by the traditional long list of repeat experiments, and some who have looked for the supposed salt imbalance have not been able to find it.

There are several reasons why this is the case. One factor is that we are in a pioneer stage, using techniques and equipment not even dreamed of a short time ago, and not all researchers are equally sophisticated in the new methods. Another reason is that we are examining things that do not hold still for our inspection. The pioneer bacteriologists had the advantage on us there. They, too, had their problems with new methods, but at least when they put something on a slide, they could freeze it or bake it there until all concerned had a look and agreed on what they saw.

Our biochemical inquiries are conducted for the most part in a very different setting, one in which critical events may come and go swiftly while leaving behind only circumstantial evidence of what has transpired.

Even the mood of severely depressed patients fluctuates from hour to hour and day to day. Almost certainly some of the crucial biochemicals fluctuate at the same time. Thus one researcher might observe something that another equally skilled investigator could not find an hour later in the same subject. The question naturally arises, Was the thing observed something fleeting and irrelevant? Or was it, perhaps, something fleeting but highly relevant? In any given case the question is again almost unanswerable. Even when the results begin to pile up, there usually remains some room for different interpretation, and conclusions usually come down in the end to a matter of individual judgment in assessing the evidence.

In regard to the question of sodium-potassium imbalance, I believe that the weight of the evidence supports the indictment, and I am not put off by the fact that it has not been found in every case. It may well be not *the* cause but only one cause among several, and present or not present according to circumstances in particular cases.

In the case of sodium-potassium imbalance we are at least lucky to have some indirect evidence to argue about. We are able to record cellular electrolyte changes, delicate though they are. We can remove a blood sample, tag the suspect substance with radioactive trace materials, and measure how much is present in the sample. In effect, we follow an atom's path through the body with the aid of a highly sophisticated Geiger counter, and we can thus attempt observation of what goes on in that volatile inner world of our nervous system. The measurable changes in brain chemistry induced by medication used for treatment have contributed greatly to the construction of our theoretical models. There still remain contradictions and omissions, but we are on our way. The most recent exciting addition has been *positron emission tomography* (referred to as PET), which utilizes short-acting rather than long-acting radioisotopes. This will allow us to visualize directly in the brain what is taking place, when it takes place, for certain substances. The work has barely begun.

In some other cases, however, we can draw only secondhand conclusions from circumstantial evidence, and that raises still a third line of objection.

The matter of circumstantial evidence arises particularly in regard to the biogenic amines. Much of that case has not been proved because we had no satisfactory means of observing these events in the living human brain. PET may provide such a method, but probably not for all the substances involved. However, we can make such observations in animal brains. Then comes the question, How much can we rely on animal results in assessing the human mechanism?

Earlier in this report I conceded that we couldn't measure human amine quantities exactly, and then proceeded to offer a rough guess. In fact, that estimate was based on a dog's brain, with adjustments for the difference in size and number of cells. There are purists who recoil from such speculative estimates. I'll agree that it's a very broad guess, a kind of in-the-ball-park figure, but until we can do better I'd rather have such an estimate than none at all.

The comparison question becomes even more critical when we turn to matters of function. In animals we can observe amine levels go up and down in the brain as a result of both stress reaction and in response to drugs. We can't see that in man, but we can measure amines and their metabolic breakdown products in man's urine and blood. The levels go up and down in the same way for the same apparent reasons. That, of course, is not proof, for the urine and blood collect these chemicals from numerous areas of the body. Theoretically, one might argue that when a particular drug is given, the resultant amine change takes place in the dog's brain but in the man's gut. Personally, I am convinced that it takes place in both brains and guts, following a rule of nature common to all the higher species.

To me, then, the biogenic-amine evidence is circumstantial but very strong, and it gets stronger when it is applied to a drug therapy that relieves the symptoms. But again, one can argue that relieving the symptoms does not necessarily prove anything about the cause.

All such arguments are valid enough in their own right, but there is a point in theoretical argument where one plus one adds up to something less than two. It has been said that logic allows us to arrive at the wrong conclusions with conviction. However, in my own view, the general outlines of biochemical malfunction are now established beyond reasonable doubt. There is much more we would like to know about the precise mechanisms, but meanwhile we have already arrived at some highly effective remedies.

6

Drug Therapy

The crudest of these methods of influencing the body, but also the most effective, is the chemical one; that of intoxication. I do not think anyone entirely understands their operation, but it is a fact that there are certain substances foreign to the body which, when present in the blood or tissues, directly cause us pleasurable sensations, but also so change the conditions of our perceptivity that we become insensible of disagreeable sensations. The two effects not only take place simultaneously, they seem to be closely bound up with each other. But there must be substances in the chemical composition of our bodies which can do the same, for we know of at least one morbid state, that of mania, in which a condition similar to this intoxication arises wthout any drug being absorbed. Besides this, our normal mental life shows variations, according to which pleasure is experienced with more or less ease, and along with this goes a diminished or increased sensitivity to pain. It is greatly to be regretted that this toxic aspect of mental processes has so far eluded scientific research.

—SIGMUND FREUD,
Civilization and Its Discontents

The future may teach us how to exercise a direct influence, by means of particular chemical substances, upon the amount of energy and its distribution in the

*apparatus of the mind. It may be that there are other
undreamed of possibilities of therapy.*
—SIGMUND FREUD,
Analysis Terminable and Interminable

*The shortcoming of our description would probably
disappear if for the psychological ones we could
already now substitute physiological or chemical ones.*
—SIGMUND FREUD,
Beyond the Pleasure Principle

THERE is sharp psychiatric controversy as to whether
drug therapy cures depression or merely relieves the
symptoms. The question is intriguing to medical scientists, though I suspect that for many patients the point
borders on being academic. Depressed patients are
usually quite satisfied with effective relief from symptoms, which is to say, effective relief from intense pain
and crippling disability.

For reasons already stated, I am convinced that the
therapy often goes beyond symptomatic relief and helps
to correct basic malfunctions. Even if that were not
the case, however, I would feel that practical considerations make drugs the treatment of choice in a great
many cases.

First and foremost among the practical considerations is the availability of treatment. When we debate
the relative merits of drug therapy and psychoanalysis,
we sometimes become so immersed in theories that we
talk as though the two choices were equally open. In
fact, they are not.

Psychoanalysis is an immensely valuable technique
in particular situations, but by its nature it is simply
not adapted to the needs of mass medicine. To put it
quite specifically, there are fewer than 2,000 psychoanalysts in the country today, and they probably treat
about 40,000 patients a year. If they were to ignore
all other emotional ills and devote themselves exclu-

sively to depression, they could see less than 1 percent of those who need immediate help.

I was trained as a psychotherapist, and before medications were available I used to treat depressed patients. Often it was a very frustrating experience: both the patient and I were doing our best but it wasn't enough.

Depressives have psychological problems—as all people do—and ideally we might all benefit to some degree from psychotherapy. Clearly that is not possible, however, and so it makes sense to reserve formal, in-depth psychotherapy of any sort for those patients in whom neurosis represents a major aspect of the illness. In my own practice, as I have stated earlier, that applies to perhaps one patient out of twenty.

There are other practical considerations from a patient's point of view. Effective analysis is often an exhaustive, and exhausting, procedure; it may require years of treatment and cost many thousands of dollars. Effective drug therapy, by contrast, has usually produced results in a matter of months at a fraction of the cost.

In sum, drug therapy is relatively quick, simple, and inexpensive, and for the great majority of patients it produces results ranging from marked improvement to complete remission of the illness. All of those attributes make it an immensely valuable procedure for dealing with an illness that is both serious and widespread. It is not, however, a magic solution to all of a patient's problems. It will not resolve any underlying personality defects the patient may have, and it will certainly not banish the stress inherent in the life problems we all have to face. What it does do is correct a particular kind of functional breakdown, so that the patient can address problems with capacities restored.

Some patients, of course, need both drug therapy and analysis. Even in such cases, however, I believe that very often the drug treatment should come first. Severely stricken depressives can become so down and out mentally and emotionally that they cannot manage the most mundane problems of everyday life. How, then, can they summon the emotional energy to confront painful and critical matters? And how can they reach sensible, practical decisions on important questions that may influence the entire future course of their lives?

My own approach is to tell patients that they have "a month's absolution" from all such matters. Later they may have to deal with difficult problems, but first they must allow themselves a mental and emotional truce while they give the medicine a chance to work. Incidentally, it is the severe neurotic who insists upon solving all problems. My friend William Sheldon propounded one of the best definitions of maturity as "the ability to tolerate conflict."

Quite often patients find that when the depression clears up, so do most of the other problems. That is, the other problems become manageable and normal instead of overwhelming. For these patients the depression itself would seem to be the basic problem, and once the malfunction is corrected, we can regard the illness as essentially cured. As one patient so aptly put it, "It isn't that I don't have all the problems I had before— but having problems isn't such a problem."

How lasting are such cures? That depends on the patient. For some a depressive attack occurs as an isolated episode and they may never experience a second bout. For others it is a more or less chronic condition, either constantly present in some degree or else recurring frequently in cyclic fashion.

The cyclic pattern is especially common in the manic-depressive form of the illness. In such cases we keep the patient on lithium, a substance we will discuss at some length. We use lithium either alone or with a low-level maintenance dosage of other drugs that are calculated to either prevent or greatly alleviate the future attacks. The condition of such patients is comparable to diabetics who require continuing medication in order to maintain a stable balance. Thus lithium and the other antidepressant drugs do not produce dependence or addiction any more than does insulin or digitalis. In those cases where there is recurrence of the depression—even though the patient is on lithium —the episodes are almost always very much milder, and antidepressant medications work more rapidly.

All questions of treatment and prognosis are intertwined with a large number of patient variables. Thus a particular drug may work quickly for some patients, more slowly for others, and for still others have little or no effect. This is not surprising. It may reflect in part the fact that the breakdowns are occurring in different though related mechanisms. In part also the varying results underscore the fact that every patient is different biochemically as well as personally.

The remarkable individuality of our bodies is suggested by the skin patterns that appear at our fingertips. All of us share a general fingerprint conformation of loops and whorls, and yet the intricate variations are so near to infinite that no two persons on earth have ever presented the exact same design. So, too, but in far more complex fashion, our biochemical systems differ one from another. Sometimes the minor biochemical peculiarities have major effects, either blocking a drug's action or transforming it into a toxic substance. It is a quite common medical problem, and we solve it by adjusting prescriptions until we find the one that gives the best results.

We now have for depression not just different medications but whole families of drugs that take effect along different pathways. The result is a flexible and potent pharmacotherapy that is highly effective for all but the most resistant cases. Thus when a patient enters my office, I begin on a note of cheerful reassurance, and in the great majority of cases that optimism is fully justified by events.

For the reasons already cited, the course of the treatment varies considerably from patient to patient. Usually there is an interval of three to four weeks before the medication begins to take hold. It is important for both the patient and the family to realize that there may be no evidence at all that the medication is doing anything useful during this period. There follows an improvement period that may extend over another month or two in fairly typical cases. As with any serious illness, it is not usually a matter of being sick one day and well the next. The typical process is one of gradual recovery, the patient gaining strength and confidence as one by one the painful symptoms fade and disappear. The progress is not always unbroken, and there are frequently good days followed by several bad ones, before the final improvement is attained.

The great majority of my depressive patients achieve that kind of recovery. For another small percentage recovery is only partial, and they remain on maintenance therapy while continuing to experience some level of distress. And finally there is a hard core of a few percent who just do not respond to the present treatments. It may be that they are suffering from some quite different type of malfunction, but in most cases what I suspect is a metabolic quirk that somehow neutralizes the drug action. I expect that continuing intensive research will resolve that problem while improving the already good results that we now get with the great majority of patients. The whole history of drug therapy for depression has been one of spectacular progress over the last twenty years, and there is no reason to believe that we have exhausted the possibilities of further discovery.

The principal current pharmacological methods of management involve four types of drugs,* designated as the monoamine oxidase inhibitors (MAOI), the tricyclics and tetracyclics, the psychostimulants, and lithium. They complement each other because they take effect in quite different ways. Let's start the explanation with MAO inhibitors, which were the first of the modern compounds. To understand what they are

---

* See Appendix for listing of MAOIs, TCAs, psychostimulants, and lithium.

and how they work we must glance back briefly at brain chemistry.

The reader will recall that dopamine, serotonin, and norepinephrine are amines that serve as neural transmitters, activating the "on" switches in the nerve cells of the brain. In the normal course of biochemical events these compounds are produced, used, and then consumed through metabolism. In order for metabolism to occur, oxygen must be added to the compound, and this is accomplished through interaction with another type of body chemical we call an enzyme.

The enzymes are fantastically specific, acting only on the particular compounds for which they are targeted. In the case of the amines the enzyme involved is one known as monoamine oxidase. A monoamine oxidase inhibitor is thus just what the name implies—a drug that slows down amine metabolism by inhibiting that enzyme. The enzyme is necessary for the amino acid to add oxygen. Such oxidation is the first step in the eventual excretion of the substance from the body. By inhibiting the enzyme, the oxidation is retarded and thus the amino-acid derivatives last and act for a longer period of time.

Marsilid had been introduced some years earlier as an experimental treatment for tuberculosis. At first it seemed highly promising. The drug checked the growth of the tubercle bacillus, the X rays improved, and the patients threw off the habitual TB lassitude. As a side effect, however, there developed an odd problem. The patients felt *too* good. They overexerted themselves and generally ignored the medical safeguards their condition required. The problem was solved by switching to a related but different drug that did not produce the euphoric effect. The only reason why Marsilid was still around was that some felt it had particular value for tuberculosis of the bone.

Marsilid's potential as a mood drug had gone largely unnoticed because psychiatrists at the time just weren't thinking along those lines. As the climate changed, however, a few researchers began to investigate it in a tentative way.

Marsilid brought about substantial relief when it was given to patients who suffered from severe depression. Here finally was a psychiatric drug treatment that produced not just marked improvement but in some cases a complete remission of all symptoms. It was the first drug cure in all of psychiatric history to act in such a manner.

I was serving at the time as chairman of the American Psychiatric Association's committee on research, and in that capacity I arranged to have a paper on Marsilid presented at an association research conference. There was an ironic little aftermath, in that the report was received with some initial skepticism by the research director of the company that produced Marsilid. It happened that he was looking for an antidepressant in a quite different chemical area, and he was a little taken aback to learn that such a drug was already on his shelf. Of course, the company rather quickly and easily adjusted to that surprise. Marsilid filled an enormous gap in clinical practice, and within a year it had been used in the treatment of some 400,000 patients.

Among those first 400,000 Marsilid patients there were some who got married, some who had ski accidents—and some who got jaundice. The marriages and ski accidents were not blamed on the drug, but the jaundice was. In fact, the case was never proved statistically, but the mere raising of the question created serious doubts.

Other evidence indicated that in certain circumstances Marsilid might produce high blood pressure. Thus after an auspicious start the drug became highly controversial.

Here I must digress briefly to put the safety question in perspective. Every drug constitutes a chemical intervention in the natural processes, and there is no such thing as an effective drug that is absolutely safe. The questions properly put are, how safe, in what doses, for what length of time, under what conditions, and for which patients? And beyond that there looms the larger philosophical question of how to weigh the risk of giving a drug against the risk of *not* giving it, i.e., the danger of the disease and the comparison with other treatment methods.

It would be much easier if we could apply risk-and-gain equations across the board. That can't be done, however, because what is safe for one person is not for another. Penicillin is a dramatic example. Generally speaking, it is a quite safe and extremely useful drug that has saved millions of lives. But it has also claimed some lives. There is a biochemical minority of perhaps one person in 10,000 who does not tolerate penicillin well, and some of them go into severe shock when the drug is administered. It's something that physicians have learned to watch for while continuing to use this potent agent. Yet in a case of meningitis caused by a bacteria susceptible to penicillin, it would be a foolhardy physician who did *not* treat the patient with the drug. Operations also involve danger, but the surgeon who does *not* operate on an acute appendix is likely to get into severe trouble. *Not* acting is often more dangerous than doing something even though it involves some risks.

The precaution problem is further complicated by the fact that reaction may arise from combination factors. Thus drug A may be safe enough, and drug B likewise, but together they may create a hazard. As a commonplace example, one may unwind with a nightcap before going to bed, or one may take a sleeping pill. It's a bad idea to take both. In medicine there are innumerable other examples where one and one add up biochemically to more than two.

Still other complications arise from particular medical conditions. There are otherwise beneficial drugs that become potentially dangerous if the patient suffers from high blood pressure or liver disorder, for example. And finally, there are complications that extend even to the reactions some people experience toward certain foods, fabrics, plant pollens. There are drugs one does not prescribe for asthmatics or diabetics.

All this is a commonplace medical problem. In the case of old, familiar drugs physicians compile long lists of caution signs, and the good physician remains ever watchful for the particular patient who doesn't quite fit the normal expectations.

With the newer drugs we necessarily proceed through some trial and error, but the precautions are very stringent. Before a new drug is released, it is analyzed quite exhaustively in regard to all the theoretical implications, and after that the possible interactions are examined by turn in test tubes, in animal experiments, and finally in carefully controlled human trials. The safety standards are all imposed by law, and the Food and Drug Administration regulations are the world's most rigorous. Even so, we never know entirely what to expect until a drug filters into medical practice. That's when all those vexing special problems crop up. So it was with Marsilid. It had been around for several years, we thought we had the toxic problems well in hand, and then something came up that no one had foreseen.

It turned out that Marsilid combined badly with, of all things, cheddar cheese. The problem illustrates the innumerable complexities that can arise in biochemistry.

It will be recalled that the drug functions as a monoamine oxidase inhibitor, building up the supply of brain amines by neutralizing the metabolic process. It happens that cheddar cheese is rich in another monoamine, a compound called tyramine, and one that may produce high blood pressure in patients taking monoamine oxidase inhibitors. Thus a combination risk appears if a patient is on this particular type of medication and then eats a lot of cheddar cheese. The consequences can range anywhere from severe headache to cerebral hemorrhage.

Questions were raised as to the drug effects in combination with other tyramine-containing foods and beverages including beer, Chianti wine, chicken livers, and pickled herring. Curiously, not all patients reacted to the combinations quite as expected, but there was a risk factor. Various estimates suggested that severe reactions might occur at rates ranging from one patient in 3,000 to one in 10,000.

No physician can lightly dismiss such risks, not when the projected rates are spread over the millions of patients who might ultimately take the drug. At the same time one cannot ignore all the suffering that depression causes and the suicides that might be prevented. In this case the Food and Drug Administration felt the risk was not justified because other antidepressants were appearing, and they posed fewer side effects. The pharmaceutical company thus withdrew Marsilid from the American market, though it is still used in some other countries.

Personally, I felt that this drug was particularly effective with certain patients, and its use might well have been retained under careful control. However, it was a close question. The FDA had a tough call to make, they called it as they saw it, and that was that. Actually, they only recommended but did not compel withdrawal. The pharmaceutical company did the rest. In a later, very similar case the FDA recommended withdrawal of a related drug, but the company resisted and the drug is still on the market.

Fortunately it was not the end of the matter. The potential of an MAO inhibitor had been demonstrated, and with that information in hand the chemical researchers knew where and how to search for other drugs of this type. The years that followed produced half a dozen MAO inhibitors, most of them closely related in chemical structure and yet different enough that one could shift them around to meet varied problems. After a checkered career our experimental drug thus sired a large and useful therapeutic progeny.

While this research on MAO inhibitors was going on, another research team was closing in on the same goal by a quite different biochemical route. The result was a separate type of drug discovered in Switzerland and announced just five months after the report on Marsilid. Such close juxtaposition was not pure coincidence. Antidepressant drug therapy was an idea whose time had finally come, and widely scattered researchers were pursuing a variety of different leads. It was still such a pioneer endeavor, however, that those who were involved often didn't know of each other's existence until discoveries converged along common paths.

The Swiss group was headed by Dr. Roland Kuhn, and they too arrived at discovery in a curious and roundabout fashion. The story is one of those serendipity affairs in which a searcher finds something he's not exactly looking for. It's sometimes called luck, but it requires, of course, the ability to search with both eyes and mind open.

Many years before, Klaesi in Switzerland had an idea that emotional illness might be treated with a form of hibernation, or sleep therapy. There was some reason to believe that deep, protracted narcotic coma might correct disturbed electrical circuits in the brain. Accordingly, Dr. Kuhn began looking for a sleep-inducing hypnotic drug, and in 1950 he conducted his first trials. The experiment failed, but in the course of it he obtained an unexpected lead on another kind of chemical agent.

Here let me explain that the properties of a compound are blueprinted in its chemical structure, if we but knew how to read the practical consequences of the code. Thus the number, type, and arrangement of the molecular chains determine what the compound is and what it does. In theory, the color and constituency of the substance, its weight in a given mass, its response to heat and cold, and hundreds of other properties are all imprinted in this fashion.

In theory, then, two look-alike chemicals ought to perform pretty much the same. In practice, they sometimes do and sometimes don't. The problem is that minor molecular wrinkles can signify drastic changes in the compound. In drug research it comes down to the fact that skilled chemists can help us sort out those substances that may share certain general characteristics. To locate some refined property one proceeds from there by a process that combines informed hunch with trial and error. It's a quest that is often full of surprises.

In Dr. Kuhn's case he set out to find an effective sleep-inducing drug and came instead upon an energizing compound that seemed to have some "antipsychotic effects." For various reasons it was not medically useful, but it suggested a new area of chemical search. That kind of research requires time, money, and sophisticated facilities, and Dr. Kuhn proposed the project to a Swiss drug company. They turned it down. As business decisions go, that one was about like an early-day oil company rejecting a geologist's suggestion to try Texas.

Fortunately Dr. Kuhn wouldn't let the matter rest. He spotted a couple of related compounds that seemed interesting, and each time he pressed the drug company to reconsider. In 1954 he finally got a go-ahead.

By then he had narrowed the theoretical field, and he started with a highly promising compound that the laboratory labeled No. G 22150. It had psychopharmacological properties just as expected, but it was not suitable. Dr. Kuhn and his research colleagues put their heads together, made some deductions, and decided to try substance No. G 22355. This time luck was with them. They had hit upon imipramine, the first of the important tricyclic antidepressants. It was the parent drug for what soon became another whole family of new medications for this disease.

A tricyclic is so named because the chemical structure contains three connected ring-like structures. Actually, the experimental modifications have moved somewhat beyond that basic formation, but the term tricyclic still serves well enough as a working description. As to mode of operation when the parent drug imipramine was discovered, no one knew quite how it worked but only that it did. That was quickly demonstrated in patient trials. Subsequent research indicates that it enhances the neural transmission agents in a special fashion.

Let's review the brain-cell sequence again. When a nerve cell discharges an electric pulse, it releases amines that then cross the synapse, or intervening gap, to prepare the next cells for signal reception. Ordinarily these transmitting agents then return to station and are reabsorbed into the cells around the synapse from which they came, a process called re-uptake.

Apparently tricyclic drugs block the re-uptake, leaving the transmitters free in the synapse, where they are more readily mobilized for service. The mode of action is thus entirely different from MAO inhibitors, but the practical effect is much the same. Either or both will replenish a sluggish circuit by increasing the amount of free amines at the nerve endings.

The tricyclic discovery was discussed at the Second International Congress of Psychiatry at Zurich late in 1957. That impressive setting, however, does not exactly convey the tone of the initial reception. Barely a dozen people thought it worthwhile to attend the session where the finding was described.

"Our paper," Dr. Kuhn wrote later, "was received with some interest, but with a great deal of skepticism."

I know exactly what he means!

That skepticism soon vanished, however, as the clinical evidence piled up. The mountainous dimensions of the evidence are suggested in the fact that tricyclics alone have accounted for some 10,000 scientific papers over the last twenty-five years.

Naturally enough, the continuing investigations have turned up some problems while extending the range of discovery. One of the expected tricyclic problems was that familiar inevitability of adverse side effects. You can count on it to occur more or less with almost any potent drug.

Dr. Kuhn ran the early trials with psychiatric hospital patients, and he found the side reactions rather easy to manage. Then the drug got into private practice for patients living at home, and we started getting complaints. The drug produced such effects as dryness of the mouth, mild constipation, and occasional "sweats." The hospital patients had generally ignored these difficulties, but it created problems with some less stoic private patients.

In the years since, we have learned to manage these side effects pretty well. One technique is the use of buffer medicines that counteract various reactions. Another and more basic control is that of fitting the individual patient to the particular antidepressant drug that suits best. That's why it is so valuable to have these families of drugs that are so alike and yet quite different. Some are more effective with one patient and some with another but together they stretch pretty well across the patient spectrum. Since then we now also have dicyclics (two rings) and tetracyclics (four rings).

The third major type of drug therapy involves the use of lithium salts. Actually it was the first treatment to be discovered, but it was almost totally neglected for nearly a decade. Then medical opinion began to change, and lithium came in a second time on the same wave that won acceptance for the other treatments.

Lithium is an extremely common natural substance that has some very interesting properties. It is the lightest of all solid elements and the hardest of all alkali metals. It is strongly attracted to water molecules, and in reaction with water it liberates exceptional amounts of energy. If the substance had been known to the alchemists, those test-tube magicians of the Middle Ages, they would have had a wonderful time with it. Lithium is a pure but extremely soft metal. When combined with carbonates, phosphates, citrates, or chlorides, it is known as a "salt," just as sodium when combined with chloride (sodium chloride) is known as a salt.

It may have been employed medically even before

its existence was identified. About 1,800 years ago the physician Galen advised treating mania by bathing the patient in alkaline springs, as well as "taking" (drinking) the water. Just for curiosity's sake I'd love to visit one of those old Roman medicinal springs and test for lithium content. If that's what the active ingredient was, then Galen's prescription was a real shot in the dark. Today lithium is used primarily to prevent recurrence of manic-depressive and depressive episodes.

Be all that as it may, the known history of lithium began in 1817, when it was identified chemically as a companion substance to sodium and potassium. About a generation passed before the new material could be produced in any quantity. After that it quickly passed into medical usage for numerous, often ill-chosen purposes.

Lithium citrate or carbonate combined with uric acid and dissolved urate deposits on cartilage in a test tube, suggesting a treatment for gout. The supposed benefits were largely neutralized by biochemical interactions with body salts, but that wasn't known at the time, and for fifty years it was used also in such conditions as uremia, kidney stones, and rheumatism. It appeared in most of the bottled "curative waters" that were so popular at the time, and in the age of the medicine show it became one of the all-purpose remedies touted from the back of carnival wagons.

In 1948 lithium chloride appeared in a new role, as a substitute for sodium chloride in salt-restricted diets. Some of the other uses had been poorly judged, but this one was a disaster. The salt-restricted diets are employed in cardiac and renal decompensation cases when fluid begins to accumulate. Unfortunately the lithium also accumulated, reaching dangerously high levels as it replaced the sodium that had been eliminated from the diet. Some deaths resulted, stern warnings began to circulate in the medical journals, and for a time all use of lithium was virtually proscribed.

I should add first of all that lithium never *causes*

heart disease but can be a problem if one particular type already exists. Today we know how to manage even that type better, and we can use lithium even in decompensation patients if the reactions are closely watched. There is no conclusive evidence that lithium produces serious kidney malfunction, but the question is being actively investigated. In 1980, Alec Coppen and colleagues at the Medical Research Council in Epsom, England, reported on two groups of patients with affective disorders. The group that had been on lithium from one to twelve years did not differ from the matched patients who had never been on lithium. Both groups did show more pathology than another matched group of 100 patients who did not have an affective disorder. For extra protection we now recommend that lithium be taken in divided doses rather than at one time.

As it happened, American medicine was preoccupied with the lithium upset in the same year that Dr. John Cade of Australia hit on a remarkable lithium treatment for manic-depressives. Later, in reminiscing, Dr. Cade described his situation thus:

One can hardly imagine a less propitious year in which to attempt the pharmacological rehabilitation of lithium. That the attempt was made by an unknown psychiatrist, working alone in a small mental hospital with no research training, primitive techniques and negligible equipment was hardly likely to be compellingly persuasive, especially in the United States.

To such drawbacks one must add that Dr. Cade was pursuing a line of reasoning that many critics would have found "simplistic." Indeed, one can say in favor of Dr. Cade's work that he got there first and the treatment worked. He was ahead of all the rest of us in a discovery that was then so far out that almost no one believed it. Few, in fact, even heard of it at the time, for the publication in an Australian medical journal didn't make much of a splash.

Dr. Cade did not begin with splendid expectations. He had no immediate idea of finding a cure for an emotional disorder and hoped merely to learn something about its cause.

He started with the premise that disturbed behavior in manics probably arose from some toxic reaction within the nervous system. He believed that the poisonous substance was probably some natural bodily agent that had run amok, and he assumed that traces of this aberrant material were excreted in the urine.

A normal substance can become aberrant, of course, if it is present in either too large or too small a quantity. Dr. Cade's particular hunch was that manic-depressives produced an excess of some biochemical agent, whereas depressives suffered a deficiency. He decided to concentrate on the manic patients by comparing their urine with that of depressives, schizophrenics, and normal subjects.

He needed very sensitive chemical tests, but he had no such facilities, and so he settled for a make-do procedure. He took urine samples from the four types of subjects, injected the material into guinea pigs, and sat back to see what would happen.

Readers who have any knowledge of modern science will recognize that the method was primitive. Dr. Cade recognized it, too. He put it thus: "Because I did not know what the substance might be, still less anything of its pharmacology for lower animals, the best plan seemed to be to spread the net as wide as possible and use the crudest form of biological test in a preliminary investigation."

Some of the test animals seemed immune to the urine injections, but others reacted violently. Typically, a stricken guinea pig was seized with severe convulsions, became paralyzed in all four legs, and soon after died. The effects occurred with urine from all types of subjects, from normal to manic-depressive, but one big difference appeared at once. Urine from some of the manic-depressives was highly potent, producing fatal results at doses three to four times less than those required from the comparison groups.

The next step was to try to locate the toxic agent. Dr. Cade distilled the urine into its constituent parts, tried first one factor and then another, and arrived at urea as the probable guilty substance. Here, however, he struck a puzzling contradiction. The manics had by far the most toxic urine, but they did not have more urea than any others. Some other factor was evidently acting as a catalyst or booster, and Dr. Cade suspected uric acid. He decided to test it by rerunning the experiment with an extra injection of that material.

What happened next was one of those wild bounces that make this kind of research both a fascinating and a humbling game. To control the potency of the uric acid Dr. Cade administered it in solution. He chose a solution of lithium salts because that is one of the few substances that readily combines with this acid.

It was just that, a convenient way to get the uric acid inside the guinea pig, and had nothing to do with the main thrust of his inquiry. It immediately introduced a new element, however, for he found that the lithium rendered all the urine injections far less toxic than before.

He pursued the side trail, injecting the lithium alone, and found that it had remarkable tranquilizing effects. A guinea pig is ordinarily an excitable little beast, and if placed on its back in the course of some experiment, it will kick and squeal as it tries to right itself. When these animals were placed on their backs, they just lay there and gazed back at the investigator with a placid stare.

It gave Dr. Cade an inspiration that he described thus: "It may seem a long way from lethargy in guinea pigs to the control of manic excitement, but as these investigations had commenced with toxin in the urine of manic patients, the association of ideas is explicable." In short, he decided that this might be just the medicine for mania.

He tried it out, using as test subjects ten manic patients, six schizophrenics, and three chronic psychotic depressives. As he had expected, he got little or no results with the schizophrenics and depressives. With the manics, however, there was dramatic change.

Dr. Cade described one typical result as follows:

This was a little wizened man of 51 who had been in a state of chronic manic excitement for five years. He was amiably restless, dirty, destructive, mischievous and interfering. He had enjoyed a preeminent nuisance value in a back ward for all those years and bid fair to remain there for the rest of his life.

The patient commenced treatment on 29 March, 1948. On the fourth day, the optimistic therapist thought he saw some change for the better but acknowledged that it could have been his expectant imagination; the nursing staff were noncommittal but loyal. However, by the fifth day it was clear that he was in fact more settled, tidier, less dis-inhibited and less distractable. From then on there was steady improvement so that in three weeks he was enjoying the unaccustomed and quite unexpected amenities of a convalescent ward.

Two months later the patient walked out of the hospital and returned home to resume normal life under a small maintenance dose of lithium carbonate. In six months Dr. Cade was disappointed to get back his "dirty little man," now as agitated as before, but the reason proved reassuring. The man had felt so completely cured that he had quit taking his medicine. The attack subsided when he resumed treatment.

Dr. Cade announced his discovery the following year. Lithium was then in particular disfavor, however, and pharmacotherapy of emotional disturbance was not generally accepted. For some years the treatment was ignored throughout most of the medical world. A few papers did appear, however, and eventually lithium found an ardent European advocate in Dr. Mogens

Schou, professor of biological psychiatry at Aarhus University in Denmark. Largely through his efforts its use began to spread throughout the Continent.

Dr. Schou began his campaign in earnest in 1957, and thus the threads all came together. In one great breakthrough year our American team brought out the first MAO inhibitor, a Swiss team produced the first tricyclic, and a Danish psychiatrist unearthed the half-buried Australian discovery of lithium. If some random circumstance had brought the lot of us together a little earlier, we would have been astonished to learn that we were all hot on the same trail.

In the 1960's lithium was adopted in some forty European, Asian, and African countries. In the United States it remained restricted to experimental use, though some of us were pressing hard for its clinical inclusion here. The situation was frustrating. We knew it was highly effective, that it was badly needed for particular patients, but we couldn't prescribe it for general use.

Meanwhile, it was being prescribed by other physicians from Argentina to Zambia, and in such places as Bahrain, Iran, Kuwait, Liberia, Madagascar, Mauritius, and Uganda. When we complained, we were informed that such countries lacked our high standards of safety. In fact, however, lithium was also being used in fifteen highly developed and medically advanced countries that had lower national death rates than our own. In my judgment it was again a case of being so cautious about the risks of medication that we ignored the risks of disease.

Finally in 1970 the ban was partially lifted. We were permitted to use lithium in the general treatment and prevention of manic states, including manic-depressive ones. We have been getting excellent results ever since. It has proved highly useful both in subduing the attacks and in either preventing or greatly easing the recurrent cyclic episodes that are so typical of this condition.

At present lithium is widely used for the prevention of all types of depression, although it is not yet "offi-

cial," and there is some debate as to how helpful it is
for these conditions. There is a current theory that
those patients who do respond are really disguised
manic-depressives, with the lows so marked and the
highs so subdued that a basic bipolar disturbance
passes for unipolar. Perhaps so. I'm inclined to believe
the drug is also useful in preventing the recurrence of
unipolar disorders as well. It's a therapy that helps
prevent recurrences in many patients we couldn't reach
before. The drug is of great use in the treatment of
manic states, although it usually takes from four to ten
days to work—so that in acute, severe cases it is combined with a phenothiazine or related drug for the
first week or two. Lithium is excellent in preventing
recurrence of both manic and depressive episodes.
Curiously, it is of much less use in bringing about a
recovery in a patient already depressed.

As to Dr. Cade and his historic experiment, he never
did get to the bottom of that uremic reaction in guinea
pigs. Meanwhile, we have reached a working hypothesis
as to how lithium achieves its effects. Probably it in-
filtrates the "ground substance" of the brain, alters the
nerve membrane, and thus influences the sodium-potassium balance, which we discussed earlier. Thus it
influences nerve-cell electric transmission by still another route. Additionally, it may work by affecting the
balance of biogenic amines. In any case, it works most
of the time.

For the sake of completeness and understanding it is
important to know about another group of pharmacological agents whose action mimics the "sympathetic,"
or autonomic, nervous system and that hence are labeled sympathomimetic. The sympathomimetic amines
are stimulants rather than antidepressants. They include the amphetamines: dextroamphetamine (Dexe-
drine), methamphetamine (Desoxyn), and methyl-
phenidate (Ritalin). This general class of drugs is
referred to as "uppers" or "speed," but only when used

illegally in excessive doses. These drugs *do* have legitimate medical functions, but their use is limited because of the tendency for tolerance to develop. Under proper supervision they are a valuable adjunct to the more important antidepressants.

Modern drug treatment has largely replaced electroconvulsive therapy (ECT), more popularly known as shock treatment. ECT still has some applications, however, and so a brief scan is required.

The original inspiration for convulsive treatment was the erroneous observation that schizophrenia was rare among epileptics. It isn't. However, it was deduced that perhaps the seizures from which epileptics suffered somehow prevented the schizophrenia. Thus, if one could produce convulsions in schizophrenics, perhaps the disease would disappear. A variety of substances was used for this purpose: camphor, Metrazol, insulin, and eventually in 1938, electric currents. It proved to have some value in the partial and temporary relief of schizophrenics and later was applied to severe depressives as well.

Understandably, electroshock is frightening to many laymen, raising such specters as the fear of electrocution. Actually, such hazards do not exist. Temporary loss of memory is one of several side effects that may occur. For such reasons we now prefer drug therapy whenever applicable. It's a more moderate and manageable procedure.

The one great advantage of ECT is that it usually brings some measure of quick relief, whereas drugs often require three weeks to produce an appreciable response. Thus in extreme emergencies we still fall back on ECT, usually combining it with drug treatment to achieve the best of both effects.

The most obvious emergency is a case where the patient is judged acutely suicidal and cannot be placed under proper protection. We will also consider ECT if we don't believe the patient will take the medication, if there are no relatives or friends to assist in supervision, and if hospitalization is impossible or refused. Still other rare occasions arise when we go to ECT after a severe depression has just not responded to any of the numerous drug treatments. As a general rule, we don't make such a decision until the alternatives have received a thorough trial of at least six months.

In sum, ECT is now regarded by many psychiatrists as unnecessary except in very special circumstances, and we rely on medication in the overwhelming majority of cases.

The theoretical explanation of electroshock presents an interesting question. When the method first appeared, some practitioners readily incorporated it into analytic theory. It was assumed variously that it helped the patient to atone for his guilt, or, alternately, that the convulsive effects provided a symbolic acting out of the death wish. Some theorists of more pragmatic persuasion suggested that the key effect might be the temporary amnesia, allowing the patient to forget what he felt guilty about. Today we are still not sure about the exact mode of operation, but it now seems reasonably clear that electroshock produces both biochemical and electrophysiological changes in the brain. Thus somewhat ironically, we begin to understand the treatment at about the period that it no longer is of such dominant importance.

7

The Medication:
A Clinical View

The old order changeth, yielding place to new;
And God fulfils himself in many ways,
Lest one good custom should corrupt the world.
                    —TENNYSON, *Morte d'Arthur*

IN describing the development of drug treatment I have necessarily condensed a great deal of technical detail relating to particular drugs. Some of the details are matters of concern for those personally involved with this illness, and so I will devote this chapter to the questions that regularly arise in clinical practice.

One of the first questions that occurs to many patients is that of addiction. Are these antidepressant drugs habit-forming and do they create dependency? The answer is no, they are not habit-forming in any sense of creating a craving. In fact, the clinical problem is quite the opposite. I often have to berate patients because they start feeling better and slack off on the medication before they are fully recovered.

In some severe cases the patient does require continuing antidepressant medication to avert a recurring attack. It is medically comparable to the situation of the cardiac patient who takes digitalis, the diabetic who requires insulin, and the patient with glandular deficiency who is maintained on thyroid extract. That, however, is a very different matter from addiction. We have found that long-term maintenance can be established without serious problems if the patients get worse when the drug is decreased or discontinued. For the great majority of patients the question does not arise because usually the treatment is comparatively short and no further maintenance is required. It is when there are frequent recurrences that lithium, antidepressant drugs, or a combination of the two should be considered.

Another major question involves risks. All potent medications involve some measure of hazard, as already noted, but the risk factor in antidepressant drugs is very low. There are some types of patients, however, for whom particular treatments are not recommended. It varies with each type of drug according to a general list as follows:

Factors against tricyclic antidepressant usage: Certain types of cardiovascular disease, thrombophlebitis, hyperthyroidism, a history of either narrow-angle glaucoma or presently increased intraocular pressure would each shift the choice away from a tricyclic, but are by no means absolute contraindications. Patients on tricyclic antidepressants have no dietary restrictions but should not use medication containing barbiturates (including Fiorinal), guanethidine (Ismelin), Larodopa (Dopar), or phenytoin (Dilantin) unless they get specific approval from their doctors.

Factors against MAO inhibitor usage: Chronic alcohol overuse, a liver disorder, or the presence of severe hypotension (low blood pressure) would shift the choice away from an MAO inhibitor. So also would pheochromocytoma, an unusual type of adrenal tumor. However, the cautions are relative rather than absolute.

Factors suggesting caution with the use of either tricyclics or MAO inhibitors: Any organic cerebral disorders should lead to a consideration of starting with low doses in either type of drug.

There are few major factors against lithium use except for patients whose hearts or kidneys function so inadequately as to allow excess fluid to accumulate in the body. Patients on completely salt-free diets are another group. Even these problems are only relative hazards. Patients with a history of thyroid deficiency should be followed a bit more closely, since at times the hypothyroidism (low thyroid function) is accentuated. If it does occur, one can continue lithium if thyroid extract or one of its equivalents is added.

Diuretics should be used only on the advice of your doctor. Spironolactone (Aldactone), triamterene (Dyrenium), chlorthalidone (Hygroton), and a number of others appear to be relatively safe drugs.

A special concern involves pregnancy. We have carried depressive women on medication from conception through delivery, and we have seen no indications that antidepressive drugs create any complications of pregnancy. However, this is a condition that always merits special consideration, especially in the first three months. Data other than our own indicates that with lithium the possibility of some birth defect, however minor, may increase from the usual 7 percent to approximately 9 percent. There is no evidence that this applies to the other antidepressant medications.

Quite often the patient is already taking the antidepressant medication when the pregnancy is recognized. The need for continuing the treatment usually far outweighs the risk.

Older patients do not present special problems as such, though they may be prey to the various conditions that rule against one drug or another. In general, we find that lower starting doses are more suitable for those over seventy. With lithium, often lower serum levels—and hence lower doses—are sufficient to prevent recurrence. Results in any case should be judged by clinical response rather than serum levels. This also holds true if there is enough tremor to interfere with functioning, gastrointestinal symptoms (lithium should be taken with food or milk), or headache.

Some important general precautions include the following:

Do not take medications other than those prescribed

without receiving approval from your doctor. Often a drug, even one that you have taken safely in the past, will act differently in combination with certain other medications. For this reason it is important to check with your physician whether additional medication is compatible with what you are already on. Above all, do not accept medication from friends whose good intentions may result in sad effects. It is not unusual for a person to be going to more than one physician, but make certain that each one knows what the other is doing by having one get in touch with the other if necessary.

Some chemicals that can be purchased over the counter or are found in food may interfere with treatment with MAO inhibitors only. The use of these substances, listed below, should be either entirely discontinued, limited, or used in great moderation. Some of the substances can be used in moderation, but not without approval of the treating physician. These same regulations do not apply to tricyclic antidepressants.

There follows a copy of the instructions we give to all our patients on MAOIs.

Patients on an MAOI (monoamine oxidase inhibitor) must beware of using certain substances while on this medication and for two weeks after stopping.

The MAOI antidepressant medications are:

Marplan (trade name)—isocarboxazid (generic name)
Nardil (trade name)—phenelzine (generic name)
Parnate (trade name) tranylcypromine (generic name)

There are a few MAOI medications used for other purposes:

Eutonyl (trade name)—pargyline (generic name)
Eutron (trade name)—contains pargyline

Furoxone (trade name)—furazolidone
Matulane (trade name)—procarbazine

FOOD (and DRINK):

Tyrosine is an amino acid found in some foods. When the food ages it ferments and under certain other conditions, it breaks down to produce tyramine. Normally tyramine in turn is destroyed by an enzyme, monoamine oxidase, but when an MAOI is given the tyramine may accumulate and cause an increase of blood pressure. A great deal depends on how much of the food is eaten and how it is prepared. A review of the literature plus our own experience has resulted in the recommendations which follow. We have not included foods when the evidence against them seemed questionable. We strongly recommend therefore that you adhere to these regulations since we have made them as liberal as possible.

Do NOT eat cheeses except those listed here.

SAFE . . . cream and cottage cheese, yogurt and cheeses labelled "processed" (those in which fermentation has been stopped). One or two slices of pizza made with no more than the usual amount of mozzarella is the limit.

Do NOT consume gravies, stews or drinks made with meat extracts or yeast extracts (Bovril, Marmite, Gravy Master).

Meat itself (including stews) and natural gravies are safe. Bakery products and other foods containing cooked yeast are safe.

Do NOT eat:
pickled herring, chicken
liver, goose liver, and
paté de foie gras,
food which has been aged
without refrigeration
(particularly meat and
poultry),

Freshly prepared frozen
or canned food is safe.

broad bean pods and
snow pea pods (as served
in some Chinese dishes).

The beans themselves are
safe.

Do NOT use alcohol
except in small amounts.
Do NOT take more than
a single glass of port or
sherry. Do NOT take
other red wines and
especially NOT Chianti.
Beer and ale should NOT
be used.

In any 3-hour period,
limit yourself to 2 glasses
of white wine (4 ounces
each) or 2 glasses (1½
ounces each) of whiskey,
scotch, vodka, etc.
Wine used in cooking is
safe.

AVOID food or drink
which has made you
uncomfortable in the past
or to which you are
allergic. Other foods may
occasionally cause a
reaction (none of them
very serious), according
to published reports.
None of our own patients
have reported such an
effect, however.

Several patients have
asked about bananas.
They are safe. The one
negative report is about a
patient who boiled the
bananas and ate the peel.
Chocolate in reasonable
amounts (the equivalent
of 2 regular size candy
bars) is safe in our
experience.

If in any doubt, first obtain your doctor's approval.

MEDICINES

Non-Prescription Drugs
Do NOT take any over-
the-counter preparations
unless you obtain your
doctor's approval except
those listed in the other
column.

SAFE . . .
Aspirin, Tylenol, Bufferin
(and their generic equiv-
alents) are safe. So are
vitamins, citrate or milk
of magnesia and enemas.

Particularly AVOID
nasal and pulmonary
decongestants such as
Contac (and its generic
equivalents). Also do
NOT use tablets, drops
or sprays used to treat
asthma, coughs, colds,
sinus conditions, hay
fever unless you check
with your doctor. The
same is true for sleeping
medications, pep-up pills,
anti-appetite and anti-
weight preparations.

Medications such as
Gelusil and Metamucil
used to reduce gastric
acidity tend to interfere
with the absorption of
other medications if taken
at the same time. Take
the medications separate-
ly an hour or two apart.

Prescribed Medications
Be absolutely certain that
each and every doctor
treating you for *any*
condition is aware that
you are on an MAOI.
Some medications such
as rauwolfia (reserpine),
l-dopa, Ismelin (gua-
nethidine), and drugs for
diabetes are usually not

If an operation is needed,
the MAOI is usually
discontinued a week or
two in advance. In case
of emergency surgery be
certain that the doctors
know you are on an
MAOI.
Injections for dental
work are safe.
Except for Demerol

used or require adjust-
ment of dosage.

Do NOT take Lomotil,
an antidiarrheal medica-
tion.

(meperidine) and possibly
morphine, most narcotics
used for medical purposes
are safe.
Your doctor (aware that
you are on MAOI) may
prescribe oral amphet-
amines and related sub-
stances in low doses but
usually will NOT give
these preparations by
injection.

CAUTION

If you DO ingest some of the foods or medications
listed, the probability is that nothing will happen if the
amount is small (except for over-the-counter medications, Chianti and certain cheeses when there will almost certainly be a reaction). Do NOT regard this as
an indication that you won't get the reaction next time.
We are not certain why, but sometimes the reaction
occurs and sometimes it does not. As a rule the reaction which occurs is a severe pounding headache (usually within a few hours). If this or some other severe
side-effect should occur, GO TO THE EMERGENCY
ROOM AT A HOSPITAL. They are much better prepared to treat you than is your doctor at your home or
even in his office. Usually prompt treatment can quickly
relieve the condition.

To serve as additional protection you will be given
a card to remind you about which foods and medications to avoid, and also what to do in case of an
emergency.

REMINDER FOR PATIENTS ON AN MAOI

Be certain to tell ALL doctors who treat you that
you are on an MAOI.

AVOID THESE FOODS AND BEVERAGES:

pickled herring
liver
aged meat or poultry
yeast or meat extracts
broad bean and snow pea pods
cheese, except cottage and cream cheese and yogurt
beer, ale, wine (especially Chianti),
alcohol in other forms except in very limited
     amounts

AVOID OVER-THE-COUNTER MEDICATIONS:

except aspirin (and similar substances), vitamins,
citrate and milk of magnesia. Other medications may
be safe, but check with your doctor.
Particularly AVOID CONTAC and similar preparations such as nasal and pulmonary decongestants for
ashthma, colds, stuffy nose, sinus conditions, hay
fever. Also sleeping medications, anti-appetite and
anti-weight drugs unless your doctor has approved.

In case of a reaction (such as a severe pounding
headache), go to the EMERGENCY ROOM AT A
HOSPITAL.

And finally there is that question of side effects. How
serious are they, and what exactly can the patient
expect? The question cannot be answered precisely
because every patient is different. There are some
general probabilities. Here's what we tell the patients
they may experience:

"Peculiar" feelings: You are taking a medication
designed to change your feelings. Should you feel
"zonked out" or "like a zombie," either the dosage of
medication or the medication itself is not the correct
one for you. There is no reason to fear that the treat-

ment will be worse than the disease. You should not be surprised, therefore, if you have a somewhat strange sensation. Usually this represents a period of adjustment that lasts only three or four days. If the feeling lasts longer, you should report it to your physician.

Change in bowel movements: Some of the medications will reduce the number of bowel movements. This is not necessarily constipation and usually not cause for alarm. Some people have the idea that there is something wrong if they do not have a bowel movement every day. Actually, the body can adjust well to movements only every three or four days or even once a week. If you do experience a reduced number of bowel movements while you are taking medication for your depression, there is usually no need for laxatives or cathartics. A mild constipation frequently adjusts itself over a period of a few weeks.

However, if after a week you do not have a bowel movement, this should be reported. In rare cases, especially among older people or those on a number of different medications, this causes a problem.

No medication other than mineral oil or enema should be taken without your doctor's advice. Most of the common treatments for constipation are safe, but check with your doctor first.

Sleep changes: A reduced need for sleep sometimes occurs for patients on MAO inhibitors as treatment progresses. This will be particularly noticeable for those patients whose main symptom has been an inordinate desire to sleep and who have spent long hours in bed. Many patients find after a time they can get along quite well on three or four hours of sleep a night. There is no proof that the body needs more than this to function healthily and efficiently. It is customary not to give the MAOIs late in the day, on the theory that they will then interfere less with sleep.

If there is a reduction in the amount of sleep or if you have trouble getting to sleep, it is of course important to let your physician know it. *But do not take sleeping medication without your doctor's specific knowledge and approval.* Certain sleeping medications can prove dangerous in combination with the drugs used for depression if they are not specifically and properly prescribed. They also may interfere with the beneficial effect of the medication.

Even if you have used a particular sleeping pill in the past without difficulty, this may no longer be true, since the medications you are taking may make the sleeping pills act in a different way or to quite a different degree. Barbiturates often act to increase certain enzymes and thus increase the rate at which your body excretes (metabolizes and eliminates) the antidepressant medication. This may counteract the effect of the antidepressant medication by making the level drop so low as to be ineffective.

If you find that you are remaining awake two or three or four extra hours a night, be grateful; as you begin to feel better, you will have time to do many things that you could not do in the past because you were too depressed. When the medicine is decreased or discontinued, your sleeping will return to its normal pattern. (Incidentally, over 35 percent of the general population, responding to an inquiry, report some sleep difficulty.)

Physical reactions: Sometimes you will experience minor but annoying reactions such as an increased amount of sweating, also dryness of the mouth. If the dryness of the mouth is too annoying, the use of a glycerine-based cough drop (like Pine Brothers) will help relieve that particular symptom. At times blood pressure decreases, which may produce some feelings of dizziness or weakness. Usually the body rapidly adjusts, but if not, there are medications to correct this side effect so that you can continue on antidepressant treatment. The use of an elastic abdominal binder also helps to maintain blood pressure.

Menstruation: Irregular or delayed menstruation is common and is no cause for concern. You should report it to your doctor, however, just as you should report any other changes.

Sex drive: Some patients experience a temporary reduction in their sex drive. When the medication is reduced or discontinued, there is complete recovery. In some cases changing to a different type of antidepressant will solve the problem. But you must tell your doctor about it or else he will not be able to help you. In any case, this also is not a cause for alarm.

In some patients in whom the depression has already reduced sexual activity, the medication may have a stimulant effect.

Blurred vision: At times blurred vision, especially when reading, results soon after starting medication. It usually disappears fairly soon, but if not, it can be corrected by using reading glasses. After you go off medication this side effect disappears. The effect is due to weakness of the muscles used in accommodation for near vision. Usually distance vision is unaffected, so it does not interfere with driving a car.

The various side effects listed above may or may not occur with any particular patient. Some tolerate the medication beautifully. Some have problems. Sometimes we can alleviate a particular reaction by switching from one antidepressant drug to another. At times we can add another preparation that will compensate for the side effect. And sometimes the patient just has to endure disagreeable reactions as the price of getting well.

Of course, all this requires a physician's close supervision. A patient should never take it on himself to increase or decrease the dosage and should never try to decide for himself which side effects are worth reporting to the doctor. Every effect should be reported.

The list that follows includes some of the cautions that should be observed in respect to drug interactions:

Tricyclics
1. Tricyclics enhance the depressant effect of alcohol.

2. Thyroid products may potentiate tricyclic activity.
3. Barbiturates, in contrast, usually reduce tricyclic action.
4. Combining tricyclics with reserpine or Rauwolfia may result in overstimulation.
5. Rarely, there may be motor impairment when combined with chlordiazepoxide (Librium).
6. The antihypertensive effect of guanethidine (Ismelin) may be reversed by tricyclics, except for doxepin (Sinequan and Adapin).
7. Tricyclics should be combined with MAOIs only under strict medical supervision.

MAOIs
1. See list of foods, drinks, and medications that may produce hypertensive crisis.
2. Diabetics on insulin may show decreased blood sugar requiring a reduced dose of insulin.
3. Meperidine (Demerol) may produce an excitatory and/or depressant reaction. Codeine or morphine is preferable.
4. Injected amphetamines and other related substances for injection are definitely to be avoided.
5. Atropine, scopolamine and related substances (as found in Contac, etc.) should not be used since they can produce hypertensive crises.
6. Neo-Synephrine is the safest type of nose drop.
7. Levodopa (Sinemet, Larodopa, Dopar) used for parkinsonism may cause a significant rise in blood pressure (usually in doses over 50 mg).
8. MAOIs should be combined with tricyclics only under strict medical supervision.

Lithium
1. Thiazide diuretics (Diuril, HydroDIURIL, Naturetin, Saluron, Hygroton, Zaroxolyn, Hydromox) should be used under strict supervision since they can increase the chance of a toxic reaction (especially in pregnancy).
2. Aldactone and Dyrenium seem to be acceptable.
3. Potassium iodide may lower thyroid function and increase the chance of getting a goiter.

And finally, the patient must be patient. We do get those marvelous cases in which the illness clears up almost immediately, but mostly the treatment takes a little time. The first three or four weeks are usually the most trying because the patient may doubt that he will ever feel better. If he stays with it, though, he has an excellent chance, and often the physician can see the change before the patient himself knows that he has turned the corner.

In a recent investigation in which both an English and a Swedish investigator (S. A. Montgomery and M. Asberg) were involved, the same ten symptoms were found most responsive to treatment. These were:

1. Apparent sadness (as seen by others)
2. Reported sadness (as experienced by the patient)
3. Inner tension
4. Reduced sleep
5. Reduced appetite
6. Concentration difficulties
7. Lassitude (apathy, fatigue, indifference)
8. Inability to feel
9. Pessimistic thoughts
10. Suicidal thoughts

Thus, when the treatment begins to work these are the symptoms that are most likely to disappear earliest.

One of my patients heard I was writing this book and we agreed that it would be most useful to include a "patient's-eye" view of the universe. Her report follows:

I went to Dr. Nathan Kline about three months ago at the suggestion of a friend of mine, who happens to be a psychiatrist on the staff of one of New York's leading hospitals. The friend knew me well and felt that I was suffering from what he called "cyclical depressions." "You should be on lithium," he said. "And the best man to handle this drug is Dr. Kline. Call and get an appointment."

I telephoned as I was told and was given an appointment, later than I would have liked. After seeing his crowded waiting room, I knew I was lucky to have one at all. As it is now turning out, I am more than lucky.

Who am I? I am a free-lance photographer in my forties, whose work has appeared in national magazines, in books, and in museums. I am also a producer and director of films for television and theatrical release. Married and the mother of three, I have a large and beautiful apartment in New York with a view of Central Park pleasing enough to satisfy the uneasiest of souls.

Some years back I had been in extensive psychotherapy with an accredited doctor of Freudian persuasion, and over the past five years I had practically become a psycho "groupie," touching base with many a well-known private and popular group therapist, trying to beat my "mercurial" temperament (as I cheerfully called my depressive bouts of emotional highs and lows). My recent depression was lasting on and off over a year, until I was almost incapacitated by the time I reached Dr. Kline.

The symptoms: unprovoked tears plummeting down my cheek at odd times and for long spells. The outgoing, often joyous nature that was me at my best became tense, withdrawn, unproductive, and silent. I stuttered when I decided to talk, but mostly I sat quietly, dreading being with people. Social life was painful.

I avoided going to my office, and when I did get there, I played the shifting-papers-from-one-side-of-the-desk-to-the-other game for days and days. I was sure I was the living example of the Peter Principle: I had overreached the top level of my capabilities, which, it seemed, was anybody else's lowest level. After all, wasn't I completely worthless? Everyone was better than I. I'd marvel at the efficiency of the people who did even the simplest of jobs. The bus driver. The doorman. The lady in the supermarket who made change so rapidly and happily. Everyone was so content and capable.

And, mostly to avoid people, I escaped to the kitchen on weekends and cooked and cried. My family did not mind my kitchen tears; they were receiving some benefits in the form of chili con carne and a few exotic recipes never tried before or, if all goes well, ever again.

Fortunately the "buck-up," "pull-yourself-to-gether," "buy-a-hat" type of bad advice was not passed on to me by close friends. They had seen me survive a tragic widowhood five days after the birth of a second son, and I had endured three operations after the birth of another some years ago. I'll refrain from further proving my mettle and stop here. Self-pity was not my standard approach in life.

But here I was, all dressed up, holding myself together, with my sympathetic husband at my side. Dr. Kline's smile was broad and reassuring in a well-tanned face, capped by startling silver hair. He studied my case-history form. (Everyone receives such a form in the mail. It asks for information as to the pills you may now be taking, your medical, psychiatric, family, and personal history.)

He was impressive as he explained the nature of depression. Mine, he thought, was probably caused by a genetic factor. This brought back memories of my mother going through an imagined "tumor" on the brain during my adolescent years, requiring me to change ice packs on her head, and of the several times she had been mysteriously "away," "resting," while I was even younger. Dr. Kline agreed. And listened.

Soon, after more conversation, he prescribed a number of different pills for me. They were to get me out of my depression. Lithium, he explained, was to help keep my depression from recurring once it was gone. Thus lithium would be given later.

The others were a combination of antidepressants of varying names, milligrams, and frequencies. I put their names and times of intake on a piece of paper to keep them straight. Cheese, liquor, beer, wine, and chocolate were taboo for a while. The length of time till I would be completely on lithium and off the antidepressants could be "three to six months," I was told.

In the meantime, my blood pressure is checked at every visit and a sample of my blood taken periodically to determine if my lithium level is correct. Two pamphlets written by Dr. Kline about patients on lithium or antidepressants bolster my knowledge in between visits about the do's and don'ts of what is happening.

I had fooled the good doctor during our first meeting; I had held myself together a bit too much. The pills were making me feel worse. During our next visit he changed my medication, its type, and strength, and I relaxed. But weeks went by. I still saw no progress. I continued cooking and crying in the kitchen. A friend even snidely referred to my new psychiatrist and his magic pills as "Dr. Feelgood." "You look terrible," she reported. "Worn, jumpy, and exhausted." I thanked her for her honesty and wept some more.

Suddenly everything changed. Or maybe it was gradual. But in the sixth week I walked into Dr. Kline's office smiling broadly, noticed the sculpture garden outside his window for the first time, and announced gleefully, "We did it. I feel terrific."

"And you were beginning to think I was quack," he said, looking almost as pleased I was.

"Not really," I answered. "But it wasn't happening fast enough." Naturally I wanted to feel better and more at peace . . . immediately. I understand from the pleasant nurses on staff that some patients call expecting to feel good after the first night.

And who can blame us? There is nothing that describes a feeling of depression, but I understand there are six million sufferers in this country. Perhaps one of them may be articulate and speak for us.

Now, I'm not all the way home. But I'm working, alive and lively and quite peaceful. And what's more, I'm sleeping through the night. It's strange, but all those guilts, fears, and self-doubts are gone. (It might be appropriate to have some therapy now, though I won't; some people do at this point, I hear, quite successfully.)

Allow me to preserve my privacy and not sign my name, but do not doubt for a moment that I am real and so is my dramatic turnaround. If pharmacotherapy and Dr. Kline have been responsible, that's all right with me. I'm grateful. I'd love to talk to you when I'm all the way home.

I'm not cooking and crying anymore.

It is now ten years since this patient began treatment. She continues to do well on lithium alone.

8

The Patient

My heart is a lonely hunter that hunts on a lonely hill.
—WILLIAM SHARP, *The Lonely Hunter*

How heavy the days are. There is not a fire that can warm me, not a sun to laugh with me. Everything base. Everything cold and merciless. And even the beloved dear stars look desolately down.
—HERMANN HESSE, *Steppenwolf*

"IN a real dark night of the soul it is always three o'clock in the morning. . . ." So wrote F. Scott Fitzgerald during a severe depression. He caught exactly the mood of most of my patients when they first appear in my office.

What stands out most vividly in Fitzgerald's description is the word "always." The depressive often feels that he is trapped in a timeless, unending nightmare, and he can visualize nothing that will break the spell. In fact, with proper treatment the dark mood will probably begin to lift rather quickly—typically in three or four weeks. Those first few weeks can be a very trying period, however, and that is especially true if the patient has little confidence in the medication.

The mental attitude does not directly affect the healing process, because the treatment is usually effective whether the patient believes in it or not. The problem is to persuade the doubting patient to stick with the program, take the medicine faithfully, and tolerate if necessary the side effects that may temporarily add to his general misery.

Interestingly enough, the prospects for recovery are also not decisively affected by the depth of the depression. Very severe cases often respond well, while an occasional rather mild case may prove resistant to the treatment. The regulating factor is the individual patient's biochemical response to the drug. The treatment either works or it doesn't—and generally it does.

I start the treatment with a medical history, laboratory tests, and a complete psychiatric evaluation. That is important in determining which of the various antidepressants may be most applicable. It also has a quite practical psychological value. In many cases the patient is suffering from both mental and physical distress. He wants, and is entitled to, an attentive medical hearing as to all his aches and pains.

Often enough the patient has discerned in his friends or relatives the opinion that his illness is "all in his mind," and he may have been told openly or by implication that things would be all right if he would just "pull himself together." He may secretly and shamefully half-agree with that verdict. Thus careful attention to the physical examination helps to reassure him. It establishes the fact that he is indeed sick and that his distress is real.

I always encourage the patient to describe his symptoms, even after the diagnosis is clear. Thus I have heard thousands of depressives tell of their sleepless nights. For the patient that was a wretched experience, perhaps frightening, and he needs to talk it out with somone who understands. At times referral for psychotherapy is most useful.

Another value of a thorough interview is that it provides a later yardstick for measuring the course of recovery. When a patient describes his symptoms, I am listening not just to his words but also to his tone, and I am observing the nuances of his posture, dress, and general manner. Perhaps he sits slack-bodied, eyes averted, reciting his complaints in a flat and distant monotone. A few weeks later he may insist that the medicine isn't helping, that he still has all the same problems, but a change in speech and manner may signal the beginning of recovery.

Some of the signals are so subtle as to be almost subliminal. When a patient is announced, I make it a practice to meet him at the door and shake hands, and sometimes I sense something of his condition from that brief physical contact, not just that his grip is firm or weak but some perception that goes beyond that. I don't try to analyze it because I might lose those moments of intuition if I thought about it too much.

It adds up to the fact that drug treatment of depression consists of much more than prescribing pills. One must treat the whole patient while dealing with many human facets of the disease.

One critical aspect is to establish a good personal relationship, so that the patient will report frankly on all his reactions as the treatment progresses. Oddly enough, a chief difficulty is that some patients are just too cooperative, too anxious to please. They will try to dredge up whatever response they think the psychiatrist expects.

One must be careful not to intimidate such patients. They may fail to report poor reactions because they think you'll be disappointed in their failure to improve. On the other hand, one can be too sympathetic. The passive, overcooperative patient may feel obliged to produce some symptoms if you keep pressing him, asking: "Are you sure you feel better?" "Do you still have those dreadful headaches?" "Are you really getting enough sleep?"

Through years of experience one develops almost a sixth sense in evaluating patient responses. Even so, I always welcome the backup support of the nurses who assist in my clinical practice. They are first-rate observers, they have the advantage of seeing the patient off-guard, and they are encouraged to report what they see and hear.

Sometimes a nurse will note that a patient behaves

very morbidly in the waiting room and then puts on a cheerful show when ushered into my office. Occasionally I am misled by such a performance, and I reduce the medication in the belief that the illness is abating. The nurse sees the change as she processes the new prescription. If she thinks something is amiss, she steps into her own office, calls me, and alerts me to the situation. If the report warrants, I may reinstate the previous prescription, and the patient may never know that we have caught on to his act. The next time he calls he just finds me more skeptical and probing as I inquire into his progress.

An opposite type is the patient who exaggerates every ill and magnifies every problem to absurd dimensions. As an example, one warns such a patient that the drug may cause the side effect of some dryness of the mouth, and shortly he reports back that he can't take the medicine at all. It has made the mouth so dry that he can't even swallow the pill! This is neurotic behavior, of course, though it doesn't necessarily mean that the depression arose from neurosis. In any case, the immediate problem is to persuade the patient to take the medicine.

Usually we coax him along while reducing the initial doses to minimal amounts, or changing from tablet to capsule—or even fluid if available. Or we may suggest that the tablet be crushed and dissolved and mixed with applesauce. If that doesn't work, we occasionally resort to the kind of tactic that is known at the poker table as calling and raising.

"I believe there is a psychological factor in your reaction," I tell the patient.

No, no, he insists, he actually can't tolerate the pill.

"All right," I say, "but let's put it to a test. It happens that we have two kinds of pills that look exactly alike. One is the drug that you have been taking. The other is a placebo—a total blank. I'll call the nurse and ask her to prepare a bottle of each. Then go out and pick one of the bottles without knowing whether it's the active medication or the placebo. Come back next week and tell me if you've experienced any effects."

We don't use that approach very often, but on occasion such treatment can be most efficacious. Although the neurotic usually concedes at this point, he'll find some other way to call attention to himself, but meanwhile he'll take the medicine.

Most depressives are not that neurotic. They regard the illness as a painful disability, they want to get well, and they try to cooperate. When they resist the medication, it is usually for a quite different set of reasons.

One type of problem involves the patient who doesn't really believe the medication will work. At other times he doesn't believe he "deserves" all the attention or "trouble" he is causing. In fact, he may believe he "deserves" to suffer. He needs constant encouragement to stay with it during the early phases of treatment, before benefits become obvious.

Another problem is the patient who starts cutting down on the recommended dosage as soon as he begins to feel a little better. This phenomenon occurs in other illnesses, by the way, and represents a rather common human foible. I believe that at bottom it involves a kind of magical thinking: it is well known that people who have to take medicine are generally sicker than those who don't; ergo, when you stop taking medicine, you must be getting well. The patient who really wants to recover will sometimes persuade himself that he has already achieved it, and as a proof to himself he starts to neglect his pills. When we find out about that, we raise a real fuss.

We usually cut down on the medicine a bit at a time as recovery progresses, but only the physician can judge the pace and amount of such reduction. Generally we continue a full medication schedule for several months after the patient is symptom-free, in order to stabilize the condition.

For individual patients the course of the treatment varies considerably. I've had cases that cleared up after a few treatments and others that stretched on for a year.

More typically, however, the treatment is completed in the course of about eight office visits, usually spaced about two weeks apart at first, then once a month or even less frequently.

The first faint sign of recovery usually occurs when the patient begins to take more interest in himself and his surroundings. Then gradually he becomes a bit more active, attending to routine things he had neglected before. A clear improvement in mood is usually the last sign to appear and indicates that recovery is well under way.

Mood changes are sometimes quite erratic in the early stages of recovery. The patient may experience brief remissions of the depression and then sink back to the former level. There may be as many as half a dozen ups and downs before the illness finally fades away.

We counsel both the patient and his family to expect occasional setbacks. The family can be very helpful just by encouraging, supporting, and reassuring the patient during the dark periods.

It does not help at all to exhort the patient to get well. Suggestions that he should "buck up" are liable to increase his guilt or hostility, as will reminders that he should "be thankful for what he's got." What is needed is simply a calm and steady assurance that he will soon be feeling better.

At times actions are even more reassuring than words. As a case in point, I remember one woman patient whose family made it an annual custom to rent a cottage at the beach. Then she was seized by a severe depression, and she felt there was no point in reserving the cottage for the next season. She knew she could never take part in the round of beach parties and social gatherings that always marked the summer holiday. Just thinking about packing up for the trip took more mental and physical energy than she thought she could summon. All she wanted to do was stay home, crawl into her shell, and endure her misery in lonely withdrawal.

I advised the family to go ahead and reserve the cottage. "Tell her she's going to feel better soon," I said, "and then act on that assumption. She'll gain confidence when she sees that you believe in her recovery.

"Don't push her," I said. "Don't try to hurry her recovery. Just show by your actions that you're sure she's going to get well.

"Of course," I added, "there's a chance that the recovery won't come in time for the summer vacation. But that's a small gamble. The most you'll lose is the reservation fee. You have a lot more than that to gain."

As it happened, she did recover in time, and the beach outing provided a happy change of scene as she again picked up the threads of life. As an added benefit, she wasn't burdened with guilt from having unnecessarily deprived the others of their pleasure.

For the most part, the early stages of the treatment are heavily concentrated on the physical aspects of the illness. We establish a medication regime, check regularly on the patient's reactions, and put off problem-solving until the patient is well enough to make decisions.

Once the treatment is well established, the typical patient visit requires about fifteen minutes. For a good many it's even quicker. They are in and out of my office in five to ten minutes, pausing just long enough to report that all is going well.

Occasionally we encounter a problem that has to be talked out, and then the visit may stretch on for an hour or more. The other scheduled patients are not too happy about that, but still it contributes to the group psychotherapy that goes on unendingly in the waiting room.

The usual brisk pace of office visits has produced a revolutionary change in the logistics of mental health. The psychiatrist who makes full use of pharmacotherapy can see in a day more *new* patients than a typical analyst may see in a year.

My own practice provides an illustration. I share a private New York City practice with a number of colleagues, and since we also have other responsibilities, we each keep office hours from one to three days a week. Even so, in one recent two-year period we were able to see and treat well over a thousand new patients.

There are those who recoil from such methods as "assembly-line medicine." In fact, it is no more an assembly-line method than is the practice of those physicians who sit in an office seeing a steady stream of patients who suffer from virus diseases, infections, and the like. The fact that treatment is often quite brisk does not thereby render it less effective. Psychiatry has labored too long under the delusion that every emotional malfunction requires an endless talking out of everything the patient ever experienced.

Of course, one does see patients whose problems can't be worked out in a handful of fifteen-minute visits. There are people who have remained enmeshed in the same basic problems all their lives, and they may or may not be able to talk it out in a hundred hours or more of intensive psychotherapy. They are the severe neurotics, and they present an entirely different case. For them neurosis often becomes a way of life rather than an illness.

If a depressive suffers also from a separate condition of marked neurosis, I advise him to enter psychotherapy. Unless the need is quite urgent, however, I will often propose that he put off that demanding procedure until an evaluation of the effectiveness of the medication used alone can be made.

There are still more difficult cases in which severe neurosis appears to be not just an aggravating factor but the basic cause of the depression. That presents an entirely different medical problem. In such cases drug therapy will not help and may even do harm. I urge such patients to go into psychotherapy immediately.

There are many other cases in which brief "reality" therapy or related treatment may be most effective in conjunction with the medication. This may help the patient to establish or reestablish effective means of functioning and of enjoying life.

Distinguishing between these various types of patients is one of the most difficult problems in diagnosis. It is not a matter that can be reduced to a checklist of symptoms, and even the overt circumstances are often susceptible to conflicting interpretations.

Consider a patient who has been plunged into a deep and protracted depression by the loss of his job. A psychiatrist of strong psychoanalytic bent might view that almost automatically as cause and effect, a neurotic reaction flaring up in response to the stresses of life. That might indeed be the case, but a psychiatrist of biochemical persuasions would at least suspect a different course of events. This may be a patient who has long suffered from a chronic low-level instability in his brain chemistry. So long as the condition was rather minor, he may have been able to hide the illness from others and even from himself. Then his condition grew worse, his steady deterioration culminated in the loss of his job, and after that his continuing decline finally forced an acknowledgment that he was suffering from mental and emotional collapse. In short, there may be a quite serious question as to whether he had a depression because he lost his job or, alternately, whether he lost his job because he was already a hidden depressive.

The theoretical question can become even more entangled if the depression is not linked to any apparent cause. Take the case of a depressed patient who is happily married, successful in business, seemingly fortunate in every aspect of life. A really determined theorist can make out that the reason for his depression is the very lack of reason. That is, he's ridden with subconscious guilt and is punishing himself for his success. If he cannot dredge up appropriate guilt responses, that becomes a denial mechanism and all the more potent evidence of the fact.

The elastic lengths to which such interpretation can be carried is illustrated by one of the psychiatric stories that psychiatrists like to collect. It is said that when you keep a psychiatric appointment you can't win, because if you come early you are anxious, if you come late you are hostile, and if you come exactly on time you are compulsive.

I am skeptical toward all the more fanciful flights of interpretation, and I would welcome eagerly a standard laboratory test that would allow us to distinguish the one type of illness from the other. I hope that we will soon develop sufficiently refined laboratory procedures enabling us to know exactly when a particular biochemical failure has occurred. Meanwhile, a number of investigators have tried to differentiate the two ills by checklisting various symptoms, but those systems just don't prove out. The criteria are so general and the assessments so subjective that the testers almost never agree on the results.

Another kind of clue is provided if the patient does not respond to medication. But again that is not definitive, because the drug action may be blocked by a metabolic quirk.

In the end we can rely only on clinical judgment. In my own practice I assume that the depression is probably biochemical at base if the patient displays only the "normal" or garden-variety kind of neurotic reactions. We all share at least a little of that. I consider that it is probably a true neurotic depression if the depression appears to arise as an integral part of the entire personality.

The judgment is again subjective, and the standard may seem broad, but the matter can be reduced to some pretty concrete observations:

If the depressive has at base a healthy personality, and if he is suffering chiefly from a biochemical breakdown, then he regards the illness as a terrible nuisance. He'd like to get it over with so that he can get back to the main business of life.

If he is at base severely neurotic, and if that's the root of the problem, then the illness *is* life. He clings to it as an essential expression of his tortured spirit.

That is a far graver illness, and it can be exorcised only by coming to grips with the underlying pathology of self-hatred and life rejection. In my opinion that type of neurotic depression is fortunately rather rare.

What one does encounter quite commonly is a depressive who also has some neurotic problems. Depending on the severity of neurotic reactions, they may or may not need some supportive therapy when the depression abates. Let's look at some typical cases of the kind that pass regularly through my waiting room.

On a given day one may find sitting side by side in the waiting room an office worker, a middle-aged housewife, and a young college dropout. They share the fact that all of them suffered a depressive breakdown. Another thing they share is that all had emotional problems that preceded the depression and will still exist when the depression is cured.

Looked at objectively, their emotional problems are of a most common and ordinary sort. They may or may not be able to look at their problems objectively. Even full self-knowledge does not guarantee that one can deal with one's problems.

Take the office worker, for instance. He's fifty-five years old, he has worked hard and faithfully for the same company for the last twenty-five years, and he thought he was in line for the next promotion. He didn't get it. He was passed over for a thirty-five-year-old "upstart," and it has brought out a lot of hostile reactions.

His objective problem, to repeat for emphasis, is extraordinarily common. There were a half dozen other people at his office who didn't get the promotion. Quite a number of them went home complaining about what a poor choice the company made. Our patient, however, has carried his disappointment to greater lengths. He has convinced himself that the company is rife with favoritism, that it's run by a pack of idiots, and that no one there appreciated his contributions.

Is he neurotic? Certainly. Does he need intensive

analysis? Not necessarily. It depends on how severe the reaction is.

I get to know this patient in the course of the treatment, and I find that his neurotic reaction involves something more than an isolated response. He is in a small way what we sometimes call an "injustice collector." When disappointments occur or problems arise, he discovers rather readily that some segment of society is engaged in a conspiracy against him. Of course, he'd be embarrassed to call it that, so he uses more acceptable terms like "office politics." It comes down to the same thing. He's sure he didn't get his just deserts. Sometimes the "conspiracy" can go back to childhood, when the patient felt that his parents always gave his brother the bigger pieces of pie—and the larger shares of love and attention.

That kind of neurosis can become severely crippling and may require protracted therapy. In the case at hand, however, I find that it is a rather minor aspect of the total personality. His persecution complex is usually exhibited in flash responses that quickly come and go, and over the years it hasn't interfered too much with his life. He has a substantial circle of friends, a fair range of healthy interests, and a pretty good relationship with his family. In spite of his present complaints he's done quite well at his job. In short, he is usually a functioning, reasonably healthy personality who has this small, persistent quirk. Right now the quirk is being magnified and exacerbated by a clinical depression. I regard the depression as his major problem, and I treat it intensively. As to the neurosis, if I find it quite incidental and rather trivial I may choose to ignore it.

It may surprise some that a psychiatrist would observe a neurosis and not make a concerted effort to deal with it. In fact, however, I do not consider that all neuroses require treatment.

It is a question of perspective. A plastic surgeon regularly observes people whose features might be marginally improved by raising the nose a few millimeters or dropping the ears. It would be expensive, time-consuming, and painful, however, and when one got through, the subject would still fall short of some theoretical standard of esthetic perfection. The procedure is generally too rigorous to justify small improvements, and so most of us settle for the visage we've got. So, too, in the emotional area, I believe that we do well to accept in ourselves and others something less than a flawless psychic profile.

In the case of the disappointed office worker, he might benefit from a little more insight. He doesn't want it, however, and indeed right now he would stoutly resist it. His neurosis does, after all, have its functional uses. It provides him with a satisfactory explanation of all setbacks and disappointments, and right now it may be protecting him from the knowledge that he just doesn't have the capacities and talents for the kind of job he'd like to have.

We all have our illusions, and if his are not really damaging, I may choose not to disturb them. I may talk to him instead about the fact that one should not seek all one's gratifications at the office. I will consider the case satisfactorily closed if he goes forth from my office with his depression cured and his ego defense mechanisms even slightly improved.

Next case: the housewife.

Her emotional problem is also of a very common sort, but in this instance it's more painful. She has lost her job—her prime role and function—and it happened at at a time when other transitions left her feeling very vulnerable.

This particular woman has had a companionable relationship with her husband, but it was her children who served as a chief focus for her being. For years she was the most important person in their lives, and they in hers, and she mothered them in sometimes overwhelming fashion. Now they're grown or nearly so, and they no longer need or want all that attention. In an objective and rational way she insists that of course she wants them to grow up, but emotionally she feels rejected and pushed aside. It doesn't help any that it happens while she's undergoing her menopause.

Some would ascribe her depression to the psychological consequences of the menopause and the related shadow cast by the loss of her mother's role. I suspect a different order of cause and effect. The menopause and the depression are, I think, two separate consequences of a physical event. She is undergoing a tremendous biochemical transition, and it is not surprising that the shock waves of change are felt through the whole system. In any case, and whatever the mixture of causes, she is suffering from both physical and emotional disturbance. The physical disturbance will subside, and the depression can be cured, but when that's done, her original emotional problem is still there waiting to be dealt with. Relief of the depression may or may not make it possible for the patient to cope with her problem.

In her, too, one can find a streak of neurosis. Perhaps she overinvested in her mother's role because she had never developed a sufficient sense of her own identity as a person. Her numerous sacrifices for her children probably contained a touch of conspicuous martyrdom, and she may have used it to obtain for herself an importance she did not know how to find in more constructive ways.

She too may resist insight into her situation or find that the insight does not automatically produce the needed change. Fortunately there are some other ways to address her problem.

Does she serve others out of her own deep need to feel needed and wanted? Well, the best way to *feel* needed is to *be* needed. There are innumerable political causes, church groups, and community organizations that will welcome with open arms anyone who really wants to help. She cannot attempt such transitions while in the depths of depression, but when the illness begins to lift, it is time to think about the psychologic adjustments she has to make. I'll talk to her, try to elicit her interests, encourage her to take part in things she hasn't had much time for up to now. If she finds a good outlet, she may even begin to forge a stronger sense of that healthy self-esteem that is necessary to us all. In any case, she may become too occupied to sit and fret because the children no longer revolve their lives around hers. She'll be on her way to an excellent adjustment when she can say to the young married son or daughter, "I'm sorry, I'd really love to baby-sit tonight, but I have an important meeting."

Next case: the college dropout.

This young man looks at the other two patients with a disdain he does not trouble to hide. He is firmly convinced that their anguish is nothing like his.

He believes that he is depressed because the world is too coarse and materialistic for his sensitive spirit. He considers himself a rebel, perhaps even a revolutionary. In fact, he's a troubled and frightened young man. He, too, is insecure.

His problem began with a father who was too demanding, or at least the young man thought so. He felt he could never live up to the father's expectations, whether spoken or unspoken.

The mother was protective, and the young man came to rely heavily on that. He never developed much confidence in his own capacities.

By the time he went off to college he was secretly convinced that he couldn't handle it, and the prophecy proved self-fulfilling. By then, however, he had discovered a splendid social rationale for his problems. The college was "irrelevant." So were all the other workaday affairs of the world. So he dropped out. His father stormed, his mother wept, and the young man sat and brooded in defiant misery.

His emotional turmoil and self-imposed withdrawal coincided with and may have helped to precipitate a clinical depression. The depression was a biochemical event, however, or at least it is responding to biochemical correction. Meanwhile, there remains his neurotic problem.

He won't give up the neurotic attitudes easily, because the neurosis is serving quite a number of needs. It has finally brought him some importance, if only as the center of an interminable family row. It allows him to express his resentment of his father while testing again and again the limits of his mother's devotion. Above all, he has found a perfect cover for all his anxieties. It not only explains his failures but also elevates them to the status of high principle. Neurotics often invoke moral reasons for their behavior.

The problem is that his reactions are not functional in any larger sense. There are some constructive and useful outlets for youth rebellion, but sitting and brooding is not one of them. At least, not for too long.

If I think the youth is being put under too much pressure, I will talk with the father about it (but only if I obtain the patient's permission). Seeing a problem is one thing, however, and solving it is sometimes quite another. The father may be quite adamant. He doesn't need counseling; the boy does. The kid has fooled around long enough. He has to shape up now or ship out.

The father's attitude may reflect some neurotic anxieties of his own. He is not my patient, however. The youth is. At some point in the proceedings I must confront my patient with some realities of his situation.

"Look," I tell him, "you have a problem with your father, but you also have a problem with yourself. You want to live as you see fit, but you also want to be protected and taken care of. I think you've about run out the string on that. If you really want complete freedom, you may have to leave home and find your own place in the world."

If the young man can nerve himself to do that, once the depression has lifted, it may jolt the father into some compromise position that both can accept. It is to be hoped that they might reach some understanding in which the youth will complete his education. But if not, if he has to go out now and struggle to sustain himself—well, that is the price of freedom. Undertaking it may induce in the young man more healthy and realistic attitudes toward life.

This kind of approach is sometimes called reality therapy. Sometimes it doesn't work with those who are really severely damaged by neurosis. It is surprising, though, how effective it can be with most ordinary cases. It is not unusual for us to refer such special cases to one of the psychotherapists who collaborate with us. At times a more analytic therapy appears indicated, and occasionally we will refer patients for this more intensive and prolonged type of treatment.

There are those who concede the value of the method while believing that it does not go far enough. They contend that the underlying neurosis will always persist, surfacing again and again, unless the patient achieves insight into the original cause of his emotional disturbance.

I do not agree. I believe that many neurotic manifestations tend to be self-healing if not continually exacebated by circumstances.

We know that our bodies have enormous self-healing capacities that extend to all but the most grievous injuries. It would seem curious to me if the psyche is the only part of our makeup that does not possess regenerative and restorative powers.

Early experiences do exert enormous influence on the psyche, but I see no reason to believe that all attitudes so formed are forever frozen. If unhealthy circumstances engender neurosis, then healthy circumstances should help to correct it. Thus for the "born loser" I know no better psychologic medicine than a little practice at winning. For sloughing off dependent attitudes there is nothing quite like the sometimes rigorous necessities of independence.

And finally, I believe we do well to remember that there is no such thing as perfect health, either emotional or physical. The pursuit of that chimera can become in itself an unhealthy obsession.

Most of us accept this readily enough in the physical area. The sensible person takes good care of his body and seeks help promptly if there is any sign that something is seriously amiss. But one need not consult a specialist for every small case of the sniffles, and there is such a thing as carrying diet and exercise to neurotic extremes. The "health nut" can become so involved in his barbells, his deep breathing, and his organic foods that he loses sight of all the good and pleasant uses for which the body is intended.

Similarly in the emotional area I think one can carry concern with neurosis to neurotic lengths. In my own practice I do not even attempt to get to the psychologic bottom of every emotional quirk. I believe that it is sufficient in most cases if one can help the patient arrive at a functional and healthy adjustment to the stresses of life, so that at least part of the time he can say, as did one famous minnesinger of the Middle Ages, "*juvat vivere*"—it is a joy to be alive.

Some perspective is required also in the matter of "solving" the existential problems. Many life situations do not yield, in fact, to perfect solutions. What is presented rather often is a range of imperfect choices.

As a commonplace example, I am consulted fairly frequently by business and professional people who find themselves overwhelmed by the stress and tension of their work. Proper medication can correct the biochemical malfunction if that is the problem. Psychotherapy can ease the emotional aberrations if that is involved. In the end, however, a considerable tension level is inexorably bound up in particular pursuits of life. The individual must decide for himself how much stress he is able or willing to tolerate and what price he will or will not pay to achieve his aims.

I do not tell my patients what kind of basic choices they ought to make. That is their responsibility. My task is to restore them to normal function so that they can make considered decisions.

Because I am not emotionally involved in their problems, I can sometimes help them to clarify the practical choices that exist. At times that involves presenting them with facts they would prefer not to face. Quite often, however, it is my agreeable role to inform them that their problems are not so harsh and unyielding as they may believe. Depressives become accustomed to seeing "through a glass darkly," and they often view matters as far more hopeless than they really are.

I recall a particular woman who created very serious problems for herself while in the grip of a depressive attack. At the time she did not realize that she was sick and knew only that life had become unbearably flat, stale, monotonous, and oppressive.

In a desperate attempt to wring some feeling from existence she turned to alcohol and sex. She left her husband and children and began touring the taverns, picking up any man she could find. She wound up sharing a motel room with several men. She was posing as a gay party girl, but in fact she was caught in a miserable trap and did not know how to get out.

Eventually she came to me for treatment. I was able to relieve the depression, and when she began to recover, we talked about the other problem. She had a good deal of insight into herself, and she felt she knew why she had gone off on her aberrant spree. She also felt that it had been the greatest mistake of her life. She told me that she would give a great deal if she could restore the marriage she had thrown away. Since that was impossible, she was prepared to start over alone, accepting it as the final cost of a very expensive illness.

"It may work out that way," I told her. "But you are overlooking one alternative."

"What alternative?"

"You could go to your husband and ask him to take you back."

She thought that was grasping at straws. She was sure he could not forgive the desertion.

"Perhaps not," I said, "but perhaps so. You'll never know unless you try. It could be that you both want to start over, but neither will make the first move—he because of pride and hurt and you because of pride and guilt.

"If putting that marriage back together is what you really want," I told her, "then it's worth a try. You would be risking rejection, but I think you're strong enough to take that now. What do you have to lose?"

She took the chance, and he agreed to try again. Whether or not they will live happily ever after I would not venture to predict. It is not a "happy ending" story, but only the story of a difficult new beginning.

I approach most patient problems in that spirit. I am a psychiatrist, not a wizard, and I have no magic wand to wave. I don't solve life's problems. I can only help people address their problems in hopeful and constructive ways.

By the same token, antidepressant drug therapy is not happiness mixed into a bottle. It does not resolve the stress and challenge of life, and it does not even abolish all psychic pain. It would be bad medicine if it did, for it would make us less than human.

Emotion is a rich part of our being, and in the nature of things it embraces both hope and fear, both sadness and joy. The antidepressant drugs do not round off all those edges of existence. They do abolish the aberrant, deranged response and restore the normal capacity to think and feel. Fortunately for many patients that is therapy enough.

9

The Aged

I pray to God that I may forget these matters
That with myself I too much discuss,
*   too much explain . . .*
Because I do not hope to turn again
Because I do not hope
Because I do not hope to turn
Desiring this man's gift
Or that man's scope
Why should the aged eagle stretch its wings?
Why should I mourn the vanished power
*   of the usual reign?*
Because I do not hope to know again
The infirm glory of the positive hour . . .
                    —T. S. ELIOT, *Ash Wednesday*

Body and mind, like man and wife, do not always agree to die together.

                    —CHARLES CALEB COLTON

Old men ought to be explorers
Here and there does not matter
We must be still and still moving
Into another intensity
For a further union, a deeper communion
Through the dark cold and the empty desolation,
The wave cry, the wind cry, the vast waters
Of the petrel and the porpoise. In my end
*   is my beginning.*

                    —T. S. ELIOT, *"East Coker"*

DEPRESSION presents a serious problem in many older people, and all too often it is either not recognized or not treated properly. Often this occurs because the depression is masked by other ills to which the aged are subject. Sometimes, too, a physician is reluctant to undertake extensive treatment because he believes that the side effects may outweigh the benefits or he uses the medication in inadequate doses because of the patient's age.

There is no justification for such neglect. I have seen aged patients who regained a full degree of both physical and mental vigor after successful treatment for depression. And if such rejuvenation does not occur, then the patient is still entitled to the alleviation of depression's anguish.

Depression in the aged is often mistaken for senility or arteriosclerosis. All three conditions inhibit mental function, but that is where the resemblance ends.

Senility results from the dying off of brain cells. The condition is not reversible and there is as yet no effective treatment. The tragedy is that elderly people are sometimes dismissed as hopelessly senile when they are actually suffering from minimal senility to which has been added a severe depression that could be relieved.

There are other cases in which the patient suffers some degree of senility while still retaining partial function and some power to compensate. In such instances it is all the more important to assure full use of such brain capacity as may be present. When I suspect a depressive factor in a supposed senile patient, I always give antidepressant therapy a thorough trial. The result is sometimes a quite gratifying improvement both in mood and in mental processes.

Depression may also interact with or be mistaken the blood flow and thus depriving nerve cells of needed for cerebral arteriosclerosis. That condition arises from the hardening and thickening of the arteries, reducing oxygen. Brain damage may result, but often function is restored as blood flow increases. We do not fully understand the functions in blood flow, nor can we exert adequate control.

Behavior patterns in cerebral arteriosclerosis and senility are sometimes much alike. A chief difference is that arteriosclerotic patients tend to have good and bad days whereas the senile response level is consistently low. Arteriosclerosis also tends to produce a reversal of the usual day-night sleep rhythms.

There are treatments available for cerebral arteriosclerosis, but in most cases I find these remedies only marginally effective if useful at all.* The point I would again emphasize is that one must be careful not to overlook a possible depressive factor in such cases. Oddly enough, a finding of depression in addition to the arteriosclerosis becomes a cause for some optimism, for it means that there is much more hope of improving the patient's condition.

The mental responses of geriatric patients may also be influenced by such illness as congestive heart failure and severe respiratory infection. Here, too, the problem is one of reduced oxygen supply to the brain. The aged often have a borderline capacity in that respect and so any additional loss is keenly felt. Relief of the congestive or respiratory problem sometimes produces quite marked improvements in mental alertness.

In general, the geriatric patient is likely to present a collection of ills and functional deficiencies. Some of the conditions may prove highly amenable to treatment, some may respond only partially, and some very little or not at all. In such a context we should try all the harder to extend as much help as we can while taking a realistic view of what constitutes a successful treatment.

Another complicating factor is that the aged patient may be taking numerous medications, some of which

---

* Piracetam, a drug still in trial and not yet on the market, does appear to be effective at times. The extent of its usefulness is being investigated.

may induce the kind of secondary depressions described earlier. This is particularly true of the Rauwolfia alkaloids, reserpine, and certain other drugs which are often prescribed for high blood pressure. This factor appears in perhaps 15 to 20 percent of the older depressives whom I encounter in clinical practice. It creates difficulties in that the patient may need the medication that is causing the depressive reaction. Fortunately it can often be solved by adjusting to a similar but slightly different drug.

Tissue alterations, metabolic changes, and other factors all render the aged more susceptible to adverse side effects from medications. That also applies, of course, to the drugs we administer as antidepressant therapy. We adjust to the problem by prescribing one of the milder antidepressants in low dosage and then building up gradually while monitoring reactions very carefully. Typically we start with a tricyclic at about half the dose that would otherwise be used. This may stretch out the recovery period, and in particular cases we have to settle for a somewhat lower level of response, but such limitations must be accepted. Age does inhibit the recuperative process in almost any illness, be it depression or a broken hip.

Despite such problems we get good to excellent results with more than half of the older depressives. On occasion we achieve dramatic transformations.

I recall one woman, the widow of a prominent statesman, who suffered a quite sudden and severe deterioration in her early seventies. She had previously been strong willed and dynamic, the kind of person who was involved in projects by the score and automatically took charge when she walked into a meeting room. Now she complained of memory failure accompanied by general loss of interest and ability to concentrate. She was plagued also by such assorted and, to her, unaccustomed ills as headaches, backaches, and heart palpitations, though the physical examination showed nothing seriously amiss. It was all the more distressing to her because she was not used to accepting limitations of any kind.

It could have been the first stage of general degeneration, of course, but what we suspected was a thinly masked depression. An exaggerated preoccupation with physical symptoms is one classic sign of the illness in older patients. We tried her on an antidepressant drug, and soon she was her old self again. The last time I saw her she was still as lively as ever and all those ill-defined aches and pains had been overcome.

Another patient was a major philanthropist who headed an important foundation. At seventy-eight he resigned his position, retired to Florida, and there sank into what seemed like hopeless senility. He was dependent on hovering attendants for his every need. He existed that way for several years and then was referred to me for treatment of a profound depression. The treatment produced a remarkable reversal not only of mood but also of supposed mental decline.

At eighty-eight this patient is back in action, serving usefully on diverse boards and committees, and putting in four-to-five-hour workdays. I am keeping him on lithium maintenance, but his general condition is so good that I see him only once every three or four months for a general checkup. The outcome of the case was especially gratifying, for he had supported some of the pioneer work in mental-health research.

Even for the senile patient who does not have a depression there are an increasing number of rehabilitative treatments that should be applied.

Neurosis occurs in geriatric depression, but the condition is often hard to define with any degree of precision. One must attempt to distinguish between those reactions that are entirely neurotic in character and those due to personality changes as a result of brain damage. One must also be aware that the aged patient is subject to many real stresses.

The aged patient cannot write off yesterday's mistakes and failures against tomorrow's hopes and dreams. If he has not achieved his important life goals, he is faced with the fact that he never will. He must deal, too, with unhappy day-to-day reminders that his physical and mental powers are fading. He may have to struggle to perform simple tasks he used to do with ease. At worst he may experience a chronic level of distress or pain. Often he is financially insecure as well. And finally he must often confront such problems alone and lonely, left stranded by the death of a mate and the disappearance one by one of lifelong friends and close associates. If the general population endured similar pressures, one would expect to see a good many anxiety reactions.

Not surprisingly, then, anxiety is quite common among the aged. In most cases I believe it is best treated by the kind of psychotherapy that addresses itself to rather immediate and practical solutions.

For many, loneliness is the most acute problem. People need a sense of community, a sense of belonging to a group that provides strength and comfort while giving a larger focus to their lives. The aged do not differ from others in that respect, but their circumstances make it more difficult to achieve.

In mental-hospital practice, therapists have had considerable success in stimulating geriatric patients through group psychotherapy. I suspect that the group aspect is much the most important element. Problems shared do not seem so overwhelming.

It is not easy to construct group approaches for the elderly who are scattered through a diverse city. Our highly urbanized, highly mobile society is often not conducive to the maintenance of strong community roots. Something can be done about it, however, and it deserves much more thought and attention than it now receives. I would like to see some foundation or public agency make a really serious effort in this vital area of public service and mental health. The Office of Mental Health, Department of Mental Hygiene of New York State, is now supporting a number of such projects, including one under our direction at Rockland Research Institute, and through our affiliations at the

Albert Einstein College of Medicine and New York University. Our particular research interest is to improve the effectiveness and cost efficiency of the program.

Too often, however, programs for the aged make the well-meaning mistake of treating the old like helpless wards. I would like to see the kind of program that involves aged people in active participation, enlisting the resources they have to offer.

In every large city there are a great many older people who sit idle, wasting away in lonely rooms, when there is still much they might contribute if they were properly encouraged and organized. Some could provide valuable services to schools, hospitals, or libraries. Some could serve community centers, teaching youngsters such things as how to cook and sew and work with tools. It would be good for them—and for the youngsters, too. In short, we ought to encourage the old to act as surrogate grandfathers and grandmothers to the community at large.

In village life that kind of thing used to occur almost automatically. In the more fragmented society of the great cities it requires conscious effort to draw the aged back into the stream of community activity. And we aren't making effort enough.

There are, of course, some old people no longer able to contribute to the kind of programs that are suggested here. Even they, however, could benefit immensely from some simple activities. They could, at the very least, be invited to communal lectures, discussions, socials, dances, and card parties, once or twice a week.

That kind of program could be arranged rather easily and at small expense if society would just take the time and trouble. For facilities there are innumerable civic, school, church, and fraternal halls that go unused more nights than not. The aged could provide their own music and entertainment, and better so. What the program would require mostly would be some administrative agency to oversee routine details, and I would think it better if the aged played active roles in the arrangements committee.

One can find programs of this sort tucked away somewhere in every big city. Unfortunately many of the aged never hear of such activities. Many more are vaguely aware that such things exist, but they need a great deal more information plus a little urging and encouragement to take part. One must remember that for the aged a long bus or subway trip may be an arduous, sometimes frightening experience, and some have to count their carfare pennies. We ought to provide a level of communal activity that would be readily accessible in every neighborhood, and every aged resident should receive a postcard invitation to every event. After all, we do manage to mail the aged Social Security checks every month. A concerned and humane society could manage additional regular mailings to provide "social security" benefits of another but equally essential sort.

We should also attempt to establish more livable communities for the aged. I have noted earlier that where practical I think it is often best for the old to remain in familiar surroundings, particularly if those surroundings still provide a viable social focus. Often enough, however, that kind of solution is just not feasible for financial or other reasons. The problem is that we have at present a very narrow range of alternate choices. Many of the aged are either on their own or else they are removed to hospitals or nursing homes. There ought to be humane and sensible arrangements for a vast number whose needs fall in between.

Public-housing agencies could contribute much by providing apartment complexes reserved for those over sixty-five, as is done in Sweden. Intelligent planning could do a great deal to make such places attractive, convenient, and comfortable for residents who really do not need or want custodial care.

The ideal project would have a pleasant community room in every building, and outside enough yard space so that every resident could tend a little garden. And somewhere on the premises there might be tucked away a sandbox and jungle gym so that the aged could sit and watch the youngsters play when the grandchildren came to call. In short, a housing project pretty much like any other except that it would be designed to promote an easy and agreeable social exchange. At rather small expense such a facility could be combined with an on-premises nursing office capable of handling the day-to-day medical problems of a minor nature.

It seems odd that in this country we have not given more attention to such needs. Scandinavia and the Netherlands do have such programs. The aged are, after all, one of our largest minority groups, and one that sooner or later we all expect to join.

We can put their mental and emotional problems in the proper perspective if we remember that we start to approach our own mental infirmities at about age twenty. From that point on, our brain cells are dying at the rate of 50,000 a day. Fortunately we have millions of brain cells in reserve, and we have great capacity to adjust and compensate as changes occur. We must learn to make the social adjustments and compensations that will allow the aged to enjoy a healthy role in the community.

10

Suicide

To die: to sleep:
No more; and by a sleep to say we end
The heartache and the thousand natural shocks
That flesh is heir to, 'tis a consummation
Devoutly to be wish'd. To die, to sleep ...
— HAMLET

SEVERE depression is too often a fatal disease, but the cause of death is not listed that way in the medical reports. It's called suicide.

There are nearly 30,000 reported suicides in the United States every year, and it ranks currently as the tenth leading cause of death. These figures are probably a vast underestimation of the reality. For religious reasons, for insurance purposes, and most often because of uncertainty, as in automobile accidents, there are much more likely 100,000 actual suicides a year. Throughout the world about 1,000 people kill themselves every day. I am convinced that there is a large depressive element in most cases. In other cases there is no real intent to commit suicide, only a search for an intermission from an intolerable situation or an attempt to elicit sympathy or attention. There are probably more than half a million such "gestures" each year. None can be taken casually, and regardless of what appears on the surface, one should suspect an underlying depression until it is definitely ruled out. Since some patients will swallow the contents of the "whole bottle," it is usually a good idea to provide

167

only enough medication to last until the next visit, or to have someone supervise its use.

One follow-up study on depressive patients done years ago found that one sixth of them eventually ended as suicides. I would add that the study does not reflect the current advances in treatment. The figure nonetheless underlines the enormous role depression plays. The one-in-six rate compares with a suicide incidence of roughly one in 2,000 among the nation's general population. Probably one of each 300 to 500 persons in the United States attempts suicide each year.

The thing that stands out sharply in suicide is that it often seems so unrelated to the apparent objective reasons. Afterward the friends and relatives ask in genuine dismay and wonder, "Why did he do it?"

Usually it is not a response to truly desperate situations. Thus every year thousands of people learn that they suffer from some incurable malignant condition that will end inevitably in slow and painful death. Some do cut short the ordeal with suicide, but the overwhelming majority do not. They cling to life, hoping for some miracle cure, and when all hope fades they still struggle to go on living as long as they can.

Thousands of others are condemned to spend the rest of their lives in prison cells. Some of them commit suicide, but again most do not. They dream of parole or escape, and if it comes down to it, they prefer life behind bars to no life at all.

The ostensible problems of the typical suicide may seem by contrast far less critical. A man loses his job, and instead of looking for a new job he goes home and kills himself. The act is so disproportionate to the presumed cause that we are tempted to search for hidden motives. In fact, however, if we view the victim as a depressive, the event becomes far less mysterious.

Even when not faced with a particular problem, the depressive feels trapped in a slough of despond. Life is flat and stale, utterly wearisome, without any redeeming hope or purpose. The job loss confirms all that gloomy foreboding while adding a heavy new layer of anxiety and guilt. Worse yet perhaps, it forces on the victim a challenge he cannot face. In his old job, surrounded by familiar routines, he may have been able to hide or half hide his growing anguish. Now he must nerve himself to go out among strangers, presenting a cheerful and confident aspect as he seeks a new job. He cannot do it. The mere thought of an interview fills him with dread. And yet, he must.

Caught between those intolerable tensions, the depressive sees death as a welcome relief. Viewed thus, there is no real mystery about his motive. He ends life because he can no longer endure it.

The conclusions just stated do not gainsay the social and psychological factors in suicide. I believe that guilt does play a decisive role but not quite in the way that is often described. In my opinion much of the guilt derives not from the unconscious but from the culture.

My view of the problem has undergone a radical change in the course of my practice. Originally I accepted the theory that guilt was intrinsic to depression and that suicide was an inherent risk. All of my clinical practice seemed to confirm the doctrine, and I overlooked the fact that my patients represented a pretty small segment of mankind. Specifically, I was treating American patients.

Later I became acquainted with a considerable circle of European psychiatrists, and I found their clinical observations to be much like my own. But they too were dealing with a special minority group, namely, European patients. Then I was invited to take part in a mental-health program in Indonesia, and I made a discovery that forced me to take a new look at the question.

I found that Indonesians suffer from depression just as Westerners do. They exhibit most of the classic symptoms except one. They do not suffer from depressive guilt, and as an apparent consequence they rarely commit suicide.

The degree of difference is quite startling. We conducted a careful review of psychiatric hospital and clinical records in Java over a five-year period, and I did not find a single case of depressive suicide. There was not even any clear evidence of a suicide attempt.

A finding of that order requires explanation. Thus I attribute most depressions to biochemical disturbance, but brain chemistry is the same basic process for people everywhere. Why, then, should the malfunction induce a fatal response in one people but not in another?

The analyst is faced with the same question in different terms. If the ruling forces are the conflicts of id and ego and latent death wish, then presumably these two are part of a common human heritage. Then why is suicide a high risk in one group of depressive patients and almost nonexistent in the other?

I believe that the explanation is psychological in a larger sense. The two patient groups react differently because all the forces of history, culture, and collective experience have produced in them very different attitudes toward life.

The Western view is deeply rooted in the Judeo-Christian ethic. It teaches that man must accept individual responsibility for all that he does or doesn't do. It commands us to resist and overcome all human weakness in ourselves, and it holds us morally responsible if we fail.

The original religious impetus no longer plays so prominent a role, but the ethical and psychological content has been preserved in a form only slightly changed. If man is not personally responsible to his God, then he is personally responsible to himself—but still personally responsible.

In such a philosophy there is no room for despair. We command ourselves to strive and reach, and if the struggle is painful, then all the greater the glory if we but stay the course. All our legends celebrate the heroes who did not turn back, would not give up. From earliest childhood we learn that this is how man conquers the wilderness, builds a city, fulfills a dream. And beyond that the triumph of unyielding spirit is sweet for its own sake, for this is how man affirms to himself his ultimate worth. The poet Percy Bysshe Shelley said it in lines ever since recited in countless schoolrooms:

> *To suffer woes which Hope thinks infinite;*
> *To forgive wrongs darker than death or night;*
> *To defy Power, which seems omnipotent;*
> *To love, and bear; to hope till Hope creates*
> *From its own wreck the thing it contemplates;*
> *Neither to change, nor falter, nor repent;*
> *This, like thy glory, Titan, is to be*
> *Good, great and joyous, beautiful and free;*
> *This is alone Life, Joy, Empire, and Victory.*

And what if there is no victory, no joy, and nothing left for which to hope? The poet William Ernest Henley told us how the brave, free spirit responds to that:

> *Out of the night that covers me,*
> *Black as the Pit from pole to pole,*
> *I thank whatever gods may be*
> *For my unconquerable soul.*
>
> *In the fell clutch of circumstance*
> *I have not winced nor cried aloud.*
> *Under the bludgeonings of chance*
> *My head is bloody, but unbowed.*
>
> *It matters not how strait the gate,*
> *How charged with punishments the scroll,*
> *I am the master of my fate:*
> *I am the captain of my soul.*

All this is deeply embedded in our culture, and the message is not confined to particular flights of poetry. The ethic has innumerable other more workaday expressions, like "Stand on your own two feet," "Stiff upper lip," and "Don't give up the ship."

The heritage has its great values, but it does create an immense psychological burden for the depression victim. For the moment he cannot summon hope, no matter how he tries, and he is hardly captain of his soul. He feels rather more like a castaway drifting helplessly in the hulk of his shipwrecked spirit. And that fills him with guilt.

He may or may not summon up other guilts from his subconscious, but in most cases I don't really think we have to dig that deep. The depressive is often quite consciously guilty, and what he feels guilty about is being depressed. He has failed in his own eyes the test of will and spirit. He blames himself for his weakness, and he assumes that others blame him, too. Indeed, he often is blamed by those around him. That I believe is the overriding guilt that impels some depressives to commit suicide. They are driven to do something about their condition, they cannot master it, and so in one final act of resolution they end the dismal struggle.

The Indonesian patient endures the same disease in a very different spirit. His history, culture, and religion have taught him not to conquer fate but to coexist with it. Nominally he may be Muslim, but the older Hindu and pagan philosophies coexist. His primary identification is as a member of a "suku" group, one of approximately 250 such ethnic and cultural tribal groupings. He thinks of himself as a member of a suku group first, then as a member of a family, and last—and almost reluctantly—as an individual. In addition to his living family all his ancestors actively exist, as do a variety of spirits. Added to this is the acceptance of magic as an everyday fact of life.

Oriental philosophies teach patience, forbearance, the submersion of the individual in a seamless web of existence. Good and bad fortune are both a part of that web, and both are accepted as a natural order of things. For every force there is a counterforce, but individual man does not pull the strings. He exists within a vast equilibrium that embraces all the cosmos.

Time takes on a different aspect in such a culture. To Western man time is a straight line from here to eternity, and each fleeting hour must be grasped and used before it forever passes by. To the Indonesian time is a great wheel forever turning, always changing and yet always the same, for all life goes back to that from whence it came. There is no great urgency about such a journey. Further, whatever happens is "insh'-allah"—the will of Allah. There is no point to contesting with Fate.

The Western patient often informs his physician that he has "no time to be sick." If it is a sickness of the spirit, then so much the worse, for he sees or thinks he sees in all eyes an accusing question, "Isn't it about time you pulled yourself together?" The Indonesian has time for everything. He can take time out to be depressed when that circumstance befalls him.

If you go into an Indonesian village to inquire about a depressive, you will be told that he is not to be found tending his field or shop. He is in his hut resting because he is not well. In fact, there are two sick men in the village. One of them has a fever. The other one mutters to himself and hides his face and sometimes acts strangely. It is unfortunate, but such things happen. Perhaps both men will be feeling better soon.

I have had other occasions to observe depression in Africa, and there too I find a fatalistic acceptance that negates the syndrome of guilt and suicide. The forms of culture vary, but the essential features are much the same.

Some Africans ascribe life's ups and downs to complicated systems of white and black magic. There are evil spirits that assault men and good spirits that protect them, and the contest goes now this way and now that. Many Westerners might find that frightening, but to the African it is comforting. He's not boxed in. Things may be going badly today, but tomorrow the good spirits will predominate. Of course, he may unknowingly break a tabu by crossing a stream at the wrong place, or accidentally hitting a tree that has a spirit in it. Or someone may cast an evil spell on him. But even so, he is not to blame for his misfortunes.

Such a view of life derives in large part from the fact

that these people still live very close to the rhythms of nature. They observe the gentle rain that nourishes their crops and the wild storms that flood the fields and bring disaster. The work of spirits, they say, but to them spirits personify the forces of nature. They accept because they must; that is the way life is. When they are stricken with tribulations of either mind or body, they apply the same reasons and the same response.

We Westerners try to control all things, including the forces of nature. We have done it so successfully that we sometimes overestimate our powers. When we encounter a problem we can't solve immediately, we are inclined to turn on ourselves and ask, What went wrong, and why am I to blame?

There would be far fewer suicides if we could accept more readily the existence of natural elemental forces that are not at all involved with our individual aspirations or egos. I sometimes tell my depressed patients that they are suffering from one of nature's forces—a kind of storm within the brain. They will ride out the storm far more easily if they do not try to invent reasons why they brought such trouble on themselves.

Many of the Afro-Asian cultures embrace a second strong factor that protects the depressive against suicide. Their way of life is essentially communal and tribal, and that too provides great support for the patient. He is not faced with total responsibility for his own affairs, for the whole tribe—and the family within the tribe—prospers or fails to prosper as a unit. Beyond that he finds both in the tribe and in the extended family much emotional support. Both joys and sorrows are shared not just with the whole community but often with the ancestral spirits who are believed to be very much present and still close around.

It is not my purpose here to romanticize these other cultures. They pay a price for their social attitudes, just as we do for ours. They endure much that we have overcome.

If I were stricken with a dangerous viral infection,

I'd rather have it in the setting provided by our society. In their society it is easier to endure an emotional illness and not turn violently against oneself. There are things we can learn from one another.

The suicide rate in the United States varies according to rather well-defined group patterns. The phenomenon seems to bear out the observation that social and psychological pressures play a very important role.

Women suffer depression twice as frequently as men, and they more often attempt suicide, but the actual rate of successful suicide is nearly three times as high among men. The male reaction may involve a glandular predisposition toward more violent response, but that question aside, there are clearly some important cultural factors.

Traditionally in our society the man of the house was responsible for supporting the family. If he failed, he and his wife shared the hardship and worry, but he alone had the responsibility—and thus the guilt.

The social and economic structure was reflected in a general view of male and female roles. Some weakness could be tolerated in woman and at times even indulged. She could be sad and languorous on occasion, and she was allowed to break down and weep. It did not threaten her womanliness. Such conduct, however, was certainly not manly. As a consequence depression presented men with a far more cruel psychic ordeal.

Today those attitudes are changing, as are the underlying social and economic roles. More and more women are asserting their personal independence and taking an active part in the business world. It is probably not coincidental that female suicide rates have been increasing over the last ten years.

Whites commit suicide about three times as often as blacks, and again that seems part of a pretty clear pattern. For generations the blacks were forced into dependent and passive roles. This did not spare them from depression, and indeed it had many harsh psychological consequences. It did, however, relieve them of personal guilt. "If you're black," said an old ghetto adage, "stay back." One could not be blamed for failing if one was not allowed to try.

That, too, is changing as black people increasingly assert their right to participate on equal terms. Inevitably they will encounter the anxieties that go with striving and sometimes failing. Hopefully, however, we will all learn to accommodate these tensions in a less self-destructive spirit.

The portrait of the suicide as a striving, self-critical, and self-demanding individual is completed by a glance at occupational patterns. Artists, businessmen, and professional people kill themselves far more often than laborers. After dentists, physicians have the highest occupational rate of all, and candor compels the admission that psychiatrists and psychoanalysts are the worst risks in the medical profession. Their suicide rate is seven times as high as the national average. Insight alone will not save the individual victim if he is not buttressed by others in time of need. The more prolonged the illness, the greater the risk, so that pharmaceutical treatment is a crucial element.

The immense value of social support is illustrated by still other patterns. We can look at people in terms of many different social connections, and we find confirmed again and again the observation that loneliness imposes very heavy and sometimes fatal burdens.

Despite all the upheavals of modern times, the family is still the core of society. And married people are far less likely to commit suicide than those who are single, widowed, or divorced.

Rural people enjoy a more intimate communal existence than most city dwellers. The rural suicide rate is markedly lower. As Francis Bacon wrote 400 years ago, "magna civitas, magna solitudo"—great cities, great solitude.

Within the metropolitan areas the rate tends to increase as one approaches the dense inner heart of the city. That requires no complex analysis. Such places teem with rooming houses and residential hotels, and a vast, floating population comes and goes under circumstances in which people acquire only nodding acquaintance with their neighbors. It is a lonely crowd in which to endure a crisis of spirit.

Old age presents a special kind of loneliness, and the suicide rate among men climbs progressively with age. The problem is less acute for those who have the good fortune to grow old in familiar surroundings, among children and grandchildren and such lifelong friends as may survive. Women usually maintain closer family relationships than do men, so that their suicide rate levels off in their fifties. But what of those who find themselves aged and alone in that furnished room in the midst of an uncaring city? Their mates are dead, their children scattered to far places, their life connections all broken off or fast disappearing. Sometimes one sees such people feeding the pigeons in the park, and one can sense by their very attitude that it is almost their only outlet. It is not enough. If they are stricken by a depressive attack, they must face the siege stripped of all support.

For those old people who really have no home the nursing home may be the only answer. The more resilient may even find new social connections in such an arrangement. That is expecting a lot, however, and we should be chary of pushing such solutions for mere administrative convenience. Wherever feasible, I encourage the aging patients to stay on in familiar surroundings, fulfilling their days among those things that give pattern, meaning, and continuity to their lives. We all need that, but the lonely aged especially.

And finally, there is the problem of the lonely young. Suicide has been rising quite sharply among the young in recent years, and while there may be several factors, I suspect that a loss of supporting connections is a major element. The stress and clamor of our times have produced in many of the young the attitudes of alienation, and that is a kind of psychological loneliness. It is far easier to endure an individual crisis, even though it is basically the result of a biological quirk, if one retains emotional connections and roots in the general society. Beyond that there is the quite specific fact that family solidity has been shaken by changing times. Those who have grown up in broken homes present much higher suicide rates than those who have not.

These social and psychological observations might seem on casual inspection to contradict some of the earlier observations on the nature of depression. In fact, however, there is no real contradiction. I remain convinced that most depressions derive from a biochemical breakdown in brain function, and I find no provable connection between the general incidence of breakdown and particular kinds of pressure. What is clearly manifest is that social and psychological forces play an important part in determining how the patient responds to the attack. Whether, for instance, he attempts suicide or accepts the consolation of family and friends. Bacon also wrote: ". . . it is a mere and miserable solitude to want true friends without which the world is but a wilderness. For a crowd is not company; and faces are but a gallery of pictures; and talk but a tinkling cymbal, where there is no love." It is particularly sad when people do have friends and loved ones whom they deny because of their depression.

Still another element in suicide is the precipitating incident. A depressive patient may endure a rather heavy load of anxiety, guilt, or loneliness and be able to contain it at some precarious level. There is a breaking point, however, and any major problem can create a crisis.

Job loss is one such event. Aside from all the psychological ramifications, it presents the depressive with a very real and immediate challenge. He is forced to gird himself up and make a major new effort, and at the moment that is the thing he is least equipped to do. The economic factor can be graphically capsuled in the fact that suicide rose about 50 percent during the Great Depression.

Another dangerous factor can be the end of a marriage by either death or divorce. In the case of divorce there are such obvious psychological factors as guilt, feelings of rejection, or sense of failure. Some would also deduce guilt in the case of death, but I think that's much more likely to embrace the sadness and weariness of trying to go on alone without someone who provided companionship and support. It is very common, however, for the survivor to feel that he or she may have been responsible because not enough was done to help the patient or some mistake was made that may have contributed to the death. Usually these thoughts are vastly exaggerated and have no real relationship to what happened. In any case, they present a severe problem for one struggling with depression.

A third and rather common precipitating factor can be a change of address. That might seem rather trivial until one examines it closely.

In those who have suffered economic failure a change of address can signify selling the house to move to poorer quarters. A big defeat.

In the aged it might mean abandoning the home of thirty years to move unwillingly into some unfamiliar place. A final defeat.

Beyond those explanations, however, the mere fact of moving can confront depressives with an emotional trial. Consider the depressive housewife who is married to an up-and-coming businessman. He gets a big promotion that requires a move to another city. To him it's an exciting opportunity. To her it's a dreadful reminder of how inadequate she feels.

She'll have to try to make new friends when she can barely face the people she's known for years. She will have to attend to the packing and moving and the new school arrangements for the children, and all at a time when she would give almost anything if she did not have to get out of bed in the morning. If she contrasts her sense of failure with her husband's success, she may despise herself. If she despises herself enough, she may attempt to kill herself.

All beginnings and new endeavors present the depressive with special problems. There are some quite startling studies that show that many suicides occur in the mornings, at the beginning of the week, and most especially in the spring.

Such are the general patterns of self-destruction. They are, of course, only general factors, and fortunately there exists in most of us a vast reservoir of survival instinct. I have known striving, self-critical, lonely, aging patients who confronted unwelcome change and yet stubbornly resisted any assault against themselves.

The form chart reversal can also go the other way, however, and one can encounter a high suicide risk in a patient who seems to present only a few of the specifications. A judgment of risk and a calculation of preventative measures must be made individually for each patient, but there is one clear and reliable sign. The potential suicide very often cries aloud for help.

For every actual suicide there are probably four or five attempts, and some estimates place the ratio even higher. Many attempts go unreported because the act is thinly masked or because the family or the person himself conceals the incident.

Whatever the exact figure, the number is unquestionably huge. At least 500,000 people make some suicidal gesture every year, and one could populate a city of several million with those who have made such attempts at one time or another in their lives.

A really determined act of self-destruction is not so easily accomplished, and thus many people accept the erroneous and highly dangerous notion that abortive efforts are not serious. In fact, every suicide attempt and every such threat should be regarded as a desperate cry for help.

It is true that many who attempt suicide do not really wish to die. They swallow a handful of pills and within five minutes they are on the phone bidding some friend or relative a tearful farewell. They are saying, in effect: "Send the ambulance, and send it quick. Please save me from myself." In its very nature, however, it is a desperate gesture. If they do it again, they may miscalculate the margin of safety. Or next time they may nerve themselves to the final act.

The most dangerous period for a suicidal depressive sometimes comes when he seems on the verge of recovery. When he is in the full grip of the illness, he may be so mentally and emotionally disorganized that he cannot make any decision, including the fatal one. Then he makes a partial recovery, but the underlying anguish is still present, and suicide may follow.

I have learned to be especially wary of the patient who "recovers" too quickly, becoming too cheerful too soon. Sometimes that's a signal that he has found a solution to his problem—to do away with himself.

Sometimes the clue is the appearance of new symptoms in a depression that appeared to have stabilized itself. The onset of insomnia, decreased sexual potency, or weight loss under such circumstances can be danger signs suggesting that the illness is taking a marked turn for the worse.

Another danger signal is seen when a normally sloppy and careless person begins "putting things in order"—destroying old letters, checking that all his bills are paid, and arranging his papers and possessions very neatly.

I discuss suicide frankly with my patients and inquire as to any such impulses they may have had. I am usually not too disturbed if they report only vague general feelings that they sometimes think they might be better off dead. It is a good deal more alarming if they have begun to think of suicide in quite specific terms. The nurses are trained to watch for that, too, and they report at once if a patient asks them even obliquely as to the lethal dose of some medication.

Some physicians are reluctant to open a suicide discussion, fearing that they may suggest the action to a depressed patient. That is a mistake. One does not implant a suicide urge by discussing it, any more than one tempts a patient to alcoholism by inquiring of his drinking habits. The problem either exists or it doesn't, and if it does, it must be examined and dealt with. Often the suicidal patient is terrified of his dark impulses, and he is relieved to talk about it with a sympathetic listener.

As stated earlier, in very rare cases we sometimes recommend electroshock therapy in an effort to achieve quick relief if suicide seems likely. For the acutely suicidal patient, psychiatric hospitalization is not necessarily the last resort. There are times when a patient wants protection from himself and his impulses. Voluntarily going into the hospital, with an agreement that he will be discharged whenever he so requests, often serves such a purpose admirably. Unfortunately, there are a good many who resist that solution with what I regard only as superstitious dread.

It is a strange attitude in our supposedly enlightened age. If a patient has a severe heart attack, he is hospitalized until the danger is past, and he and his family are grateful if he is watched closely to detect any sign of a new seizure. Why should anyone feel differently about watchful and protective psychiatric care?

But still, some do, and if an adult is not clearly psychotic, he cannot be hospitalized against his will. In the case of a minor it requires parental permission. When we encounter extreme resistance, we sometimes send a telegram warning that we refuse to take any further responsibility if hospitalization is not accepted immediately. On occasion that jolts people into facing reality. And finally, there are those cases where all persuasions fail, and we are reduced to standing by helplessly, hoping that we can obtain cooperation before it is too late.

I recall a recent case of that sort in which I served as a consultant to a colleague. The patient was a severely troubled fourteen-year-old boy. He became more and more suicidal as the treatment progressed, but he strongly resisted hospitalization.

Most of the boy's problems centered around the mother, but we could not draw her into the therapy. The father did come for consultation, and we warned him of the danger. He listened to the recommendations and then went home to talk to his wife, who apparently made the decisions. The plea for hospitalization was rejected, and for some weeks matters dragged on in that precarious condition.

As it happened, my colleague was out of town when a crisis occurred, and I was called for an emergency consultation. The boy had disappeared from home, taken a hotel room, and sat there an entire afternoon with a loaded gun in his hand. Afterward, much shaken, he confessed the episode, and I talked to him very earnestly for a long while.

No matter how it was presented to him the youth still refused to go voluntarily to a hospital. He insisted that he had gotten it all out of his system during that agonized hotel-room confrontation with himself. My colleague and I both feared a recurrence, but he would not listen.

The parents could have had him committed, but they wouldn't listen either. The dominating mother still would not come in to talk about the problem. The father came again but was as indecisive as ever. He didn't want to get into a hassle with his son or his wife. And behind it all there was a strong indication that the parents were both concerned about a family disgrace. What would the neighbors say if the police came and took away their protesting son? The sad end of the matter was that a little later the youth killed himself.

About two weeks after the death the parents called and asked if they could come in and talk about it. We said, "Of course." We met the mother for the first time then, and she unloaded on us a furious tirade. If we had handled things properly, her son would still be alive. Why hadn't we foreseen it? Why wasn't something done?

My colleague started to detail all the warnings we had given the father. That unhappy man said he didn't really remember specific warnings. My colleague is a younger man than I, and he was shocked and angry. I managed to cut the discussion short, and afterward I told my colleague why.

"Sure, papa was lying," I said. "But papa has to live with mama. They both have to live with themselves and with the disaster. They didn't come to find out what happened. They came to unload their guilt on someone else. So let them, because nothing will bring the boy back, and getting them to recognize the truth of the matter won't help at all."

Understanding the truth of such matters may help those who have to face this question in their own lives. When a suicide risk exists, it must be examined openly and honestly, and when protective measures are discussed, the one most important consideration should be the patient's safety. Damn what the neighbors think! The tragedy of such affairs is that most such suicides are preventable, often by rather brief protective confinement during the high-risk crisis stage.

I have discussed the suicidal dangers because they present a very serious hazard in some cases. I should add, however, that most depressions do not take that course. A major risk of suicide probably appears in no more than 5 percent of the cases. The important point is that they be recognized when they occur, and that requires a straight look at any hint of suicidal behavior. It is extremely dangerous to hide it in the family closet.

The other main lesson of suicide is that the risk is lessened if the subject feels in those close around him not projections of blame and guilt but warm and compassionate emotional support. All depressives need that, whether suicidal or not.

11

Alcoholics and Drug Addicts

> Drink not the third glass, which
> thou canst not tame,
> When once it is within thee.
> —GEORGE HERBERT,
> "The Church Porch"

> *O thou invisible spirit of wine! If thou hast no name
> to be known by, let us call thee devil! . . . O God!
> That men should put an enemy in their mouths to
> steal away their brains!*
>
> —*Othello*

THE problems of alcoholism and drug addiction have strong links to depression. The search for highs may often begin as a flight from lows.

Some preliminary studies indicate that relieving the depression can help to reduce or eliminate dependence on narcotics or alcohol. The samplings are still too small to warrant sweeping conclusions, but it does appear a very promising approach to the problem.

It is not surprising that chronic depressives should turn to alcohol or drugs for solace. It provides a brief respite from the incessant psychic pain and allows the user to cover his self-doubt and confusion with what seems momentarily to be a confident mask.

It is, in fact, a crude sort of pharmacotherapy for the illness. But, of course, it doesn't work for long. It is very much like getting drunk to drown the misery of an intractable toothache. The awareness of pain may be briefly reduced, but it returns as soon as the liquor wears off, and the hangover makes the total condition worse than before. The depressive who habitually seeks such refuge acquires a disastrous chain of new ills.

Clinicians who regularly treat depressives have long been aware of these factors. In recent years the empirical conclusions have been reinforced by a number of diagnostic surveys and other studies.

One important finding was made by Dr. George Winokur of the University of Iowa College of Medicine. He traced a crisscross pattern of alcoholism and depression that applied not only to the patients but also to their immediate relatives.

The subjects included a group of 100 alcoholic women. Careful diagnosis disclosed that one fourth of them were suffering from a primary depression, the illness having gone undetected because it was covered over by all the alcoholic reactions and symptoms.

The larger thrust of Dr. Winokur's survey involved family patterns. He checked 507 first-degree relatives of alcoholics and found that 73 of the relatives were depressives. That is a rate at least four times as high as the largest estimate of the national incidence. The report is significant because depression is often associated with hereditary traits.

Dr. Winokur found that in affected families the males were more prone to alcoholism and the females to depression. That, too, is interesting, for it is well established, as I pointed out before, that depression is much more common among women. The appearance of numerous male alcoholics in such families suggests the possibility that they may suffer from some related but perhaps slightly different type of biochemical malfunction. Of course, the higher alcoholic rate among males can also be explained by social factors. In any case, what stands out clearly is a large correlation between alcoholism and depression.

Alcoholism, incidentally, is far more widespread than is generally acknowledged. The average physician sees alcoholics very frequently, though he may hesitate to make that diagnosis. By general estimate there are at least nine million problem drinkers in the United States today, and cirrhosis of the liver ranks closely with suicide as a leading cause of death.

Drug abuse is less widespread, but it also presents a major problem. For social reasons it became epidemic among some young people in recent years, but it has always existed and often takes unrecognized forms. I treat some older patients who would be shocked at the assertion that they have a drug problem, though in fact they do.

A depressive can drift into drug habits without knowing it. Often he begins with increasingly heavy use of sleeping pills to combat the insomnia. Then he starts "balancing" the sleeping potions with amphetamines or other "pep pills" to pull him through that heavy feeling in the morning. He gets on a pharmacological roller coaster of "uppers" and "downers," and that plays havoc with his nervous system. His already high level of anxiety and irritability is increased, so he starts taking tranquilizers as well. There are "pill poppers" who make the rounds of doctors' offices, piling up prescriptions when what they badly need is one basic medication to relieve their depression. It should be strongly stressed that antidepressants are *not* "uppers" and do not create either dependency or addiction. They can be discontinued at any time without any craving for the drug as such. Of course, if symptoms of the depression recur the patient will be eager to get back on medication. In all of the literature, only a few cases are reported where patients took the drug for its own sake.

A considerable number of people do become addicted to narcotic drugs such as heroin, morphine, and opium. As with alcoholics, their original illness then becomes so overgrown with new effects that the basic depression is often not diagnosed.

Interestingly enough, the mechanism of narcotic addiction may be quite closely analogous to the biochemical malfunctions involved in depression. That research is still highly experimental, but it offers at least a tentative explanation of why depressives find momentary relief in such drugs as morphine.

The research was conducted in part at Johns Hopkins University under the sponsorship of the National Institute of Mental Health. The investigators, Dr. Solomon Snyder and Dr. Candace Pert, began by asking where and how narcotic effects were exerted in the nervous system and why some drug agents were more addictive than others. Another closely related question involved the means by which certain antagonistic drugs block the effects of narcotic highs.

Based on the prior research of Professor Avram Goldstein and others, they suspected the existence of certain "opiate centers" that are the sites of action of narcotic substances in the brain. Accordingly, they tagged the narcotic with radioactive trace materials and poured them over calf brain tissue. Sure enough, the drugs honed in on particular kinds of brain tissue and bound themselves chemically to the receptor sites. (Hughes and Kosterlitz in England independently had found the same receptor sites in pig brains.) The radioactive tracing was so accurate that the researchers could make close estimates as to the concentrations found around particular cells.

The drugs tested included morphine and naloxone, the latter being a morphine antagonist that is sometimes used to block the narcotic. When both were poured on the tissue, they competed avidly for bonding position at the receptor sites. Another drug that was drawn to the same sites was methadone, which is currently used in combating heroin addiction.

There was some further circumstantial evidence in the degree of reaction. The more potent substances clustered most readily around the receptor sites.

The receptor sites were particular specialized brain cells found mostly in the forepart of the brain. They are activated by acetylcholine, which is yet another neural transmitter. The question now open is just how the narcotics alter cell transmission to affect mental and emotional states.

The researchers are also pursuing leads that suggest that biologic variables may create significant individual differences in the number of these specialized receptor sites. In other words, some people may have a constitutional predisposition to become addicted easily, just as there is a constitutional predisposition toward depression. Preliminary tests are now being conducted to determine whether or not some animals acquire drug dependence more quickly than others when the same dosages are given.

All this is still speculative, but the inquiry is hopeful. If we can trace particular biochemical pathways of addiction, it may prove a long step toward more effective solutions of that problem.

The same holds true for alcoholism. That form of addiction is usually acquired over long usage, and if a predisposing biochemical factor exists, it is probably something subtle. About all we have to go on at present is the purely circumstantial evidence of familial tendency, plus the fact that some consistent drinkers become dependent on alcohol while others do not. Of course, those facts could also yield to sociologic and psychologic explanations. The question merits openminded investigation.

Meanwhile, we do know that depressives are especially subject to drug and alcohol addictions because of the insistent need to seek psychic relief. We have found that treating the underlying depression can sometimes bring significant relief of the addictive problem.

Opium is in itself a remarkably effective antidepressant, as noted earlier, but its addictive qualities make it a dangerous potion, and ever-larger quantities are required by the user. Normal brain responses become so altered that profound depression often sets in for long periods following withdrawal. Heroin also induces postwithdrawal depression. Beta-endorphin, the brain's own opiate, is repressed when outside opiumlike substances are given. When these outside sources are withdrawn, the brain has neither its own nor the outside "opiate" available, which is what appears to create the deficiency. The all-too-frequent consequence is that the patient is driven back to the drug in search of relief, and the whole cycle starts over again.

I developed a project to attempt to break the cycle by bolstering the patients with antidepressant medication during the critical period. In the first phase of the study we treated seventeen patients and compared the results with seventeen untreated patients who received placebos. All of the untreated patients experienced the typical depressive setback. Among the treated patients the results were mixed but very encouraging. We rated the responses as six excellent, six good, and two moderate, plus two failures and one who was discontinued because of side effects.

The responses appeared biochemically determined and did not correspond to either the previous addictive history or the patient's other problems. Thus one of the subjects was a thirty-nine-year-old opium-eating tailor who had also used heroin. He had begun taking drugs because of family stress. When I met him he had been addicted for six years, had dried out four times, and on each occasion had quickly resumed his habit. His response to the treatment was excellent, and he remained drug free throughout the trial.

Another patient was a workingman who had been using heroin for eight years. His habit did not begin with personal problems—he just picked it up because the stuff was around. He had a previous history of six treatments and six relapses. His response to the program was also excellent. With some others we obtained lesser results, ranging from good to only moderate, though their addiction was of much shorter duration.

As to general social factors, a scan of the patients reveals a highly varied lot. I analyzed one series of twelve subjects and found they ranged from young to middle-aged and from lower to upper class. They included three government officials, a military officer, a

businessman, a student, five workers who were variously skilled and unskilled, and one who was unemployed.

The one thing they all held in common was the
habit. The twelve of them had a cumulative total of
119 years of addiction. They had been in and out of
drug-withdrawal centers for a total of fifty times.

Half of them had begun using drugs in response to
various problems, in most cases a physical illness. The
other half had begun casually, out of curiosity or
because the practice was common among their friends.
The precipitating cause had no apparent relationship to
the extent of addiction once they were hooked.

The youngest and most recently addicted was the
student. He had taken his first dose of heroin in a
spirit of curiosity and youthful bravado, to impress his
friends. When I met him he was twenty, a habitual user
for two years, and already on his fourth withdrawal. In
our treatment program he fell in the middle range with
a response that we rated "good."

Was he able to stay off the drug when he passed out
of the clinic's scan? How many permanent cures were
achieved among all those assorted fifty-nine losers? I
don't know. I do know that we were able to help most
of them through a critical period by relieving one
particular cause of early relapse. It is to be hoped that
it was the extra boost that enabled some of them to
get over the hump.

The results were sufficiently impressive to obtain
substantial support. The National Institute of Mental
Health assigned Dr. H. Tuma to the project, and together we developed a comprehensive study plan. This
received the continuing support of the International
Committee Against Mental Illness, which had spon-
sored the earlier work. In addition, sizeable grants were
obtained from the World Health Organization, the
United Nations Narcotic Control Commission, the National Institute of Alcohol and Alcohol Abuse, the
Schering-Plough Pharmaceutical Company, and, most
important, the government of Iran. (The final data for

the project were collected only two weeks before the revolution in that country.)

The project involved 220 patients: 55 controls who received no further treatment after they were detoxified; 55 given placebos; 55 placed on methadone; and 55 treated with Mutabon (amitriptyline, a depressant, plus a very low dose of perphenazine). At this writing, we are still analyzing the data to see what relationship there is to depression, age, length of drug use, and other factors. The patients were followed in outpatient clinics for a year after discharge from the hospital. The one fact that is already very obvious is that the groups on methadone and antidepressant responded very much better (by not going back on opiates) than the control and placebo groups. The conclusion seems obvious: that before using methadone (another narcotic) treatment with antidepressants is indicated.

Recently I participated in a similar experiment with alcoholics, this one in conjunction with a Veterans Administration Hospital at Togus, Maine, utilizing our laboratories at Rockland Research Institute, Orangeburg, New York. Again the premise was that relief of depression might reduce or eliminate one cause of habitual relapse.

We selected 73 patients with well-confirmed histories of severe episodic drinking. Their behavior pattern was strongly suggestive of recurrent depressive attacks, though their symptoms were not sufficiently clear-cut to establish that diagnosis. Typically, they stayed sober for months and then went off on uncontrolled sprees that might last days or weeks.

We divided them into two roughly equal groups, treating one group with regular lithium maintenance and giving the other group similar-appearing inactive placebos for comparison purposes. They were all hospital outpatients, and aside from the antidepressive medicine, all received the same general treatment. We followed the subjects for periods of two to three years, and the results were quite encouraging. The lithium didn't solve all the drinking problems, but it certainly helped.

The comparative results:

In the group that did not receive lithium maintenance the drinking habits remained unchanged from the established patterns. About three fourths of them experienced at least one severe alcoholic bout during the period studied.

Among those treated with lithium only a quarter have experienced relapse. Moreover, those who did fall off the wagon have generally not fallen quite as hard or as often as was their previous habit.

These results were confirmed in a study done by the Medical Research Council of Epsom, England. The Veterans Administration is now planning a multi-hospital study, which will involve screening thousands of patients to determine exactly how effective the treatment is, and for which patients it is most useful.

The experiments reported here represent only small beginnings in a field that invites vigorous research. Obviously antidepressive medication is not a cure-all for either addiction or alcoholism, but I believe that it can be of great help for many who suffer from those conditions.

It can be of even greater prophylactic value if society learns to recognize depression and treat it in time. Once alcoholism or addiction becomes established, it creates its own chain of circumstances including altered biochemistry, the habits of psychological dependence, and the stress of personal problems that inevitably pile up. It may then become very difficult to reverse all the consequences just by removing the original cause. We can prevent many of those problems if we treat the depressive promptly, before he resorts to self-treatment with disastrous agents. There should be a thorough check for a depressive syndrome whenever a drug or drinking problem begins to appear.

12

Who Are the Depressives?

For this is the journey that men make: to find them-selves. If they fail in this, it doesn't matter much what else they find. Money, position, fame, many loves, revenge are all of little consequence, and when the tickets are collected at the end of the ride they are tossed into a bin marked FAILURE. But if a man happens to find himself—if he knows what he can be depended upon to do, the limits of his courage, the position from which he will no longer retreat, the degree to which he can surrender his inner life to some woman, the secret reservoirs of his determination, the extent of his dedication, the depth of his feeling for beauty, his honest and unpostured goals—then he has found a mansion which he can inhabit with dignity all the days of his life.

—JAMES MICHENER, *The Fires of Spring*

DEPRESSION is sometimes termed "the common cold of psychiatric ills." The expression is misleading in that it understates the potential seriousness of the illness. It is apt enough, however, in the sense that it describes a pervasive illness to which all of us are at least potentially subject.

The precise incidence is not really known. In part that can be ascribed to some of the diagnostic problems discussed earlier. The symptoms can be quite diffuse, and the disease often hides behind other conditions. In part also the lack of firm epidemiological data reflects the fact that psychiatry has not yet adapted itself to the needs of mass medicine. There are far too many emotionally disturbed people whom we are just not reaching. The medical gap is confirmed by innumerable spot surveys that find in sample populations a high rate of previously undiagnosed and untreated emotional ills. The Mental Health Systems Act of 1979 estimates that "between 10 and 15 percent of the population—20 to 32 million Americans—need some form of mental health service at any one time."

In such a context any statement of depressive incidence necessarily contains a considerable element of guesswork. We do know that it is a very common illness, however, and informed estimates place the annual toll at anywhere from 2 to 4 percent of the adult population. Even the more conservative figure adds up to some four million cases a year in the United States.

The most accurate surveys indicate that fewer than one and a half million patients go for initial visits involving treatment of depression. This sounds substantial until we realize it is only a third of the most conservative estimate of those in need of treatment, and more like one tenth of the more realistic figures. Millions upon millions suffer the disorder without relief.

The year-to-year cases include a large number of repeaters among those prone to recurrent attacks. Even so, the general incidence is such that an estimated 30 million Americans can expect to suffer a severe depression at some point in their lives.

Typically, the disease tends to be self-limiting and self-remitting. Somehow or other the natural balances restore themselves so that the attack sometimes subsides after six months or so even when the illness is not treated. That is a fortunate dispensation of nature, but the lack of proper treatment causes immense suffering for many victims. For many the results are not so happy and the condition can become a chronic one.

Anyone can have a depression. As with other ills, however, there are particular factors that make some groups more susceptible than others.

Women are more subject to depression than men. As

a general estimate, about one woman in six experiences a depressive episode at some point in her life. The estimate for men is about one in twelve.

The male-female observation must be qualified with a social factor discussed earlier. Men more than women tend to cover depression with drinking, and the male alcoholic population may contain a large pool of undiagnosed depressives. In general, however, women do appear much more subject to depression.

Depression is rarely diagnosed before puberty, but cases among children may be more common than we used to suspect. In the classic description, however, the age range is adolescence to old age with the peak incidence in the middle to later years. Manic-depressive (bipolar) illness follows a slightly different curve; it tends to appear earlier in the life cycle, usually before age thirty.

Numerous studies support a finding of some hereditary tendency in the illness, though there is much uncertainty on that point. As a general estimate, a history of severe depression in one parent may present about a 10 to 15 percent chance that the disease will later reappear in the offspring.

One study found an even closer concordance between identical twins. If one twin suffered a severe depression, there was a more than 60 percent chance of the disease appearing in the other twin, and often at about the same age. That's especially significant because identical twins have a very similar genetic makeup.

We do not know exactly how depressive tendencies are inherited. The ratios indicate that it is not a simple Mendelian gene, either dominant or recessive. Probably it is some combination of genetic factors that we have not yet unraveled.

Dr. Winokur, whose work was cited earlier, has conducted studies indicating that a manic-depressive can pass on either a manic-depressive or depressive tendency. If so, it indicates a combination factor involving at least two genes, and Dr. Winokur believes they are located on the X-chromosome side. That's an interesting clue. A mother can pass an X-chromosome trait to either son or daughter, but a father passes it only to a daughter. It would explain those diagnostic surveys that find depression more common in women.

In general the genetic mode is still not clear, but the fact of familial tendency is well established. That in turn strongly supports the assumption of biochemical malfunction as the basic cause. Our knowledge in this area is still too meager for specific assessments, but surely we inherit differences in biochemistry just as we do in other more prominent physical features.

For a clinician the hereditary trait provides a clue to treatment. There is tentative evidence that response to particular drugs also follows familial tendencies, and so one inquires whether close relatives have had the illness and how they fared with particular medications. The rule of thumb is that if the patient's close relative had a favorable reaction to a tricyclic, and if other considerations are equal, then that's a preferred choice. The same would be true, of course, if the family history indicated good response to an MAO inhibitor. It is not the most important factor in prescription, but it does provide an empirical approach. As our research progresses, we may find out why one patient does well on one drug, and one on another, and it may trace down to some quite specific biochemical circumstance.

Further research may also clarify other questions about the illness. We may find that it is really several diseases presenting common symptoms but stemming from different kinds of brain malfunction. It may even be that the basic disorder in some cases is not in the brain at all but in the endocrine system or even related to the ability of the gastrointestinal tract to absorb and excrete certain proteins or other substances. Even quite minor differences in the precipitating cause might prove important in regard to such matters as the severity of attack and the probability of recurrence. All that is speculative, however, and at present we can make only practical judgments in terms of symptoms and response to treatment. The only clear distinction that now exists is between pure depression (unipolar) and manic-depressive (bipolar), with the first form much the more common. There is very likely only one type of unipolar depression, which manifests itself in different ways at different times of life. In youth it is called "adolescent depression," after childbearing it's labeled "postpartum" depression, while at the time of change of life we use the term "involutional melancholia," and in later years "depression of aging."

Some studies find susceptibility to the illness conforming rather loosely to general personality types. The typical depressive tends to be a more rigid individual and somewhat lacking in energy and drive even when not suffering a depressive attack. Manic-depressives are usually more outgoing. When in the normal, or hypomanic, phases of the cycle, they may be very dynamic personalities.

There is no demonstrable correlation between depressive incidence and particular kinds of neurosis, and no evidence I know of that depressives are more neurotic than others. The percentage of those who suffer purely neurotic depressions is so small as to have no appreciable effect on that picture. When neurosis enters in, it is usually as an aggravating factor and does not change the basic nature of the illness. Of course, it does change the patient's response to the problem.

Social and economic factors are also irrelevant in terms of incidence, but play important roles in shaping response. Well-educated persons of middle- and upper-middle-class backgrounds are much quicker to admit emotional disturbance and seek psychiatric help. That's especially true in the great metropolitan centers. Unfortunately psychiatry has not put down firm roots among the less educated and especially not in the small towns and rural areas. For victims in such circumstances the depression very often goes not only untreated but also unrecognized.

A depressive may easily enough suffer through the

illness and never suspect that he has it. He displaces the symptoms into headaches, backaches, chest pains, or whatever. He complains of feeling tired all the time, and this he readily explains by the fact that he is not sleeping well. If he admits to feeling blue, he ascribes it to the poor state of his health, and in fact he's right enough in the broad sense, but he is wrong about what is causing what. The physical and emotional reactions are both common symptoms of the same illness, and the physical problems are the lesser aspect.

Unfortunately the failure to recognize depression extends to many physicians, too. Doctors' offices are filled with people who make the rounds with a list of often vague complaints, and they are rather too easily told that nothing is wrong with them and dismissed as hypochondriacs. Some of them are hypochondriacs, of course, but some are suffering from a thinly masked depression. It is a problem that ought to command far more attention both from physicians and the general public.

For depressives and their relatives the solution lies in dismissing once and for all any vestige of that superstitious heritage that places emotional disturbance in a special and somehow shameful category. A depression is a disease as natural as any other, and like most others, it is far more easily managed if recognized in the early stages.

Of course, there is also such a thing as obsessive concern with every symptom or imagined symptom, whether physical or emotional. There are some practical and sensible guidelines as to when one should or should not suspect a depression.

It is quite common to experience depressive reactions after such physically exhausting events as viral infection, surgery, or childbirth. The patient may feel wrung out physically and very dejected, but this is not true depression in the clinical sense. It usually passes within a few days or at most a few weeks. Antidepressant drugs will not help these conditions, because they are not addressed to that type of biochemical cause. The patient's best recourse is to get plenty of rest and just wait it out in the knowledge that this is a residual effect that will soon pass.

I advise my patients to take a similar accepting attitude toward occasional small fits of "the blues." We all have ups and downs in response both to the biological rhythms of life and the ebb and flow of pressures and circumstances. In particular cases these occasional blues may or may not represent minidepressions, but not every such incident requires treatment. One does not go into traction for every strained muscle or apply massive doses of antibiotics to every small infection. The body has its own splendid devices for restoring health, and a serious medical intervention should be reserved for cases of serious need.

When, then, should one consider medical treatment for a clinical depression? Only a trained physician can make such diagnosis, but the patient can and should make practical judgments as to when he needs medical advice.

Basically the test is functional. If a mood disturbance is sufficiently persistent and severe as to interfere with normal life, then it's high time to do something about it.

Such disturbance may be quite serious and still not take the classic form of mournful gloom. The mood may be just flat, heavy, dull—not so much the presence of pain as the acute absence of any pleasure. If a person feels that way all the time or even most of the time, then something is amiss. On the other hand, if he sparks up readily at some stimulating event, then probably he's not severely depressed but just bored. Caution is required even here because chronic boredom is itself usually a symptom of depression. Displacing the blame to the environment is allowable only for a short time. A healthy person does something to change the situation if it continues to be unstimulating. One hallmark of true depression is the complete inability to enjoy or even respond to things one always found pleasurable before. In fact, this lack of pleasure (anhedonia) is the most universal symptom.

The probability of depression is still further increased if there are changes in basic biological rhythms that cannot be explained by other causes. Marked disturbance of sleep, appetite, and sex drive are all classic signs that may well point to depression.

The GP shouldn't attempt to substitute for an analyst. But he can offer the depressive common-sense advice and emotional support—just as he would for some other patient who is suffering from ulcers or a heart condition. If it becomes apparent that a particular depressive patient needs more psychotherapy than that, then he should be referred to a specialist.

Drug therapy for depressives can be mastered about as easily as any other type of medication. Oddly enough, many GP's recommend sedatives and antianxiety medications rather freely, sometimes too enthusiastically, but shy away from antidepressants because they somehow feel that the whole matter is highly specialized, very difficult, and outside their province. In fact, depressive treatment is a gratifying part of medical practice because it is so often successful.

Some GP's do experiment tentatively with treating depression and then give up on it because they are discouraged by the initial results. Most commonly they make the mistake of not giving the medicine time enough. Despite the claims of pharmaceutical companies, it takes on average a good three weeks to achieve any improvement, and one should be prepared for protracted treatment in many cases. The whole value of the therapy may be lost if the physician switches impatiently from one drug to another, not giving any of them time enough to be effective.

When such medications accumulate, one should consult a physician promptly. But please note that the physician should be consulted, not advised. A doctor is properly put off when a patient sits down, announces his own diagnosis, and proceeds to prescribe for himself the latest medicine he has read about.

Of course, if the patient suspects a particular illness, then it's entirely sensible to seek out a physician with experience in that particular area. But that does not necessarily imply a specialist. It is my judgment that most depressions could and should be treated by general practitioners.

13

A Medical Proposal
for Doctors Only

In the complex business of living, both theory and practice are necessary conditions of understanding, and the method of Hippocrates, the most famous of physicians, is the only method that has ever succeeded widely and generally. The first element of that method is hard, persistent, intelligent, responsible, unremitting labor in the sick-room, not in the library: the complete adaptation of the doctor to his task, an adaptation that is far from being merely intellectual. The second element of that method is accurate observation of things and events, selection, guided by judgment born of familiarity and experience, of the salient and the recurrent phenomena, and their classification and methodical exploitation. The third element of that method is the judicious construction of a theory—not a philosophical theory, nor a grand effort of the imagination, nor a quasi-religious dogma, but a modest pedestrian affair, or perhaps I had better say, a useful walking-stick to help on the way—and the use thereof. All this may be summed up in a word: The physician must have, first, intimate, habitual, intuitive familiarity with things; secondly, systematic knowledge of things; and, thirdly, an effective way of thinking about things.
—L. J. HENDERSON,
Hippocrates and the Practice of Medicine

I have noted that at least four million persons in the United States suffer a serious depression every year, and the actual number may be from two to five times that high according to figures issued by officials of the National Institute of Mental Health.

Statistically, this would suggest that each patient saw a physician once, or just long enough to be diagnosed but not treated. But, of course, that's absurd! What actually happened was worse than absurd. The figures indicate that some 10 to 15 percent of those needing help received adequate treatment, and the rest were skimmed, ignored, or failed to follow through with treatment. This is nothing less than a medical scandal. If pneumonia, diabetes, or any other major disease entity was so often undiagnosed and untreated, the courts would be justifiably filled with patients suing for medical malpractice.

The situation is all the worse because it is so totally unnecessary. Effective treatment of most cases of depression is now readily accomplished, and any general practitioner can acquaint himself with the necessary procedures.

The basic problem is that medicine has not kept pace with its own times. Twenty to twenty-five years ago the general practitioner was quite justified in regarding emotional illness as a mysterious and difficult area, one in which he could offer little help. All that has been changed dramatically by the very rapid development of effective psychotropic medications. It is now high time to translate all the technical advances into clinical benefits available to all patients.

In short, it is now high time to turn a lot of psychiatric medicine back to the general practitioner. Therapeutically it is entirely feasible, and logistically it is the only way to solve the problem.

To accomplish it, medicine will have to overcome some of its ingrained tendencies to become ever more specialized and compartmentalized. Of course, there are virtues to specialization, and it has helped us to achieve high levels of therapeutic skill. It becomes self-defeating, however, when we become so overspecialized that we can't deliver the skills to the bulk of the patients.

To paraphrase Churchill, we have reached a point in psychiatric medicine where we can say, "Never were so few so thoroughly treated by so few." Without sacrificing the great gains we have made I believe that we can transform therapy for depression into the treatment of the many by the many.

A truly effective program would require a close working partnership between psychiatry and general medicine. There already exist some practical models for a successful approach. I have worked closely with one such project in Indonesia, and we obtained excellent results.

Indonesia's shortage of medical services is so staggering as to make our problems seem eminently manageable. Specifically, it's a country of more than 100 million people, and at the time we undertook the project it had just 32 trained psychiatrists. On a per capita basis that's about as though there were three psychiatrists to serve all of New York City, or sixty-eight for our entire country.

Working with the Ministry of Health and with Dr. Kusumonto, chairman of the Department of Psychiatry at the Medical School, we established experimental clinics and training centers in the city of Djakarta, and set about training general practitioners to take over the routine aspects of psychiatric therapy. That's less difficult than it might sound, for much psychiatric practice is as routine as any other branch of medicine once one has learned to recognize basic situations and procedures. The trained psychiatrists supervised the program and took personal charge as special problems required. A great deal of the therapy, however, was handled by the general practitioners working out of their own offices or clinics.

After a year's trial we assessed results. Mental-hospital admissions from the trial districts had declined significantly despite the fact that we were encouraging a special focus on emotional problems. In short, we were reaching and helping a lot of people before they deteriorated to the point where they needed hospitalization.

I believe that a similar approach could be employed to great advantage in our own country. A group of family doctors or GP's could agree to pool their training in regard to psychiatric problems and work with a psychiatrist who would conduct "on-the-job training" in the office of one of the doctors. That is, he'd join them in patient interviews to establish diagnosis and treatment. They would handle routine follow-up procedures, and the psychiatrist would remain available for consultation as occasion required. In such fashion he might make his special skills and experience available to five or ten times as many patients as he serves now. Moreover, as the GP's gained experience, they could take over more and more management of the ordinary cases.

Such a team approach would be bolstered still more by the addition of psychiatric social workers and other paramedical personnel. I believe it would be valuable to divert a good share of those people from the "medical housekeeping" of institutional situations and channel them into the often much more productive field of office practice. I see no reason why foundations and public-health agencies should not contribute some services as part of a general effort to extend treatment to all who need it.

In any case, the ideal situation would include backup services by a skilled social worker or nurse, and would provide also for crisis intervention in such matters as a suicide threat. This is not as difficult to arrange as it might seem. All it really means is that some trained, skilled person would be available to drop everything and get to a particular patient in a hurry if he needed help badly. Doctors and nurses do that all the time in regard to other kinds of medical problems.

Even without the establishment of medical teams, the knowledgeable family doctor or GP could rather easily take over a lot of ordinary depressive cases.

Primarily it's a matter of learning to recognize the disease and becoming acquainted with the medications and how to use them.

For instance, in cases in which there is a complaint of daytime sleepiness we have had equally good results by giving the entire dose of medication at bedtime. This may eliminate the need for a sleeping medication. At times the various tricyclics can be combined and a stimulant one given in the morning if the patient is sleepy or complains of being "hung over."

The selection of a particular tricyclic antidepressant depends on the type and degree of particular symptoms. If there is a need for stimulation, triptyline is the medication of choice. If the patient is in the mid-range, then imipramine or desipramine is the drug to use; and if anxiety is present, then doxepin, amitriptyline, or triptyline is to be preferred. There are other circumstances to be considered. Does the patient live alone, so that if he or she falls asleep with the stove on, no one is there to turn it off? Is the person's occupation such that increased nervousness or sleepiness might be dangerous (airline pilot, for instance)? Medication on the market in Europe may be available sooner or later in the United States. Therefore a list is included, together with recommended dosage.

The MAO inhibitors are used much less frequently than they deserve. Their chief problem involves the nuisance of providing the patient a list of foods and medications that should be avoided. Their virtue is that they often produce results when the tricyclics fail. There are a dozen drugs used in medicine that are much more dangerous than the MAO inhibitors—digitalis and insulin, as examples—and the even slight experience will prove most encouraging. The mildest of the MAO inhibitors is isocarboxazid. Phenelzine is much more potent, and tranylcypromine is usually reserved for hospital uses or for patients who fail to respond to other antidepressants.

Still other antidepressants will probably appear soon in general practice. One likely candidate is L-tryptophan, which is already on the market in England and Europe. In our own testing, it proved to be as effective as the tricyclic antidepressants, and when combined with an MAO inhibitor, it was superior.

We are seeking drugs that will extend the treatment range even further by producing quicker relief or more long-lasting effects. Studies are now being conducted on an experimental drug (trazodone) that is claimed to work in three to seven days. Thus we are in sight of even more effective approaches as this ancient illness yields at last to healing efforts.

Some may object to a call for broadening the base of psychiatric medicine. It will be argued that no general practitioner can possibly acquire the sophisticated experience available to one who has spent his life dealing with a particular kind of illness. And, of course, that's true. That's why we have specialists. But not every case requires the full attention of a specialist, and we cannot afford to relegate to a small corps of specialists a disease that causes great suffering to millions of people.

The psychiatrists of the country cannot begin to handle the necessary case loads. Thus as a quite practical matter we must seek out the most feasible alternative.

Aside from the sheer logistics of the matter, there are other reasons why I would think it valuable to enlist active assistance of the family doctor or the GP. He is ideally placed both to observe the early warnings of depression's onset and to conduct a continuing follow-up after the immediate crisis is past.

Finally, and perhaps most important, I feel that by working closely with other physicians we could help to demystify the whole question of emotional illness. This would have a lot of benefits.

There are today an enormous number of people who are simply not receptive to psychiatric treatment, who "don't believe in psychiatry." Oh, they may say they believe in it, but for someone else, not for themselves.

"I'm not crazy," they say. Or, in some cases, "If I'm crazy, I don't want to know about it."

Every psychiatrist knows personally of many such people. They are all the names on slips of paper that are never matched by faces in the office. They are referred by their physicians, they "get lost" on the way over, and they stay lost so far as psychiatry is concerned.

And then there are those who make one shamefaced or defiant appearance and never come back. The dropout rate at some psychiatric clinics runs 35 to 50 percent.

We psychiatrists try to allay those fears, but oddly enough, we sometimes go about it as though it were a strictly rational problem. That is, we try to resolve it by rational discussion. We might do better to view it as a psychological problem and then deal with it psychologically.

I think we can achieve much of that if we bring psychiatry out from behind its sometimes mysterious and forbidding façade and link it as closely as possible to the everyday business of medicine. In particular, I think there would be great psychological gains if we could arrange the kind of partnership approach in which the psychiatrist offers his services as a visiting consultant in the GP's familiar office. I'm sure that would make the whole problem a lot less frightening to many patients. It would make a depressive attack seem like just another of the ills with which nature sometimes afflicts us.

And I believe that's just what it is.

14

How Severe Is the Depression?

If there be a hell upon earth, it is to be found in a melancholy man's heart.

—ROBERT BURTON,
Anatomy of Melancholy

A rating scale often provides an illusion of scientific accuracy that, in fact, it does not possess. As Dr. Max Hamilton states, "The fact that they (the judgments of the observer) are recorded in numerical form instead of literary description does not improve their value, it only makes them more convenient for statistical evaluation." However, for certain purposes the scale is extremely useful. For instance, if the scale is well constructed, it does ensure that all the important areas that ought to be considered are touched upon. By using the same scale over a period of time, it is obviously possible to know whether an individual is getting better, getting worse, or remaining the same on a particular item. It also becomes possible to compare different individuals.

There are certain things scales cannot do, such as tell you if you are happily married or if your sex life is satisfactory—although a good scale will point out the things you ought to consider and allow you to estimate how satisfactory specific items are. The same is true of a depression-rating scale.

All rating scales that give a "score" must be used with caution for four major reasons:

1. The items are never equivalent. A "happy mar-

210

riage" scale would legitimately include both sex life and well-served meals. But are they of equal importance ("weight" is the technical term)? For different individuals they are different, and even for the same individual they are different at different times, so how can they be considered equivalent?

2. Many items overlap (e.g., "patient moves slowly" and "patient speaks slowly" could be different items but in part are the same and in part different). The patient might speak slowly because he is thinking slowly, or it might be purely physical. Because of this overlap, you may include more of one factor than you should.

3. Specific items may have different degrees of severity. Thus a patient may "hear voices" never, rarely, commonly, or often. How do you rate this? 0 for *never,* 1 for *rarely,* 2 for *commonly,* and 3 for *often?* The degree of change (technically, "step interval") from 0 (no hallucinations) to 1 (rarely) is not the same as from 2 (commonly) to 3 (often).

4. Most important of all, it is the pattern of items rather than any adding or subtracting that is important. For instance, if a person is very agitated, he may rate a 3 for *severe,* and another patient may not be agitated at all, rating 0. Both patients may rate 2 as far as hearing voices is concerned. Thus the first patient would rate 5 and the second patient only 2—yet we know that patients who hear voices and are agitated usually are not as sick as those who hear voices but are no longer upset about it. So in this case the scale would give us misinformation. The patient with agitation and depression, however, is "sicker" than the patient with only depression. Methods for evaluating combinations or patterns are only in their infancy.

Ratings determined by yourself or by someone else raise other questions. How reliable is the rater? Are the items worded well enough so that with practice the same rater would give approximately the same rating each time *(reliability of scale)?* Will different raters, once trained to use the scale, give approximately the same rating *(inter-rater reliability)*? Also, does the item really rate what it is supposed to rate *(validity)*?

The scale most widely used throughout the world was introduced in 1960 by Dr. Max Hamilton, now of Leeds University in England and Rockland Research Institute in the U.S. As Dr. Hamilton points out, the rating scale is designed to measure the severity of illness in patients diagnosed as suffering from primary depressive disorder. It was not intended for use as a diagnostic instrument and should not be used for this purpose. A diagnosis must be based not only on the present condition of the patient but on the course of the illness, its mode of onset, the previous history of the patient, and the family history of mental illness. A depressive illness will sometimes occur secondary to such disorders as diabetes mellitus and addisonian anemia. In that case it must be remembered that the symptoms of the primary disorder, e.g. fatigability, will overlap those of the depression, and this will make for difficulties in assessment. It is true that patients suffering from different mental disorders can be rated on the scale and given an appropriate score, but it cannot be said that such scores are comparable to those obtained from true depressives. Within the group, changes of scores may have some meaning, though their clinical significance can be determined only on external grounds.

The original Hamilton Rating Scale for Depression is not a self-rated scale, but one in which trained evaluators do the rating. In 1980 Dr. Hamilton reviewed the advantages and cautions of both self-rated and observer-rated scales. Certain items cannot be scored by the person being evaluated, e.g. degree of insight, delusions, or hallucinations. On the other hand, subjective feelings can be described only by the individual experiencing them.

Dr. Hamilton further points out certain other cautions that should be taken into account:

1. It is obvious that the rater should have adequate training in psychopathology. If he does not know what

"retardation" is and is unable to recognize it when it is present, he will not be able to rate it.

2. He should have experience with the different levels of severity.

3. The rater should also have some instruction on the use of rating scales. Information that is used for the rating of one item should not be used in the rating of another. The score on one item should not influence the scores on adjacent items.

4. Logical errors must be avoided: because a patient has lost weight, it cannot be assumed that his appetite has decreased; because he is suicidal, it cannot be assumed that he is very depressed.. The ratings on the two items should be based only on information pertaining to each.

5. The rater should avoid "central" and "extreme" biases, i.e. the tendency to prefer either middle or extreme scores. The former bias is one to which inexperienced raters are particularly prone. There are other errors and biases, but these are the most important and the most frequent ones.

Hamilton summarizes his conclusions as follows:

"Many other symptoms can be found among depressive patients but although they are of the greatest importance in the treatment and management of the individual patient, they need not be considered in the measurement of the severity of illness. A scale is designed to be used for the generality of patients, to measure their suffering and the burden of their illness. This scale has been found to be sufficient for this purpose. Despite its deficiencies, it has been found easy to use in practice and to be meaningful to clinicians. It is sensitive to the changes produced by treatment or occurring as a result of spontaneous recovery. It is primarily a research tool, but because it is concerned with the level of pathology over a period of at least a week, or even two, it is not necessarily the best scale for particular purposes or particular patients. In addition to its obvious use, it has also been found convenient in the teaching of students and even as an aide-mémoire in clinical practice. Doubtless, in due course, it will be replaced by better scales."

The Hamilton rating scale itself is included in the appendix. The Newcastle Scale helps distinguish between endogenous and neurotic depression.

There exist a number of self-rated scales, such as the Zung Self-Rating Depression Scale and that of Beck. For a variety of reasons, we have included three such scales in the appendix. One of these, published by Dr. Bernard Carroll in 1981, converts the Hamilton observer-rated scale to a self-rated scale. The others are (2) The Leeds Scales for the Self-Assessment of Anxiety and Depression and (3) The Wakefield Self-Assessment Depression Inventory. These two latter scales were devised and tested by R. P. Snaith, G. W. K. Bridge, and Max Hamilton.

15

A Public Appeal

The health of nations is more important than the wealth of nations.
    —WILL DURANT, *What Is Civilization?*

WE are in the midst of a great age of discovery in mental and emotional illness. It has already produced tremendous advances in prevention and treatment, and the long-run prospects are brighter still. Every breakthrough opens up new fields of exploration, and we are now pursuing an array of immensely promising new leads. In 1973 the medical and scientific opportunities were threatened by appalling political decisions. In the first edition of *From Sad to Glad,* I wrote: "The federal government has adopted an unannounced but quite evident policy that holds that we can afford to go slow in the conquest of mental illness. In 1973, as one evidence of such an attitude, the administration refused to spend some $80 million that Congress had appropriated for mental health. The impounded funds included $10 million needed for vital research programs, and the money was tied up until foundations and other interested parties forced its release through court action.

"If this foot-dragging attitude prevails, it will be a harsh blow to the hopes of all those who suffer from mental and emotional illness. It ought to be a matter of deep concern for all Americans.

"Something can be done about it. Elected officials do take note when the will of the people is strongly expressed. All who care about this problem should write to their Congressmen, urging restoration of the funds and continuing vigorous support of the research programs."

Something *was* done about it. The first edition of *From Sad to Glad* sold 125,000 copies and was probably read by at least half a million persons. I would hope that at least one of every 100 persons reading the book did write. Five thousand letters is an important number, especially when there is no organized campaign to exert such pressure. In any case, the budget was increased and research has continued to advance.

Great interest was aroused in the whole field of mental health by the report of the Presidential Commission on Mental Health in 1978, and by the Mental Health Systems Act proposed by the Administration in 1979 and signed just before Mr. Carter's term expired. The activities of Rosalynn Carter, the former president's wife, further stimulated interest in mental health. The contribution to the field has been significant, but there is a danger—that the publicity be mistaken for the reality!

Funds for the ADAMHA (Alcohol, Drug Abuse, and Mental Health Administration) and for the NIMH (National Institute of Mental Health) component and its research are as follows:

	1974	1975	1976	1977	1978	1979	1980	1981	1982°
			(Funding in Millions of Dollars)						
ADAMHA		789	761	885	939	1025	1026	998	458
NIMH		407	371	455	493	570	569	540	235
Research		86	88	104	111	130	145	143	145
Decrease in value of dollar since January 1, 1974				26%			44%		

°Estimated

Since the beginning of 1974, when I wrote the first edition of this book, the Consumer Price Index has gone from 133 to 236 at the start of 1981. This means that the dollar is worth only 56 percent of what it was on January 1, 1974, so that the budget of ADAMHA has decreased 25 percent, that of NIMH 30 percent, and even psychiatric research is less than it was five years ago.

The Reagan administration has dealt with the psychiatric research budget more considerately than had been anticipated. Reductions were recommended, but support is continued at about the same level as in 1980. However, congressional action may alter this. Community mental-health centers are to become the responsibility of the individual states, and support for the training of psychiatrists is to be limited or discontinued despite an anticipated shortage of nearly 8,000.

It is important to let those in power, who are there because of you, know when you think they are doing a good job as well as when you are dissatisfied. As of 1981 one could say that it is good that the importance of mental-health research has been recognized but that a great deal more needs to be done.

This is where *you* can make the crucial difference— by letting your congressman know, directly and indirectly, that you want him to back mental-health legislation.

There are many appeals for federal support of particular programs. Let me set forth briefly the compelling reasons why mental-health research deserves a top priority.

The chief thrust of modern psychiatric research is the exploration of brain processes and the corresponding search for ways to correct malfunctions. The first mass benefits were realized in 1956, when psychotropic medications were accepted for widespread use in mental hospitals. A before-and-after comparison of hospital case loads reveals the truly revolutionary progress that resulted.

In the years 1946–56 the number of American mental-hospital patients increased by almost 97,000 persons, climbing to a peak of 558,900. The steady rise reflected partly an increase in the general population base as well as a growing awareness of a problem that had long suffered from much neglect. We were recognizing and acknowledging mental illness but not yet treating it effectively, and the hospital rolls swelled accordingly. Every month the number of new patients admitted averaged from 800 to 1,000 more than those released. Indeed, for some patients commitment carried the specter of lifetime confinement to an institution.

In 1956 the psychotropic drugs were introduced into hospital practice on a sizable scale, and the steady upward curve was checked and turned down. Over the next two years the hospital case load shrank by 7,500 patients. It was a small gain, but at that period any gain at all was tremendous news. For the first time in mental-hospital history, the sign-out desk was busier than the reception center.

The years since have brought a stream of new discoveries, and with them has come an accelerated procession of former mental patients leaving the hospitals. For more than two decades, the occupancy of the wards has been decreasing at rates averaging approximately 20,000 persons a year. By the end of 1980 the case load was down to 119,000—a reduction of more than 440,000 from the peak level of 1954 (see figure for detailed comparison).

If we consider a previous upward curve of 10,000 to 12,000 more resident patients at the end of each year than there were at the beginning of the year, then the total number of additional patients by 1981 would have been over 250,000. Considering the growth in population, the number of patients in hospitals might have been approaching the 1,000,000 mark. But one need not belabor the statistical analysis. It is sufficient to know that we could populate a large city entirely with former mental patients and their families—all of them people whose lives have been transformed by the healing knowledge gained through medical research.

Our next large effort is to enable hundreds of thousands of these patients to participate productively in society so that they are no longer a burden; to have them actually contribute to the general welfare and economy. For the past few years the situation has

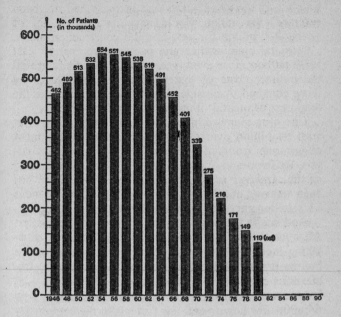

Number of resident patients in state and local government hospitals in the United States (based on USPHS figures).

stabilized: about one-fourth of all patients are cared for in hospitals, in contrast to 1955 when more than three-fourths of the patients were cared for in hospitals. The number of patient-care episodes has also stabilized at about seven million a year, in contrast to a little over 1.5 million in 1965.

And there remains another large community of those still waiting for the discoveries that can help them. It is unconscionable that their hopes should be thwarted by penny-pinching economies.

The human cost aside, the policy doesn't even make economic sense. The research programs have paid for themselves many times over in reducing the staggering costs of mental illness.

It costs an average $50,000 a bed to build a modern

hospital. If the steady case-load increase had not been reversed, the nation would have incurred a bill of nearly $10 billion for new hospital construction alone.

Hospital maintenance and patient care cost at least $500 million more every year. And finally there are all the indirect costs of lost productivity and wages by those confined. A presidential commission estimates the total cost of mental illness at $20 billion a year.

One drug alone, lithium, has made a difference of at least $4 billion over the past decade in the treatment of just one group of patients. In a conservative analysis, Reifman and Wyatt show in the April, 1980 issue of the *Archives of General Psychiatry* that there has been a saving of $2.9 billion in medical expenses and a $1.3 billion increase in productivity.

And finally there is the scientific aspect of the matter. All over the country laboratories are pursuing painstaking inquiries into the fundamental processes of the human brain. We have just begun to glimpse the tremendous possibilities that are opening before us.

In accord with the shift in patient population, new programs for how to care for patients in the community are now being proposed. Research in evaluating "enablement" (or what was formerly called rehabilitation) is essential.

It is the very nature of such research that we don't know what we'll find until we look. Often enough we can't even guess where a particular finding may lead us. Some inquiries indeed wind up in apparent dead ends. Others yield information that seems extraneous, but then several pieces of information are combined and something important emerges. Thus there is no way to look at an investigation in progress and know in advance what it will finally be worth. We do know that the sum total of effort has already been of inestimable value.

If we hamstring this program with budget cuts, we will never know exactly how much we have lost. Inquiries will be dropped before they are fairly launched, research teams will be scattered, and the work half done will be filed away in some neglected archive. It is immensely frustrating to confront such obstacles at a time when the scientific prospects are so brilliant.

The February 7, 1981 issue of *The New York Times* reported that an anticipated new military bomber would require $6.7 billion over the next two years. The entire mental-health research budget is less than 5 percent of the cost of this single bomber.

These shortsighted policies can be reversed if people care enough. The most useful and effective way to express concern is by raising the question with those who have power to do something about it.

A lot of people do care, but unfortunately they believe mistakenly that government is too vast and cumbersome to react to their appeals. In fact, as already discussed, congressmen usually respond when public opinion is clearly expressed.

And that leaves it up to us. We cannot really complain of governmental neglect if we will not take the small trouble to make our wishes known.

Recently I talked to one congressman whose district is composed mostly of well-educated and articulate people. He told me that his constituent mail averages about two hundred letters a week. If he gets even fifty of those letters on a particular issue, he pays close attention. "That," he said, "is how I stay in office."

The support of all congressmen is helpful, but some exert particular influence through membership on key committees. I am appending a list of such committee assignments with asterisks to designate further membership on a crucial subcommittee. For the reader's convenience, the committee lists are alphabetized according to state.

SENATE COMMITTEE ON LABOR AND HUMAN RESOURCES

REPUBLICANS	DEMOCRATS
Denton	Eagleton
East	Kennedy*
Hatch*	Metzenbaum
Hawkins	Pell
Humphrey	Randolph
Nickles	Reigle
Quayle	Williams
Stafford	
Weicker	

SENATE COMMITTEE ON FINANCE, SUBCOMMITTEE ON HEALTH

REPUBLICANS	DEMOCRATS
Dole*	Baucus
Durenberger*	Bradley
Heinz	Long
Packwood	

SENATE COMMITTEE ON APPROPRIATIONS

REPUBLICANS	DEMOCRATS
Abnor	Burdick
Andrews	Byrd
Hatfield*	Chiles
Rudman	Eagleton
Schmitt*	Hollings
Specter	Inouye
Stevens	Proxmire*
Weicker	

* Chairman of committee or subcommittee, or ranking minority member. If writing to a congressman not from your state, send to: U.S. Congress, Washington, D.C. 20510.

HOUSE COMMITTEE ON WAYS AND MEANS, SUBCOMMITTEE ON HEALTH

DEMOCRATS	REPUBLICANS
Ford	Duncan
Heftel	Crane
Holland	Gradison*
Jacobs	
Rangel*	
Rostenkowski*	

HOUSE COMMITTEE ON ENERGY AND COMMERCE, SUBCOMMITTEE ON HEALTH AND THE ENVIRONMENT

DEMOCRATS	REPUBLICANS
Dingell*	Benedict
Florio	Bliley
Gramm	Brown
Leland	Broyhill
Luken	Dannemeyer
Mikulski	Madigan*
Moffett	Ritter
Scheuer	Whittaker
Shelby	
Walgren	
Waxman*	
Weyden	

HOUSE COMMITTEE ON APPROPRIATIONS, SUBCOMMITTEE ON LABOR, HEALTH, AND HUMAN SERVICES

DEMOCRATS	REPUBLICANS
Dwyer	Conte*
Early	Livingston
Natcher*	O'Brien
Obey	Porter
Roybal	Pursell
Smith	
Stokes	
Whitten*	

The first persons to whom you should write are the congressmen from your own district and state. The following list (alphabetized by states) gives the local addresses of all congressmen. Those with an asterisk next to the name are especially important.

MEMBERS OF CONGRESS
BY STATE

ALABAMA

SENATORS
Jeremiah Denton—Mobile
Howell Heflin—Tuscondia

REPRESENTATIVES
Tom Bevill*—Jasper
William L. Dickinson*—Montgomery
Jack Edwards*—Mobile
Ronnie G. Flippo*—Florence
Bill Nichols—Sylacauga
Richard C. Shelby*—Woodstock
Albert Lee Smith, Jr.—Birmingham

ALASKA

SENATORS
Frank H. Murkowski—Anchorage
Ted Stevens—Anchorage

REPRESENTATIVE
Don Young*—Fort Yukon

ARIZONA

SENATORS
Barry Goldwater—Phoenix
Dennis DeConcini—Tucson

REPRESENTATIVES
John J. Rhodes*—Mesa
Eldon Rudd*—Scottsdale
Bob Stump*—Tolleson
Morris K. Udall*—Tucson

ARKANSAS

SENATORS
   Dale Bumpers—Little Rock
   David Pryor—Little Rock
REPRESENTATIVES
   Bill Alexander*—Osceola
   Beryl Anthony, Jr.*—El Dorado
   Ed Bethune*—Searcy
   John Paul Hammerschmidt*—Harrison

CALIFORNIA

SENATORS
   Alan Cranston—Los Angeles
   S. I. (Sam) Hayakawa—San Francisco
REPRESENTATIVES
   Glenn M. Anderson*—Harbor City
   Robert E. Badham*—Newport Beach
   Anthony C. Beilenson*—Los Angeles
   George E. Brown, Jr.*—Colton
   Clair W. Burgener*—Rancho Santa Fe
   John L. Burton*—San Francisco
   Phillip Burton*—San Francisco
   Gene Chappie—Roseville
   Don H. Clausen—Crescent City
   Tony Coelho*—Merced
   George E. Danielson*—Monterey Park
   William E. Dannemeyer—Fullerton
   Ronald V. Dellums*—Berkeley
   Julian C. Dixon*—Los Angeles
   Robert K. Dornan*—Los Angeles
   David Dreier—LaVerne
   Mervyn M. Dymally—Compton
   Don Edwards*—San Jose
   Vic Fazio*—Sacramento
   Bobbi Fiedler—Northridge
   Barry M. Goldwater, Jr.*—Woodland Hills
   Wayne Grisham*—La Mirada
   Augustus F. Hawkins*—Los Angeles
   Duncan Hunter—San Diego
   Robert J. Lagomarsino*—Ojai
   Tom Lantos—Hillsborough
   Jerry Lewis*—Highland

Bill Lowery—San Diego
Dan Lungren*—Long Beach
Robert T. Matsui*—Sacramento
Paul N. McCloskey, Jr.*—Menlo Park
George Miller*—Martinez
Norman Y. Mineta*—San Jose
Carlos J. Moorhead*—Glendale
Leon E. Panetta*—Carmel Valley
Charles Pashayan, Jr.*—Fresno
Jerry M. Patterson*—Santa Ana
John H. Rousselot*—San Marino
Edward R. Roybal*—Los Angeles
Norman D. Shumway*—Stockton
Fortney H. (Pete) Stark*—Oakland
William M. Thomas*—Bakersfield
Henry A. Waxman*—Los Angeles

COLORADO

SENATORS
William L. Armstrong—Aurora
Gary Hart—Denver
REPRESENTATIVES
Hank Brown—Greeley
Ray Kogovsek*—Pueblo
Ken Kramer*—Colorado Springs
Patricia Schroeder*—Denver
Timothy E. Wirth*—Denver

CONNECTICUT

SENATORS
Christopher J. Dodd—Norwich
Lowell P. Weicker, Jr.—Bridgeport
REPRESENTATIVES
William R. Cotter*—Hartford
Lawrence J. DeNardis—Hamden
Sam Gejdenson—Bozrah
Stewart B. McKinney*—Fairfield
Anthony Toby Moffett*—Unionville
William R. Ratchford*—Danbury

DELAWARE

SENATORS
Joseph R. Biden, Jr.—Wilmington
William V. Roth, Jr.—Wilmington

REPRESENTATIVE
Thomas B. Evans, Jr.*—Wilmington

FLORIDA

SENATORS
Lawton Chiles—Lakeland
Paula Hawkins—Winter Park
REPRESENTATIVES
L. A. (Skip) Bafalis*—Fort Myers Beach
Charles E. Bennett*—Jacksonville
Bill Chappell, Jr.*—Ocala
Dante B. Fascell*—Miami
Don Fuqua*—Altha
Sam Gibbons*—Tampa
Earl Hutto*—Panama City
Andy Ireland*—Winter Haven
William Lehman*—North Miami Beach
Bill McCollum—Altamonte Springs
Dan Mica*—West Palm Beach
Bill Nelson*—Melbourne
Claude Pepper*—Miami
E. Clay Shaw, Jr.—Ft. Lauderdale
C. W. Bill Young*—St. Petersburg

GEORGIA

SENATORS
Mack Mattingly—St. Simon's Is.
Sam Nunn—Atlanta
REPRESENTATIVES
Doug Bernard, Jr.*—Augusta
Jack Brinkley*—Columbus
Billy Lee Evans*—Macon
Wyche Fowler, Jr.*—Atlanta
Newt Gingrich*—Carrollton
Bo Ginn*—Millen
Charles Hatcher—Albany
Ed Jenkins*—Jasper
Elliott H. Levitas*—Atlanta
Larry McDonald*—Marietta

HAWAII

SENATORS
Daniel K. Inouye—Honolulu
Spark M. Matsunaga—Honolulu

REPRESENTATIVES
Daniel K. Akaka*—Honolulu
Cecil (Cec) Heftel*—Honolulu

IDAHO

SENATORS
James A. McClure—Boise
Steven D. Symms—Boise
REPRESENTATIVES
Larry E. Craig—Midvale
George Hansen*—Pocatello

ILLINOIS

SENATORS
Alan J. Dixon—Belleville
Charles H. Percy—Chicago
REPRESENTATIVES
Frank Annunzio*—Chicago
Cardiss Collins*—Chicago
Tom Corcoran*—Ottawa
Daniel B. Crane*—Danville
Philip M. Crane*—Mount Prospect
Edward J. Derwinski*—Flossmoor
John N. Erlenborn*—Glen Ellyn
John G. Fary*—Chicago
Paul Findley*—Pittsfield
Henry J. Hyde*—Bensenville
Edward R. Madigan*—Lincoln
Lynn Martin—Rockford
Robert McClory*—Lake Bluff
Robert H. Michel*—Peoria
George M. O'Brien*—Joliet
John Edward Porter—Evanston
Melvin Price*—East St. Louis
Tom Railsback*—Moline
Dan Rostenkowski*—Chicago
Marty Russo*—South Holland
Gus Savage—Chicago
Paul Simon*—Carbondale
Harold Washington—Chicago
Sidney R. Yates*—Chicago

INDIANA

SENATORS
   Richard G. Lugar—Indianapolis
   Dan Quayle—Huntington
REPRESENTATIVES
   Adam Benjamin, Jr.*—Hobart
   Dan Coats—Fort Wayne
   H. Joel Deckard*—Evansville
   David W. Evans*—Indianapolis
   Floyd J. Fithian*—Lafayette
   Lee H. Hamilton*—Columbus
   John Hiler—LaPorte
   Elwood Hillis*—Kokomo
   Andrew Jacobs, Jr.*—Indianapolis
   John T. Myers*—Covington
   Philip R. Sharp*—Muncie

IOWA

SENATORS
   Charles E. Grassley—New Hartford
   Roger Jepson—Davenport
REPRESENTATIVES
   Berkley Bedell*—Spirit Lake
   Cooper Evans—Grundy Center
   Tom Harkin*—Ames
   Jim Leach*—Davenport
   Neal Smith*—Altoona
   Thomas J. Tauke*—Dubuque

KANSAS

SENATORS
   Robert Dole—Kansas City
   Nancy Landon Kassebaum—Wichita
REPRESENTATIVES
   Dan Glickman*—Wichita
   Jim Jeffries*—Atchison
   Pat Roberts*—Dodge City
   Bob Whittaker*—Augusta
   Larry Winn, Jr.*—Overland Park

KENTUCKY

SENATORS

Wendell H. Ford—Louisville
Walter D. Huddleston—Elizabethtown

REPRESENTATIVES

Larry L. Hopkins*—Lexington
Carroll Hubbard, Jr.*—Mayfield
Romano L. Mazzoli*—Louisville
William H. Natcher*—Bowling Green
Carl D. Perkins*—Hindman
Harold Rogers—Somerset
Gene Snyder*—Brownsboro Farms

LOUISIANA

SENATORS

J. Bennett Johnston—New Orleans
Russell B. Long—Baton Rouge

REPRESENTATIVES

Lindy (Mrs. Hale) Boggs*—New Orleans
John B. Breaux*—Crowley
Jerry Huckaby*—Ringgold
Bob Livingston*—New Orleans
Gillis W. Long*—Alexandria
W. Henson Moore*—Baton Rouge
Buddy Roemer—Bossier City
W. J. (Billy) Tauzin*—Thibodaux

MAINE

SENATORS

William S. Cohen—Bangor
George J. Mitchell—Waterville

REPRESENTATIVES

David F. Emery*—Rockland
Olympia J. Snowe*—Auburn

MARYLAND

SENATORS

Charles McC. Mathias, Jr.—Baltimore
Paul Sarbanes—Baltimore

REPRESENTATIVES

Michael D. Barnes—Kensington
Beverly B. Byron*—Frederick

Roy Dyson—Great Mills
Marjorie S. Holt*—Saverna Park
Clarence D. Long*—Towson
Barbara A. Mikulski*—Baltimore
Parren J. Mitchell*—Baltimore
Gladys Noon Spellman—Laurel

MASSACHUSETTS

SENATORS
Edward M. Kennedy—Boston
Paul E. Tsongas—Lowell
REPRESENTATIVES
Edward P. Boland*—Springfield
Silvio O. Conte*—Pittsfield
Brian J. Donnelly*—Dorchester
Joseph D. Early*—Worcester
Barney Frank—Newton
Margaret M. Heckler*—Wellesley
Edward J. Markey*—Malden
Nicholas Mavroules*—Peabody
Joe Moakley*—Boston
Thomas P. O'Neill, Jr.*—Cambridge
James M. Shannon*—Lawrence
Gerry E. Studds*—Cohasset

MICHIGAN

SENATORS
Carl Levin—Detroit
Donald W. Riegle, Jr.—Flint
REPRESENTATIVES
Donald Joseph Albosta*—St. Charles
James J. Blanchard*—Pleasant Ridge
David E. Bonior*—Mt. Clemens
William M. Brodhead*—Detroit
Wm. S. Broomfield*—Birmingham
John Conyers, Jr.*—Detroit
Geo. W. Crockett, Jr.*—Detroit
Robert W. Davis*—Gaylord
John D. Dingell*—Trenton
Jim Dunn—East Lansing
William D. Ford*—Taylor
Dennis M. Hertel—Detroit
Guy Vander Jagt*—Luther

Dale E. Kildee*—Flint
Carl D. Pursell*—Plymouth
Harold S. Sawyer*—Rockford
Bob Traxler*—Bay City
Howard Volpe*—St. Joseph

MINNESOTA

SENATORS
Rudolph E. Boschwitz—Wayzata
David Durenberger—Minneapolis
REPRESENTATIVES
Arlen Erdahl*—West St. Paul
Bill Frenzel*—Golden Valley
Tom Hagedorn*—Truman
James L. Oberstar*—Chisholm
Martin Olav Sabo*—Minneapolis
Arlan Strangeland*—Barnesville
Bruce F. Vento—St. Paul
Vin Weber*—St. Cloud

MISSISSIPPI

SENATORS
Thad Cochran—Jackson
John C. Stennis—Jackson
REPRESENTATIVES
David R. Bowen*—Cleveland
Joe Hinson*—Tylertown
Trent Lott*—Pascagoula
G. V. (Sonny) Montgomery*—Meridian
James L. Whitten*—Charleston

MISSOURI

SENATORS
John C. Danforth—St. Louis
Thomas F. Eagleton—St. Louis
REPRESENTATIVES
Wendell Bailey—Willow Springs
Richard Bolling—Kansas City
William (Bill) Clay*—St. Louis
E. Thomas Coleman*—Kansas City
Bill Emerson—DeSoto
Richard A. Gephardt*—St. Louis
Ike Skelton*—Lexington

Gene Taylor*—Sarcoxie
Harold L. Volkmer*—Hannibal
Robert A. Young*—Maryland Heights

MONTANA

SENATORS
Max Baucus—Missoula
John Melcher—Billings
REPRESENTATIVES
Ron Marlenee*—Scobey
Pat Williams*—Helena

NEBRASKA

SENATORS
J. James Exon—Lincoln
Edward Zorinsky—Omaha
REPRESENTATIVES
Douglas K. Bereuter*—Utica
Hal Daub—Omaha
Virginia Smith—Chappell

NEVADA

SENATORS
Howard W. Cannon—Las Vegas
Paul Laxalt—Reno
REPRESENTATIVE
Jim Santini—Las Vegas

NEW HAMPSHIRE

SENATORS
Gordon J. Humphrey—Swapee
Warren Rudman—Nashua
REPRESENTATIVES
Norman E. D'Amours*—Manchester
Judd Gregg—Greenfield

NEW JERSEY

REPRESENTATIVES
Bill Bradley—Denville
Harrison A. Williams, Jr.—Newark
REPRESENTATIVES
James A. Courter*—Hackettstown
Bernard J. Dwyer—Edison
Millicent Fenwick*—Bernardsville

James J. Florio*—Camden
Edwin B. Forsythe*—Morristown
Frank J. Guarini*—Jersey City
Harold C. Hollenbeck*—East Rutherford
James J. Howard*—Spring Lake Heights
William J. Hughes*—Ocean City
Joseph G. Minish*—West Orange
Matthew J. Rinaldo*—Union
Peter W. Rodino, Jr.*—Newark
Robert A. Roe*—Wayne
Marge Roukema—Ridgewood
Christopher H. Smith—Old Bridge

NEW MEXICO

SENATORS
Pete V. Domenici—Albuquerque
Harrison "Jack" Schmitt—Albuquerque
REPRESENTATIVES
Manuel Lujan, Jr.*—Albuquerque
Joe Skeen—Picacho

NEW YORK

SENATORS
Alfonse M. D'Amato—Island Park
Daniel Patrick Moynihan—New York
REPRESENTATIVES
Joseph P. Addabbo*—Ozone Park
Mario Biaggi*—Bronx
Jonathan B. Bingham*—Bronx
Gregory W. Carman—Farmingdale
William Carney*—Hauppauge
Shirley Chisholm*—Brooklyn
Barber B. Conable, Jr.*—Alexander
Thomas J. Downey*—W. Islip
Geraldine A. Ferraro*—Forest Hills
Hamilton Fish, Jr.*—Millbrook
Robert Garcia*—New York City
Benjamin A. Gilman*—Middletown
Bill Green*—New York City
Frank Horton*—Rochester
Jack F. Kemp*—Hamburg
John J. LaFalce*—Kenmore
John LeBoutillier—Westbury

Gary A. Lee*—Ithaca
Norman F. Lent*—Baldwin
Stanley N. Lundine*—Jamestown
Donald O'B. Martin—Canton
Raymond J. McGrath—Valley Stream
Matthew F. McHugh*—Ithaca
Donald J. Mitchell*—Herkimer
Guy V. Molinari—Staten Island
Henry J. Nowak*—Buffalo
Richard L. Ottinger*—Pleasantville
Peter A. Peyser*—Irvington
Charles B. Rangel*—New York City
Frederick W. Richmond*—Brooklyn
Benjamin S. Rosenthal—Flushing
James H. Scheuer*—Neponsit
Charles E. Schumer—Brooklyn
Stephen J. Solarz*—Brooklyn
Gerald B. H. Solomon*—Glens Falls
Samuel S. Stratton*—Amsterdam
Ted Weiss*—New York City
George C. Wortley—Fayetteville
Leo C. Zeferetti*—Brooklyn

NORTH CAROLINA

SENATORS
John P. East—Greenville
Jesse Helms—Raleigh
REPRESENTATIVES
Ike Andrews*—Siler City
James T. Broyhill*—Lenoir
L. H. Fountain*—Tarboro
W. G. (Bill) Hefner*—Concord
Bill Hendon—Asheville
Walter B. Jones*—Farmville
Eugene Johnston—Greensboro
James G. Martin*—Davidson
Stephen L. Neal*—Winston-Salem
Charles Rose*—Fayetteville
Charles Whitley*—Mt. Olive

NORTH DAKOTA

SENATORS
Mark Andrews—Maplerow
Quentin N. Burdick—Fargo

REPRESENTATIVE
   Byron L. Dorgan—Bismarck

OHIO
SENATORS
   John Glenn—Columbus
   Howard M. Metzenbaum—Columbus
REPRESENTATIVES
   Douglas Applegate*—Steubenville
   John M. Ashbrook*—Johnstown
   Clarence J. Brown*—Urbana
   Dennis E. Eckart—Euclid
   Willis D. Gradison, Jr.*—Cincinnati
   Tennyson Guyer*—Findlay
   Tony P. Hall*—Dayton
   Thomas N. Kindness*—Hamilton
   Delbert L. Latta*—Bowling Green
   Thomas A. Luken*—Cincinnati
   Bob McEwen—Hillsboro
   Clarence E. Miller*—Lancaster
   Ronald M. Mottl—Parma
   Mary Rose Oakar*—Cleveland
   Donald J. Pease*—Oberlin
   Ralph Regula*—Navarre
   John F. Seiberling*—Akron
   Bob Shamansky—Columbus
   J. William Stanton—Painesville
   Louis Stokes*—Cleveland
   Ed Weber—Toledo
   Lyle Williams*—Lordstown
   Chalmers P. Wylie*—Worthington

OKLAHOMA
SENATORS
   David Lyle Boren—Oklahoma City
   Don Nickles—Ponca City
REPRESENTATIVES
   Mickey Edwards*—Oklahoma City
   Glenn English*—Cordell
   James R. Jones*—Tulsa
   Dave McCurdy—Norman
   Mike Synar*—Muskogee
   Wes Watkins*—Ada

OREGON

SENATORS
  Mark O. Hatfield—Salem
  Bob Packwood—Portland
REPRESENTATIVES
  Les AuCoin*—Forest Grove
  Denny Smith—Salem
  James Weaver*—Eugene
  Ron Wyden—Portland

PENNSYLVANIA

SENATORS
  John Heinz—Philadelphia
  Arlen Specter—Philadelphia
REPRESENTATIVES
  Eugene V. Atkinson*—Aliquippa
  Don Bailey*—Greensburg
  William F. Clinger, Jr.*—Warren
  Lawrence Coughlin*—Villanova
  James K. Coyne—Washington's Crossing
  William J. Coyne—Pittsburgh
  Charles F. Dougherty*—Philadelphia
  Bob Edgar*—Broomall
  Allen E. Ertel*—Montoursville
  Thomas M. Fogletta*—Philadelphia
  Joseph M. Gaydos*—McKeesport
  William F. Gooding*—Jacobus
  William H. Gray III*—Philadelphia
  Raymond F. Lederer*—Philadelphia
  Marc L. Marks*—Sharon
  Joseph M. McDade*—Scranton
  John P. Murtha*—Johnstown
  Austin J. Murphy*—Monongahela
  James L. Nelligan—Forty-Fort
  Don Ritter*—Coopersburg
  Richard T. Schulze*—Malvern
  Bud Shuster*—Everett
  Doug Walgren*—Pittsburgh
  Robert S. Walker*—East Petersburg
  Gus Yatron*—Reading

RHODE ISLAND

SENATORS
John H. Chafee—Providence
Claiborne Pell—Providence
REPRESENTATIVES
Fernand J. St. Germain*—Woonsocket
Claudine Schneider—Narragansett

SOUTH CAROLINA

SENATORS
Ernest F. Hollings—Columbia
Strom Thurmond—Aiken
REPRESENTATIVES
Carroll A. Campbell, Jr.*—Fountain Inn
Butler Derrick*—Edgefield
Thomas F. Hartnett—Charleston
Ken Holland*—Camden
John L. Napier—Bennettsville
Floyd Spence*—Lexington

SOUTH DAKOTA

SENATORS
James Abdnor—Mitchell
Larry Pressler—Humboldt
REPRESENTATIVES
Thomas A. Daschle*—Aberdeen
Clint Roberts—Presho

TENNESSEE

SENATORS
Howard H. Baker, Jr.—Nashville
Jim Sasser—Nashville
REPRESENTATIVES
Robin L. Beard*—Brentwood
William Hill Boner*—Nashville
Marilyn Lloyd Bouquard*—Chattanooga
John J. Duncan*—Knoxville
Harold E. Ford*—Memphis
Albert Gore, Jr.*—Carthage
Ed Jones*—Yorkville
James H. (Jimmy) Quillen*—Kingsport

TEXAS

SENATORS
Lloyd Bentsen—Houston
John Tower—Austin

REPRESENTATIVES
Bill Archer*—Houston
Jack Brooks*—Beaumont
James M. Collins*—Dallas
E. de la Garza*—Mission
Jack Fields—Humble
Martin Frost*—Dallas
Henry B. Gonzalez*—San Antonio
Phil Gramm*—College Station
Ralph M. Hall—Rockwall
Sam B. Hall, Jr.*—Marshall
Kent Hance*—Lubbock
Jack Hightower*—Vernon
Abraham Kazen, Jr.*—Laredo
Marvin Leath*—Marlin
Mickey Leland*—Houston
Tom Loeffler*—Hunt
Jim Mattox*—Dallas
Bill Patman—Ganado
J. J. Pickle*—Austin
Ron Paul*—Lake Jackson
Charles W. Stenholm*—Stamford
Richard C. White*—El Paso
Charles Wilson*—Lufkin
Jim Wright*—Fort Worth

UTAH

SENATORS
Jake Garn—Ogden
Orrin G. Hatch—Salt Lake City

REPRESENTATIVES
James V. Hansen—Farmington
Dan Marriott*—Salt Lake City

VERMONT

SENATORS
Patrick J. Leahy—Burlington
Robert T. Stafford—Rutland

REPRESENTATIVE
    James M. Jeffords*—Montpelier

VIRGINIA

SENATORS
    Harry F. Byrd, Jr.—Winchester
    John William Warner—Middleburg
REPRESENTATIVES
    Thomas J. Bliley, Jr.—Richmond
    M. Caldwell Butler*—Roanoke
    Dan Daniel*—Danville
    Robert W. Daniel, Jr.*—Spring Grove
    Stan Parris—Woodbridge
    J. Kenneth Robinson*—Winchester
    Paul S. Trible, Jr.*—Tappahannock
    William C. Wampler*—Bristol
    G. William Whitehurst*—Norfolk
    Frank R. Wolf—Falls Church

WASHINGTON

SENATORS
    Slade Gorton—Olympia
    Henry M. Jackson—Seattle
REPRESENTATIVES
    Don Bonker*—Ridgefield
    Norman D. Dicks*—Bremerton
    Thomas S. Foley*—Spokane
    Mike Lowry*—Mercer Island
    Sid Morrison—Zillah
    Joel Pritchard*—Seattle
    Al Swift*—Bellingham

WEST VIRGINIA

SENATORS
    Robert C. Byrd—Sophia
    Jennings Randolph—Elkins
REPRESENTATIVES
    Cleve Benedict—Lewisburg
    Robert H. Mollohan—Fairmont
    Nick Joe Rahall II*—Beckley
    David Michael Staton—South Charleston

WISCONSIN
SENATORS
   Bob Kasten—Thiensville
   William Proxmire—Madison
REPRESENTATIVES
   Les Aspin*—Racine
   Steve Gunderson—Osseo
   Robert W. Kastenmeier*—Sun Prairie
   David R. Obey*—Wausau
   Thomas E. Petri*—Fond du Lac
   Henry S. Reuss*—Milwaukee
   Toby Roth*—Appleton
   F. James Sensenbrenner, Jr.*—Shorewood

WYOMING
SENATORS
   Alan Kooi Simpson—Cody
   Malcolm Wallop—Casper
REPRESENTATIVE
   Richard Bruce Cheney*—Casper

PUERTO RICO: Baltassar Corrada*
         (Resident Commissioner)—San Juan
AMERICAN SAMOA: Fofo I. F. Sunia
         (Delegate)—Pago Pago
DISTRICT OF COLUMBIA: Walter E. Fauntroy*
         (Delegate)—District of Columbia
GUAM: Antonio Borja Won Pat* (Delegate)—Agana
VIRGIN ISLANDS: Ron de Lugo (Delegate)—St. Croix

The committee or subcommittee chairmen are instrumental in determining how our taxes will be spent. These are the congressmen to whom you should write next. Address them: U.S. Congress, Washington, D.C. 20510.

COMMITTEE OR SUBCOMMITTEE CHAIRMEN

SENATORS	REPRESENTATIVES
Max Baucus	Silvio O. Conte
Robert J. Dole	John Dingell
David Durenberger	William D. Gradison
Orrin G. Hatch	Andrew Jacobs, Jr.
Mark O. Hatfield	Edward Madigan
Edward M. Kennedy	William H. Natcher
William Proxmire	Daniel Rostenkowski
	Henry A. Waxman
	Jamie L. Whitten

David Stockman, the Director of the Office of Management and Budget, has a great deal to do with recommending to Congress how money should be spent. His opinion will be particularly important in deciding whether psychiatric disorders are to be included under any national health insurance or equivalent programs. In the past, when Mr. Stockman was a congressman from Minnesota, he introduced a bill in which mental-health services were *not* included as basic health care. Possibly in his new position he will have a different point of view. Certainly if enough taxpayers write to him it may help influence his decision. If you believe that psychiatric disorders are as important as physical illness, and that some form of government support should help pay the cost of psychiatric treatment, then it is crucial that you let the Director of the Office of Management and Budget know how you feel. Write to David Stockman, Director, Office of Management and Budget, Washington, D.C.

Two organizations in Washington play an important role in representing *you*. One is the National Committee Against Mental Illness. Write to Mr. Mike Gorman, Executive Director, National Committee Against Mental Illness, 1101 17th Street, N.W., Washington, D.C. 20036. The other is the National Association for Mental Health, 1800 N. Kent, Arlington, Va. 22209.

When representatives of these groups appear before the congressional committees that determine budgets or speak to those in the Bureau of the Budget, the number of letters they have that indicate interest on the part of the public are of great importance. Almost all of those in the Congress and administration who are involved *want* to do what *you* think ought to be done. But if you don't let them know, they'll never find out. Don't feel it is not worth the trouble. You *can* get results from even *one* letter.

Should important legislation be pending and if time is short, Western Union provides a special service at reduced rates. Phone them and say you want to send a Personal Opinion Message. Western Union has on file the addresses of each of the legislators, and the name and address are not counted as part of the message. Twenty words of text cost $3.50 from anywhere in the country.

If each reader were to write even *one* letter, it could bring to attention a whole new realization of how important the public considers the problem to be; how greatly we need to learn new ways of more effectively treating—and preventing—mental illness. It would make it possible to set up programs for teaching the primary-care physician—your family doctor—how to make use of what we already know. *Please write.* And encourage others in your family or even your friends to write—or at least to sign your letters. Writing takes only a few minutes and may help a loved one, a friend, a fellow worker, or even you yourself. If this book has been informative or helpful, you know how important I feel it is to send even one letter. *Thank you for writing.*

Appendix 1

COMMON MEDICATIONS

FOR the convenience of the reader who is interested in detailed information, I have listed some of the more common medications.

The *Monamine Oxidase Inhibitors* (MAOIs) on the market in the United States are:

Generic name	Trade name	Recommended official use
isocarboxazid	Marplan	antidepressant
phenelzine	Nardil	antidepressant
tranylcypromine	Parnate	antidepressant
pargyline	Eutonyl, Eutron	blood-pressure stabilizer
furazolidone	Furoxone	antibiotic
procarbazine	Matulane	anti-cancer (research only)

The *Tricyclic Antidepressants* (TCAs) on the market in the United States are:

Generic name	Trade name
nortriptyline	Aventyl, Pamelor
amitriptyline	Amitril, Elavil, Endep, Amitid, Amitriptyline, SK-Amitriptyline
amitriptyline plus perphenazine	Etrafon, Triavil
plus chloridiazepoxide	Limbitrol
amoxapine	Ascendin
desipramine	Norpramin, Pertofrane
imipramine	Tofranil, Antipress, Imavate, Imipramine, Janimine, SK-pramine, Presamine

244

Generic name	*Trade name*
protriptyline	Vivactil
doxepin	Sinequan, Adapin
trimipramine	Surmontil

The *tetracyclic* on the market in the U.S. is:

maprotiline	Ludiomil

The *psychostimulants* are:

amphetamines, including dextroamphetamine	Benzedrine, Biphetamine, Dexedrine, Obetrol
(combined with prochlorperazine)	Eskatrol
methamphetamine	Desoxyn
methylphenidate	Ritalin
pemoline	Cylert

Other medications with some antidepressant action are:

thiothixene	Navane
chlorprothixene	Taractan
thioridazine	Mellaril

Lithium appears under a variety of trade names:

Eskalith
Lithane
Lithium Carbonate
Lithobid
Lithonate
Lithonate-S
Lithotabs
Pfi-Lith

Appendix 2

RATING SCALES

The Hamilton Rating Scale for Depression is an observer-rated scale. Individuals with depressions generally score 15 or more.

HAMILTON PSYCHIATRIC RATING SCALE FOR DEPRESSION*

INSTRUCTIONS: For each item select the one "cue" which best characterizes the patient.
See *special instructions* that precede rating.

1. DEPRESSED MOOD (*Feelings of sadness, hopelessness, helplessness, worthlessness*)
   0=Absent
   1=These feeling states indicated only on questioning
   2=These feeling states spontaneously reported verbally
   3=Communicates feeling states non-verbally—i.e., through facial expression, posture, voice, and tendency to weep
   4=Patient reports VIRTUALLY ONLY these feeling states in his spontaneous verbal and non-verbal communication

2. FEELINGS OF GUILT
   0=Absent
   1=Self-reproach, feels he has let people down
   2=Ideas of guilt or rumination over past errors or sinful deeds

---

* Printed with permission of Dr. Max Hamilton.

3=Present illness is a punishment
4=Hears accusatory or denunciatory voices and/or
   experiences threatening visual hallucinations. Other
   delusions of guilt

3. SUICIDE
   0=Absent
   1=Feels life is not worth living
   2=Wishes he were dead or any thoughts of possible
     death to self
   3=Suicide ideas or gesture
   4=Attempts at suicide *(any serious attempt rates 4)*

4. INSOMNIA EARLY
   0=No difficulty falling asleep
   1=Complains of occasional difficulty falling asleep—
     i.e., more than ½ hour
   2=Complains of nightly difficulty falling asleep

5. INSOMNIA MIDDLE
   0=No difficulty
   1=Patient complains of being restless and disturbed
     during the night
   2=Waking during the night—any getting out of bed
     rates 2 *(except for purposes of voiding)*

6. INSOMNIA LATE
   0=No difficulty
   1=Waking in early hours of the morning but goes
     back to sleep
   2=Unable to fall asleep again if he gets out of bed

7. WORK AND ACTIVITIES
   0=No difficulty
   1=Thoughts and feelings of incapacity, fatigue or
     weakness related to activities, work or hobbies
   2=Loss of interest in activity, hobbies or work—
     either directly reported by patient, or indirect in
     listlessness, indecision and vacillation *(feels he has
     to push self to work or activities)*
   3=Decrease in actual time spent in activities or
     decrease in productivity. In hospital, rate 3 if
     patient does not spend at least three hours a day

in activities *(hospital job or hobbies)* exclusive of
ward chores

4=Stopped working because of present illness. In
hospital, rate 4 if patient engages in no activities
except ward chores, or if patient fails to perform
ward chores unassisted

8. RETARDATION *(Slowness of thought and speech;
impaired ability to concentrate; decreased motor
activity)*
0=Normal speech and thought
1=Slight retardation at interview
2=Obvious retardation at interview
3=Interview difficult
4=Complete stupor

9. AGITATION
0=None
1=Fidgetiness
2=Playing with hands, hair, etc.
3=Moving about, can't sit still
4=Hand-wringing, nail-biting, hair-pulling, biting
of lips

10. ANXIETY *(Psychic symptoms)*
0=No difficulty
1=Subjective tension and irritability
2=Worrying about minor matters
3=Apprehensive attitude apparent in face or speech
4=Fears expressed without questioning

11. ANXIETY *(Somatic symptoms)*

0=Absent	Physiological concomitants of anxiety, such as
1=Mild	Gastro-intestinal—*dry mouth, wind, indigestion, diarrhea, cramps, belching*
2=Moderate	Cardo-vascular—*palpitations, headaches*
3=Severe	Respiratory—*hyperventilation, sighing*
4=Incapacitating	Urinary frequency Sweating

12. **GASTRO-INTESTINAL SYMPTOMS**
    0=None
    1=Loss of appetite but eating without staff encouragement. Heavy feelings in abdomen
    2=Difficulty eating without staff urging. Requests or requires laxatives or medication for bowels or medication for G.I. symptoms

13. **GENERAL SOMATIC SYMPTOMS**
    0=None
    1=Heaviness in limbs, back, or head. Backaches, headache, muscle aches. Loss of energy and fatigability
    2=Any clear-cut symptom rates 2

14. **LOSS OF LIBIDO**
    0=Absent
    1=Mild
    2=Severe

15. **HYPOCHONDRIASIS**
    0=Not present
    1=Self-absorption (bodily)
    2=Preoccupation with health
    3=Frequent complaints, requests for help, etc.
    4=Hypochrondriacal delusions

16. **LOSS OF INSIGHT**
    0=Acknowledges being depressed and ill
    1=Acknowledges illness but attributes cause to bad food, climate, overwork, virus, need for rest, etc.
    2=Denies being ill at all

17a. **LOSS OF WEIGHT** *(estimated)*
    When Rating By History:
    0=No weight loss
    1=Probable weight loss associated with present illness
    2=Definite (according to patient) weight loss
OR (Do not score both 17a. and 17b.)

17b. LOSS OF WEIGHT *(actual)*
    0=Less than 1 lb. weight loss in week
    1=Greater than 1 lb. weight loss per week
    2=Greater than 2 lb. weight loss per week

18a. DIURNAL VARIATION *(occurrence)*
    Note whether symptoms are worse in morning or
    evening. If NO diurnal variation, mark none
    0=No variation
    1=Worse in A.M.
    2=Worse in P.M.

18b. DIURNAL VARIATION *(severity)*
    When present, mark the severity of the variation.
    Mark "None" if NO variation
    0=None
    1=Mild
    2=Severe

19. DEPERSONALIZATION AND DEREALIZATION
    (such as *feelings of unreality or nihilistic ideas*)
    0=Absent
    1=Mild
    2=Moderate
    3=Severe
    4=Incapacitating

20. PARANOID SYMPTOMS
    0=None
    1=Suspicious
    2=Ideas of reference
    3=Delusions of reference and persecution

21. OBSESSIONAL AND COMPULSIVE SYMPTOMS
    0=Absent
    1=Mild
    2=Severe

The [Hamilton] scale provides a simple way of assessing the severity of a patient's condition quantitatively, and for showing changes in that condition. It should not be used as a diagnostic instrument. A set of items to be so used should include not only those which will show the presence of the symptoms that the patient has, but also those which the patient has not, for a diagnosis not only includes the patient within a certain category but also excludes him from others. It is possible that the scale may have other uses, e.g.: predicting outcome and selection of treatment, but these have not yet been worked out.

Ratings can be done in a number of ways, depending on the purpose, but whatever this may be it must never be forgotten that the scores are merely a particular way of recording the rater's judgment. Other things being equal, the value of the ratings therefore depends entirely on the skill and experience of the rater and on how adequate is the information available to him. This scale was devised for recording the severity of symptoms of a patient (apart from minor and temporary fluctuations) and therefore questioning should be directed to his condition in the last few days or week. It is desirable to obtain additional information from relatives, friends, nurses etc. and this should always be done whenever there is doubt about the accuracy of the patient's answers. A question frequently asked concerns the length of time required to make a rating, i.e. for how long should the patient be interviewed in order to obtain sufficient information on which to base a judgment. This will obviously depend on the skill of the rater and the condition of the patient. Sick patients cannot think quickly and they should never be hurried. An adequate interview will surely be not less than half an hour, for that gives an average time of about two minutes per item, which is not really sufficient.

The following points about interviewing will be obvious to the skilled interviewer, but it does no harm to emphasize them. The patient should not be pressed and should be allowed sufficient time to say what he wants to say; but he should not be allowed to wander too far from the point. The number of direct questions should be kept to a minimum and such questions should be asked in different ways and, in particular, both in positive and negative form, e.g. "How badly do you sleep?" and "How well do you sleep?" Questions should be asked in language which the patient understands and ordinary words should never be used in a technical sense. It must not be forgotten that patients sometimes misuse technical words. Patients should be helped and encouraged to admit to symptoms of which they are ashamed. Normal people do not talk freely about themselves to strangers, and this is true of patients; it is therefore helpful to delay a detailed assessment to a second interview.

When ratings are repeated they should be made independently. The interviewer should not have previous ratings in front of him and should use a new form on each occasion; this may seem a trivial matter but experience has shown that it is important. As far as possible he should avoid asking questions relating to changes since the previous interview. In order to increase the reliability of ratings, it is advisable for two interviewers to be present, one of them conducting the interview and the other asking supplementary questions at the end. The two raters should record scores independently and then sum them after the interview to give the rating for the patient. Discussion can take place after this. A discrepancy of one point on any item is of no consequence but a difference of 2 points requires careful consideration. Experience has shown that a preliminary training done on about a dozen patients should produce close agreement. A difference of 4 points on the total score is the maximum allowable, but in practice, the difference is rarely more than 2 points. There is a great practical gain from having two raters: occasionally one of them may not be available and then the other can do the rating (and double his scores). With increasing experience, a rater can learn to give half points, but summed scores from two raters should be converted into integers for each item.

Symptoms are rated finely or coarsely; the former are on a five-point scale (0-4) where the numbers are equivalent to absent, doubtful or trivial, mild, moderate and severe. The latter are on a three-point scale (0-2) equivalent to absent, doubtful or mild, and obvious, distinct or severe.

THE RATING OF MALE PATIENTS

1. Depression (0–4). Depressed mood is not easy to assess. One looks for a gloomy attitude, pessimism about the future, feelings of hopelessness and a tendency to weep. As a guide, occasional weeping could count as 2, frequent weeping as 3, and severe symptoms allotted 4 points. When patients are severely depressed they may "go beyond weeping." It is important to remember that patients interpret the word "depression" in all sorts of strange ways. A useful common phrase is "lowering of spirits."

2. Guilt (0–4). This is fairly easy to assess but judgment is needed, for the rating is concerned with pathological guilt. From the patient's point of view, some action of his which precipitated a crisis may appear as a "rational" basis for self-blame, which persists even after recovering from his illness. For example, he may have accepted a promotion, but the increased responsibility precipitated his breakdown. When he "blames" himself for this, he is ascribing a cause and not necessarily expressing pathological guilt. As a guide to rating, feelings of self-reproach count 1, ideas of guilt 2, belief that the illness might be a punishment 3, and delusions of guilt, with or without hallucinations, 4 points.

3. Suicide (0–4). The scoring ranges from feeling that life is not worth living 1, wishing he were dead 2, suicidal ideas and half-hearted attempts 3, serious attempts 4. Judgment must be used when the patient is considered to be concealing this symptom, or conversely when he is using suicidal threats as a weapon, to intimidate others, obtain help and so on.

4, 5, 6, Insomnia (initial, middle and delayed) (0–2). Mild, trivial and infrequent symptoms are given 1 point, obvious and severe symptoms are rated 2 points; both severity and frequency should be taken into account. Middle insomnia (disturbed sleep during the night) is the most difficult to assess, possibly because it is an artifact of the system of rating. When insomnia is severe, it generally affects all phases. Delayed insomnia (early morning wakening) tends not to be relieved by hypnotic drugs and is not often present without other forms of insomnia.

7. Work and interests (0–4). It could be argued that the patient's loss of interest in his work and activities should be rated separately from his decreased performance, but it has been found too difficult to do so in practice. Care should be taken not to include fatigability and lack of energy here; the rating is concerned with loss of efficiency and the extra effort required to do anything. When the patient has to be admitted to a hospital because his symptoms render him unable to carry on, this should be rated 4 points, but not if he has been committed for investigation or observation. When the patient improves he will eventually return to work, but when he does so may depend on the nature of his work; judgment must be used here.

8. Retardation (0–4). Severe forms of this symptom are rare, and the mild forms are difficult to perceive. A slight flattening of affect and fixity of expression rate as 1, a monotonous voice, a delay in answering questions, a tendency to sit motionless count as 2. When retardation makes the interview extremely prolonged and almost impossible, it is rated 3, and 4 is given when an interview is impossible (and symptoms cannot be rated). Although some patients may say that their thinking is slowed or their emotional responsiveness has been diminished, questions about these manifestations usually produce misleading answers.

9. Agitation (0–4). Severe agitation is extremely rare. Fidgetiness at interview rates as 1, obvious restlessness with picking at hands and clothes should count as 2. If the patient has to get up during the interview he is given 3, and 4 points are given when the interview

has to be conducted "on the run," with the patient pacing up and down, picking at his face and hair and tearing at his clothes. Although agitation and retardation may appear to be opposed forms of behavior, in mild form they can co-exist.

NOTE: The scale points printed on the original adult packet are 0–2. Dr. Hamilton states that the original range (0–4) was abandoned when severer forms of agitation could not be found. He has since found that more severe cases of agitation do occur—particularly in countries other than Great Britain. The author prefers the 0–4 range, but the packet was printed before this instruction could be inserted. Subsequent editions of the adult packet will contain the 5-point scale, and raters are urged to employ the 5-point scale for this item.

10. Anxiety (psychic symptoms) (0–4). Many symptoms are included here, such as tension and difficulty in relaxing, irritability, worrying over trivial matters, apprehension and feelings of panic, fears, difficulty in concentration and forgetfulness, "feeling jumpy." The rating should be based on pathological changes that have occurred during the illness, and an effort should be made to discount the features of a previously anxious disposition.

11. Anxiety (somatic symptoms) (0–4). These consist of the well-recognized effects of autonomic over-activity in the respiratory, cardiovascular, gastro-intestinal and urinary systems. Patients may also complain of attacks of giddiness, blurring of vision and tinnitus.

12. Gastro-intestinal symptoms (0–2). The characteristic symptom in depression is loss of appetite and this occurs very frequently. Constipation also occurs but is relatively uncommon. On rare occasions patients will complain of "heavy feelings" in the abdomen. Symptoms of indigestion, wind and pain, etc. are rated under Anxiety.

13. General somatic symptoms (0–2). These fall into two groups: the first is fatigability, which may reach the point where the patients feel tired all the

time. In addition, patients complain of "loss of energy" which appears to be related to difficulty in starting up an activity. The other type of symptom consists of diffuse muscular achings, ill-defined and often difficult to locate, but frequently in the back and sometimes in the limbs; these may also feel "heavy."

14. Loss of libido (0–2). This is a common and characteristic symptom of depression, but it is difficult to assess in older men and especially those, e.g. unmarried, whose sexual activity is usually at a low level. The assessment is based on a pathological change, i.e. a deterioration obviously related to the patient's illness. Inadequate or no information should be rated as zero.

15. Hypochondriasis (0–4). The severe states of this symptom, concerning delusions and hallucinations of rotting and blockages, etc., which are extremely uncommon in men, are rated as 4. Strong convictions of the presence of some organic disease which accounts for the patient's condition are rated 3. Much preoccupation with physical symptoms and with thoughts of organic disease are rated 2. Excessive preoccupation with bodily functions is the essence of a hypochondriacal attitude, and trivial or doubtful symptoms count as 1 point.

16. Loss of insight (0–2). This is not necessarily present when the patient denies that he is suffering from mental disorder. It may be that he is denying that he is insane and may willingly recognize that he has a "nervous" illness. In case of doubt, inquiries should be directed to the patient's attitude to his symptoms of Guilt and Hypochondriasis.

17a. and 17b. Loss of weight (0–2). The simplest way to rate this would be to record the amount of loss, but many patients do not know their normal weight. For this reason, an obvious or severe loss is rated as 2 and a slight or doubtful loss as 1 point.

18a. and 18b. Diurnal variation (0–2). This symptom has been excluded from Hamilton's factors as it indicates the type of illness, rather than presenting an addition to the patient's disabilities. The commonest form consists of an increase of symptoms in the morning, but this is only slightly greater than worsening in the evening. A small number of patients insist that they feel worse in the afternoon. The clear presence of diurnal variation is rated as 2 and the doubtful presence is 1 point.

The following three symptoms were excluded from Hamilton's factors because they occur with insufficient frequency, but they are of interest in research.

19. Derealization and Depersonalization (0–4). The patient who has this symptom quickly recognizes the questions asked of him; when he has difficulty in understanding the questions it usually signifies that the symptom is absent. When the patient asserts that he has this symptom it is necessary to question him closely; feelings of "distance" usually mean nothing more than that the patient lacks concentration or interest in his surroundings. It would appear that the severe forms of this symptom are extremely rare in patients diagnosed as depressive.

20. Paranoid symptoms (0–3). These are uncommon, and affirmative answers should always be checked carefully. It is of no significance if the patient says that others talk about him, since this is usually true. What is important in the mild symptom is the patient's attitude of suspicion, and the malevolence imputed to others. Doubtful or trivial suspicion rates as 1, thoughts that others wish him harm rates as 2, delusions that others wish him harm or are trying to do so rates as 3, and hallucinations are given 4 points. Care should be taken not to confuse this symptom with that of guilt, e.g. "people are saying that I am wicked."

21. Obsessional symptoms (0–2). These should be differentiated from preoccupations with depressive thoughts, ideas of guilt, hypochondriacal preoccupations and paranoid thinking. Patients usually have to be encouraged to admit to these symptoms, but their statements should be checked carefully. True obsessional thoughts are recognized by the patient as coming from

his own mind, as being alien to his normal outlook and feelings, and as causing great anxiety; he always struggles against them.

THE RATING OF FEMALE PATIENTS

The same general principles apply to the rating of women as of men, but there are special problems which need to be considered in detail.

1. Depression (0–4). It is generally believed that women weep more readily than men, but there is little evidence that this is true in the case of depressive illness. There is no reason to believe, at the moment, that an assessment of the frequency of weeping could be misleading when rating the intensity of depression of women.

7. Work and interests (0–4). Most women are housewives and therefore their work can be varied, both in quantity and intensity, to suit themselves. Women do not often complain of work being an effort, but they say they have to take things easy, or neglect some of their work. Other members of the family may have to increase the help they give. It is rare for a housewife to stop looking after her home completely. If she has an additional job outside the home she may have to change it to part-time, or reduce her hours of work or even give it up completely. Women engage in hobbies less frequently than men. Loss of interest, therefore, may not be as obvious. Patients may complain of inability to feel affection for their families. This could be rated here, but it could be rated under other symptoms, depending upon its meaning and setting. Care should be taken not to rate it in two places. It is a very valuable and important symptom if the patient mentions it spontaneously but could be very misleading as a reply to a question.

11. Anxiety (somatic) (0–4). These last three symptoms appear to be more common in women than in men.

13. Somatic symptoms (general) (0–2). It is not

uncommon for women to complain of backache and to ascribe it to a pelvic disorder. This symptom requires careful questioning.

14. Loss of libido (0–2). In women whose sexual experience is satisfactory, this symptom will appear as increasing frigidity, progressing to active dislike of sexual intercourse. Women who are partially or completely frigid find that their customary toleration of sex also changes to active dislike. It is difficult to rate this symptom in women who have had no sexual experience or, indeed, in widows since loss of libido in women tends to appear not so much as a loss of drive but as a loss of responsiveness. In the absence of adequate information of a pathological change, a zero rating should be given. Disturbed menstruation and amenorrhea have been described in women suffering from severe depression, but they are very rare. Despite the difficulties in rating, it has been found that the mean score for women is negligibly less than men.

For clinical evaluation on the Hamilton Scale, *only* the first 17 items are to be used. A score of 6 is usually regarded as "within normal limits." Anything above that indicates that depression is present. Do *not* include items 18–21 in the score.

THE NEWCASTLE SCALE

After the diagnosis of depression has been established, the Newcastle scale, as described by Carney, Roth, and Garside in the *British Journal of Psychiatry*, 1965, helps distinguish between endogenous (unipolar, primary) and neurotic (reactive) depression. Anyone with a score of 6 or more is probably an endogenous depressive. According to Alec Coppen, those patients with scores in the mid-range —from 6 to 9 or 10—respond best to antidepressant medications.

The 10 specific items that follow give results just as useful as the full scale of 35 items. If an item is not present, score it 0.

	Weight	Score
Adequate personality	+1	
No adequate psychogenesis	+2	
Distinct quality	+1	
Weight loss	+2	
Previous episode	+1	
Depressive psychomotor activity	+2	
Anxiety	−1	
Nihilistic delusions	+2	
Blaming of others	−1	
Guilt	+1	

5 or less=probably neurotic depression
6 or more=probably endogenous depression

The authors help clarify the meanings of specific items by giving the following definitions.

Adequate Personality. That of subjects who are free from any history of neurotic breakdown and without disabling neurotic symptoms or serious social maladjustment.

No Adequate Psychogenesis. No psychological stress or difficulty continuing to operate after the onset of symptoms and adequate to explain perpetuation of the illness.

Distinct Quality. Some patients may describe their depression as similar to "normal" sadness or gloom, differing in degree only; others describe their mood as having a quality quite distinct from the depression with which they normally react to adversity. This feature refers to the latter type of depression.

Depressive Psychomotor Activity. This term is used inclusively to describe any objective evidence of psychomotor slowing, stupor, or agitation.

Nihilistic Delusions. Delusions of doom, imminent destruction, somatic dissolution, or poverty of the patient and/or his or her family.

CARROLL RATING SCALE OF DEPRESSION (SELF-RATED)*

Complete *all* the following statements by *circling* YES or NO, based on how you have felt during the *past few days.*

* Printed with permission of Dr. Bernard Carroll.

1. I feel just as energetic as always — Yes No
2. I am losing weight — Yes No
3. I have dropped many of my interests and activities — Yes No
4. Since my illness I have completely lost interest in sex — Yes No
5. I am especially concerned about how my body is functioning — Yes No

6. It must be obvious that I am disturbed and agitated — Yes No
7. I am still able to carry on doing the work I am supposed to do — Yes No
8. I can concentrate easily when reading the papers — Yes No
9. Getting to sleep takes me more than half an hour — Yes No
10. I am restless and fidgety — Yes No

11. I wake up much earlier than I need to in the morning — Yes No
12. Dying is the best solution for me — Yes No
13. I have a lot of trouble with dizzy and faint feelings — Yes No
14. I am being punished for something bad in my past — Yes No
15. My sexual interest is the same as before I got sick — Yes No

16. I am miserable or often feel like crying — Yes No
17. I often wish I were dead — Yes No
18. I am having trouble with indigestion — Yes No
19. I wake up often in the middle of the night — Yes No
20. I feel worthless and ashamed about myself — Yes No

21. I am so slowed down that I need help with bathing and dressing — Yes No
22. I take longer than usual to fall asleep at night — Yes No
23. Much of the time I am very afraid but don't know the reason — Yes No
24. Things which I regret about my life are bothering me — Yes No

25.	I get pleasure and satisfaction from what I do	Yes No
26.	All I need is a good rest to be perfectly well again	Yes No
27.	My sleep is restless and disturbed	Yes No
28.	My mind is as fast and alert as always	Yes No
29.	I feel that life is still worth living	Yes No
30.	My voice is dull and lifeless	Yes No
31.	I feel irritable or jittery	Yes No
32.	I feel in good spirits	Yes No
33.	My heart sometimes beats faster than usual	Yes No
34.	I think my case is hopeless	Yes No
35.	I wake up before my usual time in the morning	Yes No
36.	I still enjoy my meals as much as usual	Yes No
37.	I have to keep pacing around most of the time	Yes No
38.	I am terrified and near panic	Yes No
39.	My body is bad and rotten inside	Yes No
40.	I got sick because of the bad weather we have been having	Yes No
41.	My hands shake so much that people can easily notice	Yes No
42.	I still like to go out and meet people	Yes No
43.	I think I appear calm on the outside	Yes No
44.	I think I am as good a person as anybody else	Yes No
45.	My trouble is the result of some serious internal disease	Yes No
46.	I have been thinking about trying to kill myself	Yes No
47.	I get hardly anything done lately	Yes No
48.	There is only misery in the future for me	Yes No
49.	I worry a lot about my bodily symptoms	Yes No
50.	I have to force myself to eat even a little	Yes No
51.	I am exhausted much of the time	Yes No
52.	I can tell that I have lost a lot of weight	Yes No

A "yes" response counts for 1 point and a "no" response for 0, except for the following items: 1, 7, 8, 15, 25, 28, 29, 32, 36, 42, 43, and 44. For these twelve, a "no" response counts for 1 point and a "yes" response scores 0.

A score of 11 or higher usually indicates the presence of a depressive disorder.

WAKEFIELD SELF-ASSESSMENT DEPRESSION INVENTORY

Read these statements carefully, one at a time, and underline the response that best indicates how you are. It is most important to indicate how you are *now*, not how you were, or how you would hope to be.

To score:
    a=3
    b=2
    c=1
    d=0

NOTE: Reverse scoring procedure for items 2, 5, and 7. Total score is simply the addition of all items scored.

1. I feel miserable and sad
    a) Yes, definitely
    b) Yes, sometimes
    c) No, not much
    d) No, not at all ——

2. I find it easy to do the things I used to
    a) Yes, definitely
    b) Yes, sometimes
    c) No, not much
    d) No, not at all ——

3. I get very frightened or panic feelings for apparently no reason at all
    a) Yes, definitely
    b) Yes, sometimes
    c) No, not much
    d) No, not at all ——

4. I have weeping spells, or feel like it
    a) Yes, definitely
    b) Yes, sometimes
    c) No, not much
    d) No, not at all ——

5. I still enjoy the things I used to
    a) Yes, definitely
    b) Yes, sometimes
    c) No, not much
    d) No, not at all ——

6. I am restless and can't keep still
    a) Yes, definitely
    b) Yes, sometimes
    c) No, not much
    d) No, not at all ——

7. I get off to sleep easily
   without sleeping tablets
   a) Yes, definitely
   b) Yes, sometimes
   c) No, not much
   d) No, not at all ——

8. I feel anxious when I go
   out of the house on my
   own
   a) Yes, definitely
   b) Yes, sometimes
   c) No, not much
   d) No, not at all ——

9. I have lost interest in
   things
   a) Yes, definitely
   b) Yes, sometimes
   c) No, not much
   d) No, not at all ——

10. I get tired for no reason
    a) Yes, definitely
    b) Yes, sometimes
    c) No, not much
    d) No, not at all ——

11. I am more irritable
    than usual
    a) Yes, definitely
    b) Yes, sometimes
    c) No, not much
    d) No, not at all ——

12. I wake early and then
    sleep badly for the
    rest of the night
    a) Yes, definitely
    b) Yes, sometimes
    c) No, not much
    d) No, not at all ——

Total score ——

Only 3 percent of depressed patients score less than 15.
Only 7.5 percent of normal individuals score more than 14.

THE LEEDS SCALES FOR THE SELF-ASSESSMENT OF ANXIETY AND DEPRESSION

Score each item from 0 to 3, as follows:
    0=not at all
    1=not much
    2=sometimes
    3=definitely
Write the answer in column *A* or *B* as indicated.
Next reverse the ratings of numbers 2, 5, 7, and 13 (as
listed in column *B*) so that:
    0=3
    1=2
    2=1
    3=0

List the new rating for these four items in column C.
Combine the totals of columns A and C.
A score of 6 or less would place the individual in the "healthy" group, whereas 1 or greater would lead one to suspect a problem.

		A	**B**	**C** *(reverse of B)*
1. I feel miserable and sad.	1)	——		
2. I find it easy to do the things I used to.	2)		——	——
3. I get very frightened or panic feelings for apparently no reason at all.	3)	——		
4. I have weeping spells, or feel like it.	4)	——		
5. I still enjoy the things I used to.	5)		——	——
6. I am restless and can't keep still.	6)	——		
7. I can get off to sleep easily without sleeping tablets.	7)		——	——
8. I feel anxious when I go out of the house on my own.	8)	——		
9. I have lost interest in things.	9)	——		
10. I get tired for no reason.	10)	——		
11. I am more irritable than usual.	11)	——		
12. I wake early and then sleep badly for the rest of the night.	12)	——		
13. I have a good appetite.	13)		——	——
14. I feel in some way to blame for the way I am.	14)	——		
15. I get bad headaches.	15)	——		
16. I feel life is not worth living.	16)	——		
17. I get palpitations, or a sensation of "butterflies" in my stomach or chest.	17)	——		
18. I often think I have done wrong.	18)	——		

19. I feel sleepy during the 19) ——
    day.
20. I get dizzy attacks or feel 20) ——
    unsteady.
21. I feel scared or frightened. 21) ——
22. I feel tense or wound up. 22) ——

Totals   ——   ——
Total of columns A plus C= ——

THE LEEDS SELF-ASSESSMENT OF DEPRESSION SPECIFIC SCALE

Only if the score on the previous test is 7 or more, proceed to the following test, using the scores already obtained.

		A	B	C (reverse of B
Items				
1. (Sadness of mood)	1)	——		
5. (Loss of enjoyment)	5)		——	——
9. (Apathy)	9)	——		
12. (Delayed insomnia)	12)	——		
13. (Loss of appetite)	13)		——	——
16. (Suicidal thoughts)	16)	——		

Total of columns A and C = —— (depression total)

THE LEEDS SELF-ASSESSMENT OF ANXIETY SPECIFIC SCALE

Next add the following items:
Items

3. (Panic)   ——
6. (Restlessness)   ——
8. (Agoraphobia)   ——
11. (Irritability)   ——
17. (Palpitations)   ——
21. (Fearful mood)   ——

Total= —— (anxiety total)

Subtract the anxiety total from the depression total.

If the score falls at +5 or more, the diagnosis is "Depression."

If the score is −5 or an even larger negative number, the diagnosis is "Anxiety."

Scores between +4 and −4 are diagnosable as anxious or agitated depressions.

Author's Note

I receive many inquiries about where a person can get the type of treatments described in this book. My strong recommendation is, wherever possible, to seek advice locally from a qualified physician.

We (myself and nurses or psychiatrists on my staff) are not in a position to recommend one or another local physician, but we are quite agreeable to working with such a doctor. We do this by seeing patients in consultation at our office in New York or by occasionally seeing the patient locally if one of us is lecturing or consulting in the area. Our address is 425 E. 61 St., New York, N.Y. 10021. Our phone number is (212) 249-1900.

Index

About the Author

In 1953, together with a handful of other pioneers, Dr. Kline introduced into clinical use in the United States the first of the modern psychotropic medications. In 1956, in collaboration with his staff, he was among the first to introduce antidepressant medications. Several years ago, he and his colleagues also published the first paper on the management of alcoholism with lithium carbonate. For each of the first two investigations, Dr. Kline received an Albert Lasker Clinical Research Award. In the intervening periods, he was deeply involved in the introduction and evaluation of at least a dozen more new medical substances.

Dr. Kline received a B.A. degree from Swarthmore College, having majored in Philosophy. As a result of graduate studies at Harvard, Princeton, and Clark University, he received a Masters Degree in Psychology. His Doctor of Medicine degree is from New York University. Internship and residence were at St. Elizabeth's Hospital in Washington, D.C. For approximately two years during the Second World War, Dr. Kline served as a physician in the U.S. Public Health Service, detailed to the Navy.

Organizational affiliations include appointment to the Expert Committee on Mental Health of the World Health Organization, fellowship in the American College of Physicians, fellowship in the American Psychiatric Association, former presidency of the American College of Neuropsychopharmacology, and founding fellowship of the Royal College of Psychiatrists in England and subsequent election as an Honorary Fellow.

Dr. Kline's activities in the field of international health have been recognized by decorations and awards from the governments of Liberia, Haiti, Japan, Colombia, and Indonesia, as well as the Serenissimi Military Order of Saint

Mary the Glorious with the rank of Knight Great Cross by Master's Grace.

His publications in the medical and related fields number more than 450.

After the war he served on the staff of the Veterans Administration, was director of research at Worcester State Hospital and, for the past 29 years, has been director of the Rockland Research Institute, New York State Office of Mental Health. For more than 35 years, Dr. Kline has concomitantly maintained a private practice in psychiatry.

At present he is Clinical Professor of Psychiatry at New York University and Permanent Visiting Professor at the University of California, San Diego.

Psychology Bestsellers from BALLANTINE

Before there was est, before there was assertiveness training, before anyone thought about whether or not they were OK, there was Dr. Eric Berne and the *Games People Play*.

16

Learn to live with somebody... *yourself.*